LONDONERS
on the
Western Front

This book is dedicated to

Lieutenant-Colonel Percy John Preece
24th Middlesex and 8th London Regiment (T.D)
1874 - 1921

and

Lieutenant Llewellyn 'Bo' Preece
Royal Naval Volunteer Reserve
1866 – 1918 (10 November)

LONDONERS
on the
Western Front

*The 58th (2/1st London) Division
in the Great War*

David E. Martin

Pen & Sword
MILITARY

First published in Great Britain by
PEN AND SWORD MILITARY
an imprint of
Pen and Sword Books Ltd
47 Church Street
Barnsley
South Yorkshire S70 2AS

ISBN 978 1 78159 180 2

A CIP record for this book is available from the British Library.

Printed and bound in England by
CPI Group (UK) Ltd, Croydon, CR0 4YY

Typeset in Times by CHIC GRAPHICS

Pen & Sword Books Ltd incorporates the imprints of
Pen & Sword Books Ltd incorporates the imprints of Pen & Sword
Archaeology, Atlas, Aviation, Battleground, Discovery,
Family History, History, Maritime, Military, Naval, Politics,
Railways, Select, Social History, Transport, True Crime, and
Claymore Press, Frontline Books, Leo Cooper, Praetorian Press,
Remember When, Seaforth Publishing and Wharncliffe.

For a complete list of Pen and Sword titles please contact
Pen and Sword Books Limited
47 Church Street, Barnsley, South Yorkshire, S70 2AS, England
E-mail: enquiries@pen-and-sword.co.uk
Website: www.pen-and-sword.co.uk

Contents

Appendices

Foreword

It gives me triple pleasure to write this foreword. First, because I retain fond memories of the author's father teaching me at Shrewsbury School many years ago. I subsequently met David Martin, who has written this fine volume, on the Somme when he was guiding groups over the battlefields, a vital qualification for any successful military historian. Secondly, as the grandson of a Territorial officer – albeit from the 46th (North Midland) Division, who also fought on the Western Front – and a serving Territorial officer myself, with my own overseas operational service, I can readily identify with the London Territorials about whom Martin writes so movingly. Finally, I am delighted to see so a complex subject as the First World War history of a British division addressed with such good sense and depth. Good sense, because some of what is written about the First World War serves only to reinforce myths which are much better dispelled. And depth, because what David Martin has given us here with *Londoners on the Western Front* is a most unusual and solidly-researched narrative.

It is easy to forget the backgrounds of Great War soldiers and Martin has taken the trouble to examine their social origins and remind us of what their relatives endured as civilians back in London throughout the 1914-18 war. This is important because tales of rationing and bombing trickled to the front in letters from home, whilst after writing of the 58th Division's Passchendaele battles in 1917, we travel back home on leave with some of Martin's eye witnesses. The cameo of hundreds of civilians greeting casualties at Charing Cross Station at *3am* 'cheering and throwing cigarettes and flowers into the ambulance' is as unexpected as it is heart-warming.

We have the boredom and frustration of training in England, the sobering experience of joining the fighting on the Gallipoli Peninsula in late 1915, where the Londoners suffered their first battle casualties, and the grim fighting of the Third Ypres 1917 campaign, which saw the division endure massive casualties. The instance in 1918 of three medical officers being successively appointed to a single battalion *on the same day*, due to casualties, is chilling. Importantly, and unusually, for such insights are usually neglected, Martin also takes us beyond the infantryman's battle to the work of the medics, signallers (and their dogs), engineers and railway troops, who enabled and sustained the war at the front.

The 58th (London) Division was much battered in the March-April 1918

German Spring Offensive, and whilst operating alongside Australian units, we have the fascinating report of seeing a British cavalry unit, 'gallop into action with swords and lances drawn'. Not a usual picture of the Western Front. Later, the Londoners were part of the iconic battle at Villers-Bretonneux which witnessed the world's first tank-versus-tank battle, before seeing more action in the Battle of Amiens on 8 August 1918, 'the black day of the German Army', beginning the final advance to victory in which the 58th also played a full part.

It is easy to get side-tracked into debates about the poor generalship of Britain's First World War commanders, or simply agree with the shorthand of 'senseless slaughter' adopted by many of the 1914-18 war poets – neither viewpoint I happen to subscribe to. The spectre of the Somme will forever cast its long shadow, but Martin has not given us an 'officer's war', which was the hallmark of all early divisional histories. In these, the 'other ranks' rarely qualified for a mention unless winning a VC. Whatever our view of their endeavours, Martin's Londoners would have wanted to know they had fought professionally and earned a reputation on their battlefields. In this, David E. Martin has done them a great service, even if they have had to wait nearly a century for this account to honour their service and sacrifice.

He has chosen his division well – or perhaps it chose him. He has given us a compelling story, written through the eyes of its soldiers, of a British division which participated in most of the key battles of 1917-18. Above all, Martin gives a sense of positive *progress*. He demonstrates how 'his' Londoners learned in each battle to adapt their tactics and deployments. This was a division that matured through the mincing machine of the Western Front. Despite suffering many of their leaders killed and wounded, by 11 November 1918 the 58th (London) Division had emerged as a very potent fighting formation, with a reputation to match.

Just as British forces operate with coalition partners in modern battle, the Londoners fought alongside the French, Canadians, Australians and Americans, bringing a very contemporary feel to their war. The technology may change, but the soldier does not: the unwritten subtext of *Londoners on the Western Front* is that good leadership was as necessary then to maintain the resilience and spirit of the British army as it is today.

Peter Caddick-Adams TD, PhD, FRHS
Lecturer at UK Defence Academy

Illustrations

Maps

Acknowledgements

With many thanks to staff at the following archives: The National Archives, Kew; The British Postal Museum and Archive; The Trustees of the Liddell-Hart Centre for Military Studies; The Imperial War Museum archive and photographic archive and sound and film archive; Australian War Memorial, Canberra; The National Monuments Record, Swindon; Suffolk Archaeological Services and Suffolk County Records, Ipswich; The National Library of Scotland, Edinburgh; L'Archives Departmentals d'Aisne, Laon; The In Flanders Fields Document Centre.

At the IWM Archive, the copyright holders of private papers of Ackrell, Anonymous, Bertram, Borseberry, Chapman, English, Harper, Holt, King, Maile, Maxse, Morris, Page, Patterson, Rawley, Wagner, and Young; The Council of the National Army Museum for the papers of Howard Hicklenton; the National Library of Scotland for the diaries of Field Marshall Sir Douglas Haig; the Trustees of the 58th Division (BEF) Memorial Trust Fund.

Individuals to be thanked include the following families; Browne, Cardoen-Descamps, Maxen, Martin and McKinnon. The following individuals: Anne Walsh, Sue Maxen, Helen McPhail, Sarah Poppy, Adrian Goldsworthy, Michael Ling, Edmond Thewles and Irene Moore, Denis Dillon and Mick Moreton and the BFPO for the initial leads on the VC action and Mike Dudding as well as many others who have helped, inspired and understood. Special thanks to Peter Caddick-Adams for writing the foreword. Thanks to the Australian Army for permission to use war diaries.

Preface –

Distant Thunder

Thunder rumbled around the lofty mountain tops, ancient cannon occupied old gun pits at another half forgotten battle in the cradle of European conflicts, the Balkans. This was my first battlefield visit as a young child at the site of the Battles of the Shipka Pass (1877-78) in the mountains of Bulgaria. After visits to Verdun and the Chemin des Dames and Ypres my introduction to the Great War started with reading the memoir *With a Machine Gun to Cambrai* by George Coppard. Most of the physical remains of the Great War have disappeared, but the battlefields of France and Flanders are covered with memorials and cemeteries where so many of these men lie. Great War veterans, some of whom I had met, were men who if they talked of the war, talked of mud, death and horror. Many of the men did not know where they were on the front, still less of the objectives and reasons for their being there. My task was to find out some of the military history and reality of the Great War. It seemed unlikely I could get close, but in doing so I found a whole division with no written history as one formation.

The result of a university thesis on the memorials and museums of the Ypres Salient in the First World War was that I found a highly ritualised 'memorial landscape' of gravestones and memorials to the war. Like any archaeologist I wanted to find the real history of the British in the battles and it was some family medals that started me on the path to finding out a family history and a divisional history that was largely unknown. At this stage my studies were of heritage interpretation, specialising in battlefield interpretation. Later as a tour guide I was tasked with telling the history and bringing the battlefield alive for the visitor. This was restricted by time and often the tour of a battlefield can become too generalised.

I have two ancestors who served in the Great War. It is to their memory that this book is dedicated. Two brothers came from a family with links to Post Office engineering. Their father, Sir William Preece, was an eminent engineer and the British colleague of G. Marconi. The younger son, Colonel Percy John Preece, had been commissioned in 1892 and served in the Boer War. He was briefly taken prisoner at Roodewal by a Boer Commando attack, released and returned home.[1] He then served in the new Territorial Force where he was a major at the outbreak of war, became a colonel in the second line Territorial Force from 1915-1917. Percy died in 1921. His brother Llewellyn served for a few years in the Royal Naval Volunteer Reserve, having previously travelled to America to look at telegraphs and wireless and then returned to work in the Admiralty on early submarine detection devices until his general bad health told on him and he died on 10 November 1918 of Spanish flu. They are both buried in the family tomb in Llanbeblig churchyard near Caernarfon in North Wales. Llewellyn is listed on the Commonwealth War Graves Comission database and Percy is on the same certificate.

I unearthed the medals belonging to Colonel Preece, and when I eventually traced his service, it was to discover that he served in the 2/8th (Post Office Rifles), which was in 58th Division. This was a second line Territorial division from London and based on the post-1908 Territorial system established by Haldane. A soldier in the Post Office Rifles, Sergeant Alfred Knight, won the Victoria Cross at Hubner Farm on 20 September 1917. It was largely due to luck that I became interested in this attack, as I was visited by a captain in the Royal Engineers wanting to do a tour of the battle for some of his personnel. We promptly did a tour of the Wurst Farm Ridge in the pouring rain and mud, as well as visits to trench sites, cemeteries and museums on the usual tourist route. This led to further research at the British Postal Museum and Archive, at The National Archives and the Imperial War Museum.

This all wetted my appetite for more research and it was through a series of fortuitous circumstances that I was able to write this book. I was able to discover the real wartime history of the 58th London Division from the outbreak of war to home service, to some of the most hard-fought battles in the campaigns of 1917 and 1918. I also include a chapter on communications during the Third Battle of Ypres. It is quite common for a divisional history to include a specialist chapter on a particular topic such as artillery or communications so I have followed this format. It was the Third Battle of Ypres that was the crucible that formed the 58th Division into the fighting force it was in 1918, so this occupies about a third of the book.

This has been an interesting task and I hope a valuable contribution to the history of the British Army on the Western Front. It bears out the self-sacrifice and task that faced the men as individuals, but not just as men, as Londoners and as Territorials, in a division fighting an appalling war. They faced adversity and overcame it with the best of Edwardian engineering and military skill to convert an Edwardian army into a modern army capable of achieving a final victory.

Introduction

In writing a history of 58th Division I have approached the project as a chance to look again at the most crucial engagements that the division was involved in. This is to ensure that this often forgotten contribution is explained and its place in the wider history ensured. The story involves the wartime history of the formation and its twelve infantry battalions, with some reference to the artillery, medical services and other formations within the division. I have brought out its importance in some of the greatest battles of the First World War – Bullecourt, Ypres, the German offensive of 1918, Villers-Bretonneux, Amiens, and the Advance to Victory. The division was crucial in many of the battles on The Western Front in France and Flanders. My interests in history, battlefield interpretation and archaeology, have combined to produce an account of the division from 1914 to 1918, the first time such a history has been published in one book. Although individual battalions have histories, they are focused on the battalion rather than the whole division.

I found that the division had, in some places been somewhat neglected, and in others hardly mentioned. In many battles only the most successful troops are remembered, but the story of a battle is understood by looking not just at the victories of the leading troops, but also those on the flanks. The 58th Division fought on the flank at some of the most crucial battles of 1917-1918, Passchendaele, Villers-Bretonneux and Amiens. A history covering solely the divisional attacks would suffer for it and I think that it is important to look at brigade, battalion and company level as well. There are times when it is necessary to look at a small unit such as a platoon, and at other times the division or corps can give the fuller picture.

Researching the history of the Third Battle of Ypres I found the lines of communication that ran back to Essex Farm and Duhallow Advanced Dressing Stations. I also found that access across the landscape was improved to make provisioning the troops easier in the dreadful conditions of the Salient. This led to a significant improvement in the ability of the British Army to attack, even in the event of increasingly awful weather. Researching the attack on 20 September 1917 I found the triumph and tragedy of that attack and the days following that earned the division the right to change the name of Wurst Farm Ridge to London Ridge. Then there followed the briefly successful attacks at Poelcappelle and the disastrous attacks of the end of October 1917. The tribulations of the Third Battle of Ypres led not only to many casualties, but also a change of leadership within the division that was echoed right up the army command structure.

The campaign at the end of 1917 was countered by the German attacks at the beginning of 1918. The London Division was now astride the Oise River in France, south of St Quentin. The impact of this placement was that the division largely avoided the massive impact of the German advance. This had a lasting impact on the important battles around Villers-Bretonneux in the early summer of 1918, where they were involved in combat with tanks, and it was a battle where numbers counted against the waning flow of German attacks. In the defence of Amiens the Londoners had a crucial role on the flank of the Australian forces in the Battle of Amiens on 8 August 1918. They continued fighting along the bluffs of the River Somme until Peronne was taken in September. They then moved again, to their final major battle at Epehy, not far from their first battle at Bullecourt the previous year. In the final 100 days of the war they began their final advances across a series of canals and rivers where they faced hazardous assault crossings against defended positions. They ended the war with the liberation of some of the occupied territories outside the devastated zone, where civilian populations still lived.

The military history of the campaigns in France and Flanders is a topic much covered. In the course of research I discovered the parts of the division that had been sent off to Gallipoli in 1915 while the rest of the division was based in Suffolk. Two years on the home front had been filled with trench digging, marching and a major struggle to get them fit to fight in the bedlam of the Western Front. This home front history was just as interesting as anything in France or Flanders and showed how they were trained for the battles in a different way to the Regulars or New Army divisions. When the division was not fighting on the front it was resting, providing labour for the work of the Royal Engineers or training for the next attacks. There was a final twist in the history when the division was resurrected as a phantom unit in Operation Fortitude.

58th (2/1 London) Division

The Infantry Battalions
173 Brigade (2/1 London Brigade)*

2/1st City of London (Royal Fusiliers) replaced by renamed 3/1st Battalion 1915

2/2nd City of London (Royal Fusiliers) replaced by renamed 3/2nd Battalion 1915

2/3rd City of London (Royal Fusiliers) replaced by renamed 3/3rd Battalion 1915

2/4th City of London (Royal Fusiliers) replaced by renamed 3/4th Battalion 1915

2/24th County of London (The Queen's) temporarily joined 11th September 1918

174 Brigade

2/5th City of London (London Rifle Brigade)
2/6th City of London (City of London Rifles)
2/7th City of London (London Rifles)
2/8th London Regiment (Post Office Rifles)

175 Brigade

2/9th London Regiment (Queen Victoria's Rifles)
2/10th London Regiment (Hackney Rifles)
2/11th London Regiment (Finsbury Rifles)
2/12th London Regiment (London Rangers)

Pioneer Battalion (1918 only) – 1/4th Suffolk Regiment

* 2/1 London Brigade went to Malta, Gallipoli and then Egypt 1915, returning to France in 1916 when it was broken up to provide reinforcements, mostly for 47 Division.

Note:
A battalion is composed of four companies of 120 men (8 companies until 1914) up to 1,000 men. A brigade is four battalions. A division is composed of three brigades, plus Royal Artillery, including support troops, Royal Army Medical Corps, Army Service Corps, Machine Gun Corps, and Headquarters staff.

For the purposes of this history I will refer to the battalions by their number, i.e. 2/5th Battalion becomes 5th Battalion. But also by their adopted name i.e. 10th Battalion is also Hackney Rifles.

Chapter 1

Londoners
1914–1918

The make up of the London territorial was imbued with a sense of identity that was peculiar to London. In his comprehensive social study of London, Paris and Berlin in the war Jay Winter states that to be a Londoner in the late nineteenth century meant, for most, to be born there and have one's sense of identity emerge from a particular urban environment, the rhythms of which were perhaps more settled than an immigrant city, such as Berlin or Paris.[2] The men in the battalions of the Royal Fusiliers, London Regiment or City of London Regiment were often from a particular neighbourhood, work environment or even one company. Such a unit of the latter was the 8th Battalion formed of men solely from the Post Office. Others were from particular districts such as Hackney or Finsbury.

In the aftermath of the Haldane Act of 1908 the Territorial Force had reinforced the twelve battalions that formed what became the 58th (London) Division. The first four battalions of the London Regiment were formed of men from more working class backgrounds. The London Rifle Brigade has some existing attestation papers that give a brief breakdown of the background of 318 of the recruits to this 5th Battalion. Of the men enlisting fifty-eight were student teachers, six were council workers from Kilburn Town Hall, five from the Port of London Authority, six from railway depots, and three from the Buenos Aires Railway Company offices. Seven are listed as being in family business, three from the Continental Type Company, and four were unemployed.[3] These were mostly lower middle class men at the grade of a clerk. Sixty-eight men put their address as City or East City. The 6th Battalion mostly attracted men from the printing industry.

The men of the 8th Battalion, Post Office Rifles, came from far and wide across Britain. Of 816 deaths analysed, 457 came from London boroughs and 359 from outside London, therefore fifty-six per cent were Londoners. Far the greatest number of London attestations came from Camberwell and Islington with five per cent, Bermondsey, Fulham, Peckham with three per cent, Battersea, Stoke Newington, Stratford, Paddington and Walthamstow with two per cent, and Kentish town and Lambeth not far behind. The rest were spread across London, from Kensington to Wimbledon. Outside London there are some surprises as thirteen per cent came from Scotland, twelve per cent from south-west England, seven per cent from each of Ireland, Yorkshire, Lancashire and Lincolnshire, six per cent from the Midlands and five per cent from Wales. With a national organisation it is not surprising that this should be the case. It would seem that these were men who also worked as clerks or delivery men for the Post Office.

The 10th Hackney Battalion had a quite different background and before 1912 had been part of the 7th Battalion Essex Regiment. When that battalion was moved to Essex that year, after some soul searching and appeals to Sir John Cowans, the director-general of Territorial Forces, it had taken on the number of the redundant 10th (Paddington) Rifles. One of the most cogent reasons for not drilling in Essex was that the men could simply not afford the train fare or the time to go that far to drill. The companies of the 10th were split between different districts of Hackney. In the eight company pre-war makeup of a battalion, companies one to four were from Hackney, five to eight from Bethnal Green, Stoke Newington, Dalston and Homerton.[4]

The choice of a man wanting to join the army in 1914 was threefold: he could become a Regular and perhaps train for a commission at Woolwich or Sandhurst, he could join the Territorial Force and opt for home or foreign service or he could join the New Armies and serve as a Regular for the duration of the war.[5] It actually did not matter which route one took, as soon as war was declared and the soldier volunteered for Imperial service he was in the army. For the sake of history it is easier to follow the division as a unit and understand the history of the men in this unit under the banner of the Territorial Force which put them on a different course than the Regular Army or New Army Divisions.

For a number of Regular soldiers the army was a means of escape from piecemeal work and crowded housing for a reliable income and a chance to travel. Those in the Territorials before the war were often in a job or profession but found a way of supplementing that income by spending their weekends at drill amongst friends. The highlight of the year was the annual camp in somewhere as idyllic as Devon or Sussex. Many of the officers came from the middle class layer of society. They were from areas which were more middle class in outlook and architecture to the west of London. Those who worked as clerks were able to give up their positions with the prospect of finding another job at the same grade after hostilities ceased. In fact their position as second line Territorials meant that after the declaration of war on 4 August 1914 they were able to spend months training and fitting themselves out whilst living at home and many did not leave for France until 1916 or 1917. Some were sent as drafts to the first line Territorials so this was by no means a certainty. The late departure was partly due to their position as Territorials and partly to the fact that they were severely lacking in rifles, kit and even uniforms. The best kit went to the Regulars, first line Territorials, the New Army and then the second line. This delayed the time when the division would leave for the front, and was caused by a political rift at the very highest level.

The late organisation of 58th Division was due to a struggle in High Command between Lord Kitchener on the one hand and Sir Ian Hamilton and Lord Esher on the other over the purpose of the Territorial force. Lord Kitchener wanted to circumvent the Territorial Force altogether, and expand the Regular Army, hence his build up of the New Army divisions. Kitchener with one action bypassed Lord Haldane's reforms of 1908 and formed his own army. He also bypassed the county-led structure of the army changing the control to the War Office. With this decision the Territorial Force was going to be used either to reinforce the New Armies or to relieve the Regular Army on foreign garrison duty.

Until the outbreak of war 58th (London) Division did not exist with this title, but rather as a second line of the three London Brigades of the 1st London Division, and in this regard it would be a wartime phenomenon, passing with the armistice into oblivion. The core of this division were the brigades listed in the introduction.[6] The Regular Army in 1914 was made up of enough professional soldiers to make up eight divisions, so a force of around 100,000 men, plus fourteen territorial divisions. Wartime growth would see that rise to seventy-four divisions, so a multiplication of nine times, up to 5.7 million men. These were organised into divisions and of these four were London Territorials. In the pre-war numbering system these were the 1st London Division (wartime 56th Division), 2nd London Division (wartime 47th Division), 2/1st London Division (wartime 58th Division), and 2/2nd London Division (wartime 60th Division). The wartime numbering has more to do with the date that they were organised into fighting units and 58th Division was fairly low down the list. All of the New Armies were organised and saw action long before 58th Division, although 47th Division saw action in 1915 and 56th Division in 1916.[7] This is a history of 58th Division, but never without reference to those units fighting beside it.

The August Bank Holiday weekend of 1914 was to be remembered for a very long time, for it was the weekend that Europe went to war. The cause of the war was due to a system of alliances around Europe that were mutually dependent; the assassination of the Archduke Ferdinand in Sarajevo was the spark. The crisis had been brewing throughout July 1914, but problems had been evident for a number of years, including the Moroccan crisis of 1911. There was no immediate reason why this should cause a war including Britain and her empire so there had been no threat large enough to change the summer plans of the Territorial Force.

The August Bank Holiday weekend found the battalions not in London but dispersed and on their way to their annual camps in the south and west of England, the Territorial Force of the first line leaving for their summer camp over the weekend of 1-3 August 1914. The departure of these units had been delayed so that holiday traffic to the south coast could take precedence. The first line Territorial units were leaving for a two week sojourn near Eastbourne on Sunday morning 2 August. The 4th Battalion had left for Wareham and arrived at 2.30pm. Half an hour later they were ordered to return to London which they reached at 1.30am on 3 August where they were ordered to return home and await orders. The 5th Battalion had likewise reached their camp and was ordered home at 5.30pm.

Not all units could return at once as it was hard to find space on trains and track to accommodate all the units moving around. The 6th Battalion was marching into their camp at Cowgate, Eastbourne, when they were ordered to return home. The 7th Battalion arrived at Eastbourne at 4pm and was back in London by midnight. The 8th Battalion were luckier, in that their two trains were en-route to Eastbourne, but were stopped at East Croydon and Three Bridges respectively; they returned to their drill hall at Bunhill Row and thence home. The 9th and 11th Battalions were at Wool station in Devon and likewise returned to London. A party was to stay at the camps to dismantle the bell tents and these were to be sent to Southampton on the railway.[8] An assumption is that the tents and equipment were to be sent to France to form the base camps for the British Expeditionary Force (BEF) at Le Havre. The soldiers who were quite looking forward to seeing the camps in the summer of 1914 would actually see their 'summer quarters' in the vast rest camps above Le Havre in a sea of mud.

The Territorial Force received their mobilisation orders a day after returning to London on the evening of Monday 3 August. The 9th Battalion had made a day of it since it was short of things to do, having not enjoyed any of its summer camp. They marched to Ealing and back and started to mobilise on 4 August. There was nowhere to billet the thousands of

Territorials for the moment so they lived at home, reporting daily for inspections, and training in London parks and drilling where they could. This was the core of the Territorial Force at the outbreak of war.

Like some latter day Cromwell setting out to save the nation, Lord Kitchener made an appeal to Parliament on 6 August 1914 for 100,000 men to serve in his own army, the New Army, and the press published it on the next day. Many men who had served in the pre-war period rejoined their old units. One of the soldiers who served in the 8th Battalion, Patrick Patterson, did not join this New Army. 'I had previously served four years in the 8th London Regiment from 1908-11 and rejoined on the 7 September 1914. We waited for hours before taking our turn to go through the formalities. The days following were pleasant enough.'[9] The new recruits billeted at home and drilled in Regent's Park, with plenty of breaks for refreshments. There were no uniforms for the men except for the officers who were often regulars, a few of the men bought their own uniforms but on the whole they paraded in their civilian dress. This rapid mobilisation filled up most of the strength of the first line battalions within a day or two. It was during this period of mass recruiting that the scenes that many ascribe to the outbreak of war took place with thousands thronging the recruiting offices in London and other cities.

Lord Kitchener was a lone voice who surprised many by predicting at least a three year war; he was one of the few who saw the size of the storm approaching and asked for, and got, 500,000 volunteers for his New Army. For the moment the second line Territorials, who were still forming, were to be used mostly for home defence, whilst the Regulars, first line Territorials and New Army would see action before them, notably at the Somme in 1916. In this battle the 'Pals Battalions' would be decimated and towns lose a generation of young men in just a day. Lord Kitchener would not live to see his army lost in a few months of attrition. He drowned in 1916 when the ship in which he was travelling to Russia struck a German mine.

Most of the Territorials signed immediately for foreign service, although many could, if their conscience demanded, sign for home service only. These men would be assigned to one of the provisional battalions then being formed, as would men unfit for foreign service because of ill health or a wide variety of other reasons including some resistance to serving abroad. There had been considerable social unrest before the war targeted at institutions and the establishment. The government was able to some extent to channel this towards foreign enemies and which fuelled the anti- German riots. It was the war itself and the appalling casualties that would bring about the social change that many yearned for. The first line of the Territorial Force was already mobilised, but many more men joined them in the second line battalions as the first line battalions were already full. In the way of the British Army the county regiments expanded their regular battalions into service battalions. The London Regiment had no regular force, this role being fulfilled by the Royal Fusiliers. A second line was formed to provide reinforcements to the first line, many of these second line battalions were also filled very quickly. Of course it was not always as easy as just signing up: many employers did not want to lose their staff, sometimes of many years experience. To agree on conditions of service in the army or navy that suited both employee and employer was sometimes a matter of long negotiation. The Post Office at first banned men from serving overseas until official permission was granted but then let men serve in the 8th City of London (Post Office Rifles) or the Royal Engineers Postal Service. Pat Patterson of the 8th Battalion remembered that: 'This was understandable as a tremendous number of postal employees were army or naval reservists and, as far as London was concerned, the first battalion was already mobilised for the annual training.'[10] Employers wanted men to stay in the workplace; otherwise the country would grind to a halt if too many men went away to war. This was an ongoing problem as the army sought ever more men to serve, indeed many ongoing infrastructure projects would be re-evaluated during the war.

Once war was declared and the army had the Territorial soldiers on its pay, it had to think of ways to toughen them up, give them the edge over the Germans and use their time to the full. Since Lord Kitchener had ignored them, those that were not sent to garrison duty overseas had to be used somehow. The easiest way to do this was to hold a series of competitive marches for which battalions sent teams, an annual event since before the war. The most well known route was the London to Brighton march, a competitive march, the quickest time so far was about fourteen hours to do the seventy-odd miles. This in a strange way echoed the epic retreat of the British Expeditionary Force from Mons that summer and autumn. Other battalions filled their time by asking for men from provincial post offices, especially for musicians, to form a band, and certainly E. Rawley joined on this pretext, as previously he had been forbidden to enlist due to staff shortages. He was one of ten men in the band, including 16-year-old Bobby Maders, who played a memorable cornet solo at Cuckfield. The band was broken up though when a level of military thoroughness was applied to their recruiting.[11]

September 1914 saw the battalions of the London Rifle Brigade, based around their drill halls in London, using various miniature rifle ranges for practice, drilling in establishments as diverse as the Merchant Taylors' School, Middle Temple gardens, the Archbishop's Park at Lambeth and the City of London School. For larger manoeuvres they utilised Regent's Park and Hanwell Park. Billets were not always easy to find and the Rangers of the 12th Battalion found themselves at White City, West London which was the exhibition site of the period. Officers were housed in the Fine Art Hall, other ranks in the Machinery Hall. The men found this apt and fitting, as they saw their role in the army as becoming machines for war. Some battalions, amongst them the 4th Battalion, were put on guard duty on the London and South Western Railway line from Waterloo to Bentley for the rest of August 1914. This was a difficult duty for the men to perform and it was not long before accidents claimed their first casualties, the men not being aware of dangers on the railway line. Lance-Corporal Trant of the 12th was one of the first deaths when he walked in front of an express train in fog and smoke.[12]

Colonel Shipley of the 1/9th London Regiment complained bitterly in October 1914: 'We guard the line from Farnborough through here [Winchester] to just short of Eastleigh and from Basingstoke to Reading. It's a damned nuisance and an infernal shame as the whole brigade was shaping well and we had just started battalion training, but now all training is knocked on the head.'[13] Other uses were found for the men when defences were to be dug for the defence of London at Ongar and also at Loughton for the Rangers. The Londoners were to become avid, if unwilling, trench diggers. Just because they were on the Home Front does not mean they were not becoming used to digging. The first line Territorials of 47th Division eventually concentrated at St Albans and Watford, performing manoeuvres at Gorhambury Park.

When it was decided what to do with the second line Territorials they were sent to the South Downs in Sussex to dig trenches as part of an anti-invasion scheme. This would provide a defence for London should the Germans break through in France and invade Britain. This was interspersed with periods of railway guard duties. The brigades of the London Division were based around Crowborough, Midhurst and Burgess Hill. In 1901 General Sir Ivor Maxse had written a paper on the defence of southern England, identifying positions that could be defended, one of these was the Silver Hill position, based around Bodiam Castle in East Sussex.[14] This position was part of the South Downs line and its westward continuation was defended by the London Territorials in 1914. Home defence was the use to which the second line Territorials would be put until July 1916.

The pressure to join the colours was great in 1914. The men at the core of the Territorial Force were of course divided between their profession and their soldiering. Society questioned the loyalty of men if they did not join the Army or Navy. The ultimate disgrace was to receive a white feather, but there were many men in good, secure professions who feared having to give them up, never to recover them when the war finished, as everyone believed and hoped it would be over before Christmas. The thought that the war might be over so quickly was short sighted and perhaps a hangover of Queen Victoria's little wars: although certainly the precedent of the Boer War proved a different reality. There were those who had not joined up and had received the ire of their family, friends or colleagues. There are few sources on the question of loyalty and duty as anti-war sentiments are not often mentioned.

> 'Sir, May I ask those of your readers who are conferring the Order of the White Feather upon those young men who they see still at home to think twice. Some of us are government servants, and as such have to choose between stopping at home and throwing up our situation. Since the latter means eking out an existence for the rest of our lives in some unskilled occupation one has to think twice about enlisting.'[15]

It would be difficult to survive the horror of being branded a coward by family and friends.

There were opposing voices in wartime London, in the very streets that men serving in 58th Division inhabited. The most patriotic were some streets in Hackney which the Queen visited in August 1916. Here scrolls had been placed in the houses which had sent the most men into the forces. The Reverend B.S. Batty had encouraged the residents to decorate the streets with the scrolls recording the number of men voluntarily enlisting for service. There were nine streets with scrolls, the Queen visiting five. The visit was meant to be a secret, but word leaked out and the event turned into a Royal procession. Palace Road had provided 111 men out of a total of seventy-seven houses; in Balcorne Street 180 names were shown. Here the Queen spoke to a widow who had already lost her husband in May 1915. The Royal procession was welcomed by relatives of those serving in the forces.[16] Other streets visited by the royal party were Havelock Road, Frampton Park Road, Park Road, and Eaton Place. This truly was loyalty.

Politically there were movements for and against the war. The Suffragettes were an active force before the war, as an organisation it was rent with inner divisions. It is a surprise that the movement, under the leadership of Emmeline Pankhurst, came out in favour of the war and wanted men to enlist. They changed the name of their magazine to *Britannia* from *The Suffragette*. Despite their leadership's position on the war, many members formed anti-war movements such as the Peace Crusade under Sylvia Pankhurst, and other radical socialist ideas flourished.[17] The movement had been at fever pitch in the years before the war, even carrying out a bombing campaign across Britain in militant attempts to further its cause. In the years leading up to the war the number of arrests had increased then decreased, on the other hand the seriousness of offences had increased. The Home Secretary, Mr Reginald McKenna, stated that 'the highest aggregate of offences reached was in 1912, when a body of infuriated women, armed with hammers concealed in muffs or various other parts of their dress, broke shop windows indiscriminately in the principal business streets of West London'.[18] The militancy had increased to terrorist proportions but tailed off before 1914. It was the war itself that would eventually bring about the change they sought so their support for the war at least helped to achieve their objectives.

There were socialist objectors that railed against the war, such as the various pamphlets produced against the war in North London. They circulated anti-war literature entitled 'Don't be a soldier!' This became more of a factor when conscription was brought in 1916, as before that all the soldiers were volunteers of one sort or another. If they could survive the social pressures to join before 1916 they were faced with the inevitability of conscription. Against this background there were conscientious objectors who served prison sentences for their beliefs. Mutinies also occurred between 1917 and 1918, but do not feature in this history as they are, not surprisingly, unrecorded in London Division documents of the time, having taken place at the base camp at Etaples, not at the front. The only evidence of reaction to possible mutiny are some of the orders despatched in the later stages of the Third Battle of Ypres. There were rumours of an escape route to the United States to avoid conscription and safe houses in London.[19] Others who were pacifists gave honourable service as non-combatants, often taking up the role of stretcher bearers at the front, or served in Home Service battalions. All the pressures of the war caused a hot bed of social reform. The war led to social unrest amongst professionals and workers, leading to Trade Unions taking up the fight. Amongst the first signs of the strain of social unrest were seen in May 1915 as Tram workers went on strike at the Holloway and Archway Depots in London.[20]

Other professions were also affected; after various grievances in December 1915 Islington Borough Council workers went on strike in January 1916. There was a strike amongst 10,000 workers at the London Omnibus Company in May 1916 and a national engineers' strike in May 1917 affecting 200,000 workers. In 1918 even women omnibus workers working in positions vacated by the men going off to war went on strike, which affected most of London. This action started at Willesden Omnibus depot and spread to Hackney, Holloway, Archway and Acton. By 23 August 1918 it had spread as far South Wales and Birmingham affecting 18,000 out of 27,000 women employed nationally at these depots until August 25. This spread to male workers as well and affected Tube staff in London until 28 August.[21] To add insult to injury 6,000 policemen went on strike in 1918. None of this affected the men at the front except what they heard in letters and newspapers. The reserve 3/8th Battalion of the Post Office Rifles were called upon to counter social upheaval, in this case travelling to Newport in South Wales to deal with strike action 'without bloodshed' in 1918, when they were based at Aldershot.[22] The factors affecting the strike were the five shilling war bonus and equal pay; the slogan was 'equal work, equal pay!'

The winter of 1917-1918 was very severe and cold, everyone was affected by control of gas, due to the rationing of coal, which was used to make 'coal gas' locally in most towns and cities. Coal was produced nationally but was at a premium and an essential for the war industry and the navy. Special coal trains, 'Jellicoe Specials' ran from South Wales to the fleet at its war stations, especially Scapa Flow in the Orkney Isles. Beer prices, a staple of working life, had increased 300 per cent since 1914, bread was adulterated with barley, rice, maize, beans and, up to an eighth part, potato. All these caused great social tension and for the worker at home there were the added strains of fear and loss of relatives, family and friends at the front. The common sight of soldiers returning with horrible wounds, disease and mental strain, added force to the government's desire to keep the lid on the pressure cooker of social reform. All had to be forsaken for the period of the war.

It was not just lack of food that was a problem but also stockpiling by the wealthy. A lady of good family, Mabel Temple-Gore, was fined £80 for stockpiling food unnecessarily. Police found 54lb of tea in the servants' hall and 71lbs upstairs. Also 35lb of coffee, eleven tins of syrup, twelve tins of condensed milk, 23lb of currants, 20lb of sugar, 7lb of raisins, 4½lb of sultanas. The result, beyond the fine, was to confiscate 103lb of tea.

What was all this social reform to the soldier in the trenches, or in the camps of the east coast? The general feeling that comes out is that he did not care much for the social problems of the population in comparison to his condition under constant threat of death or injury. One soldier wondered at the posters that were displayed in London, declaring of soldiers: 'He's Happy, Are you?' This when he complained his rations that day at the front were 'a piece of dry bread for breakfast and tea, a wee piece of fat bacon and a piece of cheese and some ditch water for dinner'.[23] Having just endured a three hour long bombardment near Bullecourt this soldier could not understand the omnibus drivers' strike; 'what's wrong with the 'bus drivers in town, what are they striking for?'

London in 1914 had been expanding, and various projects had to be shut down in the war years. These occupied hundreds of men who, it was thought, could be better employed in the trenches, or under them in the underground war. Various large scale national projects then underway included the Post Office underground railway, the Great Northern Railway extension from Cuffley to Stevenage, the London and North Western Railway widening at Watford and a series of reservoirs near Staines.[24] Projects of the size of the latter were being called into question as the demand for men for the Army rose. As early as 10 September 1914 the Post Office Railway was being called into question. The problems of shortages of manpower and budget had to be weighed against losing the parliamentary powers of compulsory purchase after 1916 and losing the powers of the Post Office Railway Act of 1913 if it was not finished by 1918. The tunnels of the Post Office Railway were perceived as being superfluous to the war effort. Colonel Norton-Griffiths, in charge of mining operations on the Western Front, complained on 28 September 1915: 'Stop cutting the Post Office Tube, to my certain knowledge every man working on it is not only wanted, but urgently needed at the front.' This raised eyebrows and the Right Honourable H.J. Tennant MP asked in the House of Commons: 'I should like to know in confidence what authority from the military authorities either here or in France Norton-Griffiths has in connection with the engagement of men to undertake mining operations at the front.'[25]

It was extremely difficult to find men for the army as most men still not in the forces were employed in jobs that were crucial to the country. So every company was scrutinised for spare men of the right age to serve in the forces. This included the contractor for the Post Office Railway, Mowlem and Company. In the year ending 31 March 1917 the project employed 435 men, of whom it was found that while 354 were over military age, 51 were of military age. Of the men here 93 per cent were married, 74 per cent over age and 7 per cent of single men were medically unfit for military service. At the top of the pits dug for the tunnels there were 74 men, 60 of them over military age. Of the 306 men working in the tunnels, 51 were of military age, which was quite a number which could be released for service at the front. There were a further 55 men in the surface works employed as foremen, engineers, and maintenance staff and of these 39 were over military age. News of this trawling of engineering companies for men to serve reached Tom King at the front. 'I hear that 83 men have been cleared off the works for military service.'[26] Any men pulled off the works were not sent to the infantry, but to the Tunnelling Companies of the Royal Engineers, but even they would see surface fighting later as the nature of the war changed.

The Army was scratching around anywhere for men to serve and most were over age. It was the same story on the Willesden and Chalk Farm works on the London and North Western Railway at Watford and the route of the Great Northern Railway at Cuffley. It was eventually left to the military to decide what to do, as so many men were over age for military service. The outcome on the Post Office Railway was that the only work to be continued was the digging of the tunnels which was nearly completed in July 1916. Contracts did not always end this amicably and the Court of Appeal took on the case of the contractor Dick Kerr and Company versus the Metropolitan Water Board over the abandonment of building reservoirs in Littleton, Middlesex. Elsewhere railway companies were closing small stations to release staff for war work and even branch railway lines were closed to take the track itself for lines in France.[27]

The consequences of the number of casualties, especially on the Western Front where 58th Division was fighting, were so great that huge swathes of London could be affected by deaths from just a few hours of fighting. In a city as large as London there were more battalions and so the casualties could be absorbed more easily, but every casualty had an impact. Some of the battalions of the division were based on professions, such as the Post Office Rifles, which were national organisations. Others were community based, such as the Hackney Rifles, and these would have been harder hit from casualties. Ken Weller, the author of *Don't be a Soldier*, a socialist view of anti-war protests in the Great War, states that he had heard 'recollections of times after heavy battle when nearly every other house in North London had the blinds drawn in mourning'.[28] The result in streets such as Palace Road in Hackney that had provided so many men for the services must have been much the same. The number of other ranks army deaths that appear for the district of Dalston in Hackney was 508; Hackney itself provides 1,119 names and Finsbury 523 names.[29] The wounded may have added hundreds to the casualty list, and officer deaths would have increased the total. Add to this Royal Flying Corps (later RAF) and naval deaths and the number would have been much higher still.

The London of the Great War period was a place of extremes, from overt loyalty to extreme objection to the war. On the whole the man in the street was prepared to do his duty to his country as perceived by the standards of the time. As the casualties continued to rise and the effects of bombing brought the war to the very streets of London, the mood hardened and the effect of conscription sent more and more Londoners to the front. This liberated women to work they could not have dreamt of five years previously as well as unthought of social change. It provided a counterpoint to the nights of worry for menfolk at the front and the dread of the telegram delivery during the day.

Lieutenant-Colonel Derviche-Jones had this to say of the London Territorials,

'Born and bred in a large city, where his wits have been sharpened from his earliest days by the strenuous competition for existence, he is brimful of common sense, and quick to learn and to respond to anything which appeals to his intelligence. The drill sergeant's monologue of interminable detail bores him to the to tears; he requires to be shown how to hold his rifle, and why he has to hold it in this way or that; once this is explained to him intelligently, he has got it, and rarely forgets. This applies with even greater force to his tactical training. Let him have a clear reason for any job that he has to carry out, and why it has to be done in a particular way, and he can be trained for any enterprise, however complicated, in a very short space of time.'[30]

This was the Londoner of the Great War and the society that bred him, all this however, was not enough to prepare him for the war that he marched off to fight in.

We have seen some of the influences that affected Londoners in the Great War and the opposing voices in London, the loyalty of the majority and the dissent of a minority. From socialists to trade unionists, all were affected by the war. The price of living and the standard of living were influenced by events in France and at sea, with the blockade reducing imports. The gulf between those at home and those on the front increased but the war was also bringing new forms of menace to the streets of London, as bombing raids wreaked a new type of vengeance on the civilian populace. All this moved the soldier at the front, but he felt that those at home were living happily compared with his lot where wounds and death were a daily occurrence. This was the experience of Londoners, the families of the men of the 58th Division, all this while the men were training in camps in Suffolk far from the front line.

Notes

1 The Commando raid on Roodewal railhead looted and destroyed 20,000 bags of mail including money, gold, bread, cakes etc and was a severe blow to the morale of British forces

2 Winter and Robert, 1997 Capital Cities at War, (Cambridge) p.30

3 Mitchison, K.W. *Gentlemen and Officers*, p.40

4 Fenton-Jones, 1917 *The Story of the 10th Battalion 1917*, p.7

5 Holmes, R. 2005 *Tommy*, (London) p. 137

6 See also Appendix I for the Order of Battle

7 Middlebrook, M. 2000 *Your country needs You*, (Barnsley) p.122ff

8 Cuthbert-Keeson, 1923 *The History and Records of the Queen Victoria's Rifles* (London) p.2

9 IWM archive, MISC 139/2/2165 The papers of Patterson.

10 IWM archives. MISC 139/2/2165 The papers of Patterson

11 IWM archives. MISC 139/2/2165 The papers of Rawley

12 Wheeler-Holohan, A. *The Rangers Historical record*, p. 23

13 Cuthbert Keeson, C.A. 1922 *The History and Records of the Queen Victoria's Rifles*, 1792-1922, (London) p.4

14 IWM archive, 65/53/1 The Papers of Sir Ivor Maxse

15 BPMA, POST 115/21 The Civilian, 14 August 1914

16 Online source blog.maryevans.com

17 Other streets visited by the Royal party were Havelock Road, Frampton Park Road, Park Road and Eaton Place.

18 online source The Lamp.co.uk; *Women's Suffrage*, the Morning Post July 13th 1914

19 Weller, K. 1985 'Don't be a Soldier' The radical anti-war movement in North London 1914-1918 (London) p.51

20 Weller, K. 1985 (London) p.29

21 Weller, K. 1985 (London) p.31

22 Messenger, 1982 *Terriers in the Trenches* (Chippenham) p.64

23 IWM archive 89/7/1 papers of W.T. King

24 POST 30/3210A 31st December 1915

25 BPMA POST/30/3231A The Post Office Tube Railway papers

26 IWM archive 89/7/1 The papers of W.T. King

27 Gittins, S. 2010 *The Great Western Railway in the First World War,* (Stroud) p.92

28 Weller, K. 1985 *'Don't be a Soldier'* (London) p.51

29 Soldiers Died in the Great War CD-Rom

30 Derviche-Jones, A.D. in *The Post Office Rifles*, (1919) Aldershot p1

Chapter 2

The Lost Division[31]
England
1915–17

The journey of 58th Division to war was a long one, with initial mobilisation in August 1914 followed by time in camps in the London region, defensive duties in Norfolk and Suffolk, and final training in Wiltshire in 1916. This was a time of home defence work, training as a unit, trench digging, manoeuvres, and endless parades. The war diaries give a sense of the constant movement of men in and out, desertion, courts martial, deaths and transfers of men to other units. Second line Territorial units such as our division were kept on home defence, whilst being trained and providing much needed drafts for the front. Artillery units became responsible for training horses for artillery units at the front. The training of the 58th Division involved trench digging, fitting out units, and defending against the threat of invasion on the east coast.

Men of the first line 47th Division who did not sign for foreign service would have been transferred to their second line counterparts, trained by such men as Major Percy Preece, who went on to command the 2/8th Battalion for two years. It was Major Preece who led the initial training on Hampstead Heath of the 2/8th Battalion, with most of these men going to the first line Territorials in France via the first line division. In turn the 'reserve' second battalions sent men to create the third line battalions of the depot battalions. Their experience was needed to train recruits and to make up a core of experienced military men. Others not suitable for active service would be transferred to the 100th Provisional Battalion which was based at Aldeburgh for coastal defence; the first line of defence in the case of an invasion and in that respect not an easy task for home service men. The twelve battalions that concern us here initially formed the Reserve Battalions until March 1915 and in that period formed drafts for the first line units. After that period this route was closed and the battalions were to form their own complement of personnel for 58th Division.

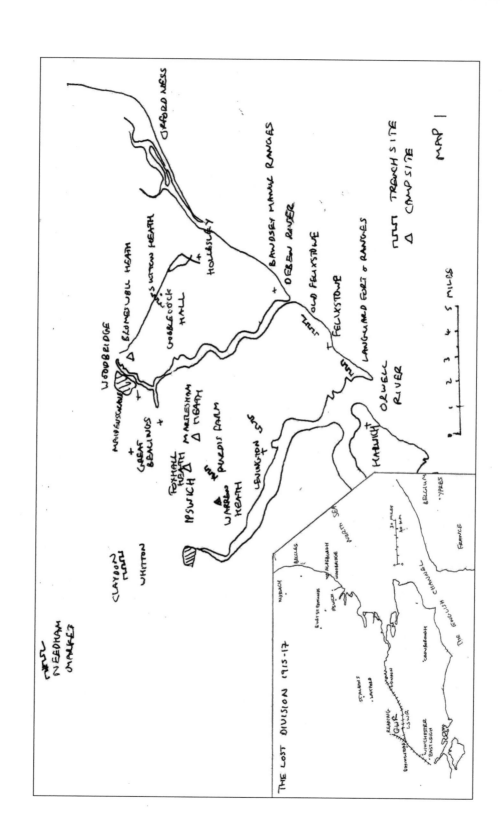

NEEDHAM MARKET

ORFORD NESS

CLAYDON
WHITTON

WOODBRIDGE

BLAXHALL HEATH

SUTTON HEATH

CRABBECOCK HALL

HOLLESLEY

BAWDSEY MANOR RANGES

DEBEN RIVER

MARTLESHAM HEATH

FOXHALL HEATH

PURDIS FARM

IPSWICH HEATH

WARREN HEATH

GREAT BEALINGS

MARTLESHAM HEATH

LEVINGTON

OLD FELIXSTOWE

FELIXSTOWE

LANDGUARD FORT & RANGES

HARWICH

ORWELL RIVER

■ TRENCH SITE
△ CAMP SITE

MAP 1

0 1 2 3 4 5 MILES

THE LOST DIVISION 1915-17

NORBACH

BURY ST EDMUNDS

IPSWICH
WOODBRIDGE

NORTH SEA

STALBANS
HATFIELD

READING
BROOKWOOD
GWR
LSWR
WINCHESTER
EASTLEIGH

SURRY

30 MILES
40 KM

THE ENGLISH CHANNEL

BELGIUM
YPRES

FRANCE

The division suffered the loss of four complete battalions in early 1915; the 2/1st, 2/2nd, 2/3rd and 2/4th Battalions were sent off to join the Mediterranean Expeditionary Force over Christmas 1914, which became embroiled in the final stages of the Gallipoli campaign covered in chapter three of this book. This split was achieved with some resistance and the division was cut by a third. The third line Royal Fusiliers were brought into their place and redesignated as second line eventually becoming some of the few third line battalions to see foreign service. The 'old' second line battalions were broken up as reinforcements for the 47th and 56th Divisions when they returned to France in March 1916.

After the loss of a third of what would become 58th Division over Christmas 1914, the General Officer Commanding, W. Fry, had to some extent start from scratch, and all the while provide drafts for the first line units. The next step in forming the brigades together would be in May 1915 when Brigadier-General E.J. Cooper took over, moving with the division to Norfolk in June and then Suffolk where the soldiers were based around Ipswich from late July. The division, part of defence units on the east coast under Central Force, pulled in units from far and wide. Artillery units were brought in from Shropshire, Suffolk and Glamorgan, and drafts of men came from London, Suffolk, and Devon, with all men being volunteers at this stage. Horses were also drawn in from the army remount depots such as those at Ormskirk (Liverpool) and Shirehampton (Avonmouth) whose horses originated from north and south America. These four-legged recruits were conditioned by the artillery units and then passed on to their front line units in France. The four battalions of Royal Fusiliers sent off to the Mediterranean embarked without many of their horses, as no facility had been made available for their transport.

The three London Infantry Brigades had shifted to Ipswich in late July 1915, where they remained for ten months until June 1916. Here the troops were at first billeted upon local residents in Ipswich and Woodbridge, an arrangement that seems to have been accepted with good grace and not caused too much upheaval as many local men were already away on service, and many large villas in the north of Ipswich were able to provide adequate accommodation. Summer camps were made at Warren Heath, Ipswich; Bromeswell Heath and Grove Farm, Woodbridge, to house some of the units.

The war had left the British Army fully committed in France and Flanders, with many of its Regular battalions at distant Imperial bases taking months to return to Europe, whilst the Territorial units replaced them like some enormous game of strategy. There was a real threat of invasion on the east coast of England with German forces so close at Zeebrugge, just across what had until recently been called the German Sea, now newly renamed the North Sea. The British Army response was to picket the east coast of England, but it was not only a full German invasion that was feared. The nature of the coastline and its remoteness and closeness to Germany led to many spy scares.

In October 1914 espionage was declared a military offence, therefore punishable by court martial and ultimately death. A German 'spy' had been arrested at Needham Market, Suffolk in 1913 and given two years in prison.[31] From the ancient tumuli at Sutton Hoo to the bleak shores of Orford Ness, Suffolk has a coastal area full of mystery which lent weight to stories of spies and invasions. Spies were caught during the war and were summarily tried and shot. On 5 November 1914 the spy Karl Hans Lody was shot at the Tower of London, followed in May 1915 by Anton Kuepferle, who managed to hang himself before the sentence was carried out. In June 1915 Carl Mueller, another spy, was shot. There were plenty of stories in the press about spies, as in July 1915 it was announced that in addition to five spies who had been convicted, some of whom had been shot, another ten had been arrested.[32]

The stories such as the novel *The Riddle of the Sands* by Erskine Childers (1903), then circulating, did not help the spy paranoia. The naval actions off the English coast in 1914 and the constant presence of Zeppelins all fed this fear of invasion. All that was needed for a German invasion was a breakthrough in France and Flanders, a 'Hun trick' such as the gas attacks at Ypres in April 1915, a change in the naval battle order. As General Sir O'Moore Creagh put it at Leeds in early 1915: 'This country is not free from the danger of invasion, and it is the duty of every man of military age to join one of the volunteer training corps.'[33]

Territorials were employed to man barricades and road blocks, whilst the Cyclist Battalions were sent on night time reconnaissance to look for breaches of the blackout, report on 'strange occurences'. Erskine Childers, in *The Riddle of the Sands*, makes the German invasion occur in Essex and The Wash, threatening Norfolk and Suffolk, and therefore not too far from Ipswich and the ports at Harwich and Felixstowe. Spies would surely be the precursor to an invasion and this was the necessity of these night-time patrols. Reading their war diary sounds like a 'Boys Own' adventure – in X town 'a light was seen revealed every evening in a way that might be guiding a German Zeppelin or spy' – and was no doubt the product of a fruitful imagination.

Relations between the military and the public were not always what they might have been and genuine businessmen seem to have fallen foul of military law. One such was a Mr Horace Rowland, a travelling conjuror and photographer, invited to a Royal Horse Artillery camp in Suffolk to take portraits of a section. He was arrested while setting up his camera to take a picture of the camp, breaching Section 19 of military law: 'Attempting to take or taking photographs at His Majesty's Defences with the intent of benefitting the enemy.'[34] It seems that he was genuinely trying to make a business venture, and we know that portraiture of soldiers was very popular at this time. Of course it was not always the public who were found at fault by the military. The soldiers also got in trouble for breaking blackout restrictions.

The soldiers, as part of Central Force, were based around Ipswich for its defence and were linked to the defences of the ports on the coast. The core strategy at the time was to defend commercial ports against sea and land attacks. Thus the soldiers at Woodbridge and Ipswich could have defended the bridges there. On the east coast 300,000 troops were deployed, the equivalent of twenty-four divisions.[35]

A force of this size gives the impression that the east coast of England was a bastion of steel against the threat of invasion, but the paper strength of the defences was, it appears, just that as a proper inspection of the regions found the Home Defence forces to be severely lacking in everything. Colonel Repington, visiting the Home Force commanders, states that General French had 'said I had been quite right in warning him that I would find chaos; he had done so. He had found an immense mass of troops, something like a million and a quarter or half, but with no organisation worth the name, and most indifferently armed. Out of his Central Forces under General Rundle, nominally 170,000 strong, he declares there are only 30,000 armed.'[36]

The generals in charge were sacked, except Hunter at Aldershot, and instead four favoured and trusted commanders, Paget, Bruce-Hamilton, Lawson and Ewart were put in charge of a sector each. So the soldiers may have felt they were doing something useful, but according to hardened military men, they were still quite lacking and had there been an invasion it is unlikely that any sort of defence could have been mounted, maybe only something worthy of the Home Guard in the Second World War.

General, E.J. Cooper reorganised the division under this new command structure. Ipswich based billets were shifted to summer camps and improvements made, and whilst living under canvas could be pleasant in summer, in winter it was not, so some billets were again used. The real training of the division now started. The practice of sending drafts for the front was stopped, the men were put to work digging, marching, parading and testing their equipment. The division was made up of infantry battalions, artillery brigades comprising gunners, artillery pieces and horses, and all the army organisation of engineers, field ambulances, Army Service Corps, signals and pioneers, machine gunners and veterinarians, the employment companies and the divisional train. It was now that the march of the division to war began in earnest.

The first step was to toughen up the men with route marching, trench digging and military manoeuvres all over Suffolk. The infantry brigades were concentrated between Ipswich and the coast, with camps built and improvements made. The brigade camps were established before early 1916 at Warren Heath, Martlesham Heath and Foxhall Heath. The brigade camp at Foxhall Heath was described in a poem by Rifleman Chapman.[37]

For the artillery the route to war was different again. The units of the London Brigade Royal Field Artillery was sent to the following war stations, 1/1st to Newcastle-upon-Tyne, the 2/1st to Hull, the 3/1st to Dover and the 4/1st to Edinburgh. All these units were disposed on these coastal defence duties until 12 December 1915 when they joined the 36th (Ulster) Division after which they joined the 56th (1st London) Division on 25-26 February 1916.[38]

Artillery in the period was horse drawn, certainly in field artillery batteries. Horses were the mainstay of the British Army in 1914 and indeed of any European army. They were used for artillery, supplies and mounts for officers. At the beginning of the Great War horses were the norm and other forms of transport often were only secondary or still developing, although this changed with the static nature of the war. The artillery was one of the units of the army that was forced to modernise the most for its part in an infantry division engaged in the stalemate of trench warfare.

Horses were imported into the south-west of England to one of the main depots at Avonmouth docks. The main object of the Shirehampton (Avonmouth) depot was to retain animals for fourteen to twenty-one days, get them clean and as fit as possible, and then pass them onto reserve outfits for further training. The scale of this process is seen in the numbers of animals imported: 11,855 horses and 1,550 mules were landed here in 1914, 97,867 horses and 101,767 mules in 1915, 13,483 horses and 23,348 mules in 1916. This was just one depot of several in the United Kingdom. There was also one at Ormskirk (via Liverpool), receiving the huge number of horses required for the army at home and on the Continent.[39]

While the unit at Shirehampton was originally manned by civilians, it was given a military structure in 1915 with NCOs and all men under military orders. Horses were received by 58th Division in Suffolk from remount depots. The divisional artillery, the 290 Brigade Royal Field Artillery (formerly the 2/1st London Brigade RFA) was heavily involved as a reserve unit in transfers and training of horses to send to the first line 47th Division in France. A brief analysis of these units shows a constant stream of horses being brought in for conditioning. In October 1915 twenty-five NCOs and men went to Kettering to assist in loading horses now being used by No 3 Training School, and in addition one officer and fifteen NCOs and men were still at Kettering, awaiting leave to bring back horses, guns and equipment of the 2/2nd Battery, which had taken over from the 1/2nd Battery, now overseas. On 30 October sixty-two horses were brought from Kettering, on 31 October twelve horses from Wembley. On 1 November fifty horses were brought from Shirehampton, on 6 November forty-five more and on 13 November thirty-three horses came direct from Avonmouth.[40] This continuing stream of horses being trained by the second line for the first line Territorials in France, mostly for the artillery and also general use, shows the importance of horse drawn transport, the reliance of the field artillery on horses, also presumably the horrendous losses of these animals, as well as the expansion of the army and field artillery.

One particular section of the artillery had a different origin and was not London based. One battery of the divisional artillery was originally from Shropshire. In 1914 the 1/1st Shropshire Royal Horse Artillery was based at the Territorial Depot in Coleham, Shrewsbury, but the two sections of the unit were split between Wellington and Shrewsbury, both in Shropshire. The Shropshire ammunition column was based in Church Stretton near to their ranges on the Long Mynd, 10 miles to the south.

The 1/1st Shropshire RHA stayed in Shrewsbury for ten days and then marched north for two days to join the rest of the Welsh Border Brigade at Chester, but the artillery battery did not go overseas with the Welsh Brigade, instead it went by train to Norwich with a 14-mile ride to Beccles where they remained with outlying units of 58th Division on coastal defence duties. There were four guns in a Royal Horse Artillery battery, split into two sections, left and right; this was increased to six guns when the unit became Royal Field Artillery in 1916.

This unit was amalgamated along with the Shropshire ammunition column and became the Medium Trench Mortar Batteries, numbered X.58, Y.58 and Z.58. The Heavy Trench Mortar Battery, V.58, was briefly in 58th

Division until being moved to become Fifth Army troops. Trench Mortar Batteries were very important for short range artillery support, bunker busting, and general psychological warfare on the enemy, and were the equivalent of the German Minenwerfer.[41] They had to change their whole formation to equip themselves for modern combat in the trenches, and this was typical of the move to siege conditions from the Edwardian army that had gone to war in 1914.

Some of the London Territorial Artillery was based for a period at Framlingham in Suffolk. Elements of the division were positioned in the south of the county, in proportion to the size of the town or district that could billet it, thus Ipswich could quarter a brigade of infantry and smaller towns only a battalion or artillery brigade. The London Division was spread all over Suffolk in mid 1915 and the artillery units were no different. The visits of the Assistant Divisional Veterinary Officer give us the sites of many of these units. The divisional artillery was at Ipswich, the 1/2nd London Brigade Royal Field Artillery (RFA) was at Saxmundham, the Divisional Veterinary Hospital at Bury St Edmunds, the 1/3rd London RFA at Framlingham. The following units were at Warren Heath, Ipswich: 1/1st Brigade RFA, 1/4th Howitzer Brigade, RFA and 1/1st Royal Garrison Artillery. The 2/3rd Field Ambulance was at Woodbridge. The artillery was split up between small villages and towns in Suffolk. This was still true of the division whilst it was forming. The major problem and reason for this was not only billeting the troops but finding adequate fodder and grass for the horses.

The immediate task of the infantry battalions was to toughen up the soldiers and adapt to the rigours of warfare, including continuing route marches and trench digging. Competitive route marches had been going on since the early days of the war. Trench digging on such a scale would be an art that was specific to the Great War, see photo.

The Londoners dug many trench sites in Suffolk for training purposes. This is the first time these trench areas have been linked as a whole to 58th Division, and the entire time spent in Suffolk by the division researched. The sites identified near Ipswich are at Purdis Farm, Blackheath at Woodbridge, various parts of Sutton Common, Needham Market water meadows and some other sites at Claydon and on the Norwich road north of Ipswich.[42] The 100th Provisional Battalion dug trenches at North Warren near Aldeburgh just inland from the coast. The site at Purdis Farm was made up of two lines of trenches facing each other each connected by two communication trenches. These trenches were dug for training purposes, to get troops used to trench life, going over the top and attacking, and the general acclimatisation of soldiers going to France and Flanders.

Several of these sites have been mapped archaeologically, and by cross-referencing with the battalion histories can be matched to individual battalions. B Company of the 6th Battalion dug trenches at Needham Market, Suffolk. Other companies of this battalion dug sites at Claydon and to the north of Ipswich. The 9th Battalion used the Martello towers on the coast as positions and were digging in on the sea wall at Alderton, Suffolk, but the next day the local authorities objected, so they had to fill in the holes.[43] The men were heard to comment; 'the first we would hear of any invasion would be when we heard their boats grating on the beach.'[44]

Trenches alleged to have been dug at Upper Hollesley Common are linked to the Rangers of the 12th Battalion. These sites do not really form any sort of cohesive system, and although they occupied some high ground, would not have formed much of a defence in the event of an invasion, although forces would then have held, where possible, the bridges and other defensive positions. Above Warren Heath the golf course was the site of positions dug to spot Zeppelins and aircraft at Broke Hall, near Ipswich, which are visible in aerial photographs taken in 1943. These fortifications must have been very minor as one night they were only manned by one officer and six men.

The 7th Battalion history makes no mention of digging trenches near Ipswich, nor trench life until they encountered it at Yarnbury Castle, near Warminster, yet it seems odd that all the other battalions were digging trenches and this battalion was not. The war diaries of the 7th Battalion record a different story, stating that 'much useful work has been done in trench digging. A large piece of private ground has been placed at disposal of the battalion for this purpose, and two opposing lines of fire trenches constructed with communication and cover trenches. These have been occupied all night by companies of the battalion and useful instruction has been delivered by this means.'[45] Not only were they digging trenches, but they were living in them for short periods as well for acclimatization and hardening the soldiers to the outside life.

Most of the Suffolk trench sites are dug in heath land. The advantage of this was the ease of digging, good drainage and that the land was not needed for agriculture. Most were dug between November 1914 and the end of 1916; between the end of the First Battle of Ypres, when trench warfare was established, and the end of the battle of the Somme. Of the sites I have found around Ipswich that relate to our division three at least were on heath land, one in clay pits on industrial land so no trace would exist today, and one in water meadows near the River Orwell south of Needham Market. Many heaths were lost to either agriculture or airfields in the Second World War so these sites rarely survive, except where heath land has essentially been preserved through golf courses or nature reserves, or they are on moorland such as Salisbury Plain. It was not just in Suffolk that the division left its mark on the landscape. A brigade of 58th Division was on Salisbury Plain in 1916 and 'was camped near Imber to dig trenches for an artillery practice range.'[46]

The 58th Division almost certainly dug all the sites around Ipswich with the exception of some at Felixstowe Fort and those at Levington Heath which are unattributed. However, when they moved down to Heytesbury in 1916 there were already trenches there, so it was just a matter of repairing them and using them for training. One of the biggest factors in military service is long periods of boredom. It is quite certain that the commanders of Central Force did not want bored troops, so the practice of trench digging fulfilled several useful weeks for many battalions still forming up or being used for home defence. The Rangers at Woodbridge dug trenches on Hollesley Heath, marching past a house named Gobblecock Hall, which was endlessly parodied. It is not just archaeology and battalion histories that provide the evidence that links the Londoners to these trench sites.[47]

It is easy to feel the mood of the soldiers who dug these trenches as the road from Bromeswell Heath Camp to the trench site near Hollesley is dead straight and would have felt punishing to march along for three miles. They would have had to carry tools and possibly barbed wire and wooden revetments to add to their troubles.

Ipswich was proud of the part it played in providing recruits for the division. These might end up either in the Suffolk regiment or the London Regiment. The local newspaper sang the praises of these local recruits. 'Ipswich, as usual, was not behind other towns in its endeavours to help in securing recruits.'[48] The army played its part in entertaining the townspeople and providing a dramatic march past in October 1915, a local journalist wrote 'the first portion consisted of 2,000 men from the various troops stationed in the district, and comprised artillery and infantry, light and heavy guns were represented, and the crowds were particularly impressed with the excellent horsing of these [units]'[49]

The troops stationed in the district, a military secret at the time, were of course the Londoners. As in London local businesses were scrutinised to allow men where possible to join up, and men were freed from the

Corporation Tramways Department to enlist, whilst an equivalent number of twenty-six women were employed in their place. The men were obliged to join the London Division if there was no need for reinforcements in the Suffolk Regiment.

This recruitment drive had started early and one of the ways was to impress the locals with the sporting side of life in the army. On Whit Monday 1915 the 12th Battalion staged a sports meeting at the Murray Road recreation ground which proved to be the start of a summer of sport and involvement in the local community. As part of its training the division played games and provided many a football team to play in local leagues in Suffolk. When the new football season started in the autumn of 1915 teams are mentioned in the local papers. Although professional football had been terminated in July that year for the duration of the war, local leagues were organised, including the London combination and the Southern League.[50] This allowed football to continue, especially within the military, but on a more ad hoc basis and would not interfere with professional footballers who wished to join up.

Various military teams played against teams called 'The Explosives', presumably a munition workers' team. In the *Evening Star* photographs appear of the teams of the 'F' Company RE of the 1st Battalion, versus the Explosives, also Ipswich Corinthians versus the 2/1st Heavy Battery RGA at Gippeswyck Park. There are photos of the teams of the Signal Company of 58th Division, the 9th, 12th, 7th, and 6th Battalion Suffolk Cyclists.[51] It is not stated whether these were well attended matches, but certainly the events and parades organised elsewhere appear to have been.

The camp at Warren Heath boasted a YMCA hut, at which a concert was performed on 2 August 1915 attended by 400 people. On 3 August the 1/3rd County of London Field Artillery made a display of the duty and work of artillerymen. The local reporter again sang the praises of the Londoners' artillery drive 'whether as gunners, drivers or members of the Ammunition Corps, those who represented their batteries in Monday's competitions could not have done better had they been Regulars with the advantage of several years training.'[52]

A reminder of the closeness of the war occurred when Zeppelins bombed the small town of Woodbridge in Suffolk, and photographs show soldiers, maybe those based in the town or at Bromeswell Heath, parading with a band for the funeral of the civilian deaths from this raid. It had been decided in October 1915 that no warning would be given to the public in London of the approach of Zeppelins, for fear of provoking panic, but the soldiers forming the air defences were often well alerted to their presence. The government felt that the fear would be disproportionate to the damage caused by these bombing raids.[53]

Other distractions were made including marking the anniversary of the start of the war, and a sixteen-carriage Great Eastern Railway Ambulance train which was displayed at Liverpool Street Station in London on 4 August and then at Ipswich station on 10 August, all six pence fares at the London viewing going towards the war relief fund.

In 1915 the full horror of the war had yet to hit home, but the list of killed, missing and wounded in the local papers grew every day. Hospital facilities in the county of Suffolk were soon full to bursting with war wounded from France and Flanders. It was policy to repatriate all those recovering from wounds severe enough to bring them back to Britain. Some of the men of the Suffolk regiment wounded in 1914 and 1915 would have come to Suffolk hospitals and convalescent homes. Despite this the army was well known for sending convalescents far away from their home county. The Suffolk and Ipswich Hospital built a new ward on the site of the tennis courts, a loss that would 'have to be borne'. This helped with forty-seven new beds and a general increase of beds in the hospital by 110. The Broadwater Hospital overlooking the river Orwell provided another forty beds for patients from 21 October 1915. Healthy eating was the order of the day for convalescing soldiers, especially fresh vegetables and rabbits were sought.[54]

It was hard to get subscriptions to war relief funds or hospitals. Many wealthy people seem to have given quite substantial amounts of money but the editor of the local newspaper was critical of the part the rest of the community played in setting up relief for wounded soldiers: 'there ought really to be a large number of small subscriptions for such an object as is now put before the public in this appeal, as the soldiers do not get their wounds merely in the protection of the rich folk, they are fighting for the honour and freedom [of all].'[55]

There was of course a more sinister reason for keeping so many troops in Britain, not only to counter any invasion plans of the 'dastardly Hun' but also to keep public order. In early 1915 the continuation of the war meant thousands of people were losing relatives, sons, husbands, and fathers. The result was a tide of anti-German feeling, riots and general disorder that spread across the country, affecting most large cities.

Anti-German riots in London seem to have started in May 1915, due to the German Zeppelin bombings, and spread to Deptford, Islington, Finsbury, and even on to Gateshead and Manchester. In London a local reporter described that '3,000 to 4,000 persons were in the high street, and four alien-owned shops were wrecked. Not a single street where a German shop was situated escaped. One hundred and fifty shops were damaged in Camden and fifty persons who were injured required treatment at Poplar hospital.'

In Southend where German Zeppelins had just bombed the town a public meeting was held and, according to the local paper, 'at the conclusion of the meeting the crowd swarmed up Queen's Road to the residence of a German, smashed his windows and wrecked the premises. Soldiers were called out to hold the thoroughfare but they were unable to deal with the situation. Two hundred special constables were called. An army captain then ordered the troops to sweep the Queen's Road and the crowds swarmed down the High Street. This was a somewhat unfortunate proceeding as because at the lower end of High Street, near the sea front, there are a number of shops occupied by Germans which were also wrecked.'[56]

Only two people were arrested. Obviously a lot had to be learnt on how to control crowds and mobs. The riots do not seem to have affected Suffolk, but the news of this disorder in the next county would have brought home to the people of Suffolk the impact of the war on civilians at home. It had also shown the need to have troops on the home front as reassurance from air raids, spies and riots. The war was spreading in its consequences and scope and as 1915 waned the new year promised but did not provide much hope; 1916 was a defining year in the war and everything changed. Kitchener was dead, the Germans attacked at Verdun and the New Army launched an offensive at the Battle of the Somme which would add significantly to the lengthening casualty lists.

A year after the first Zeppelin raids the German High Seas fleet sallied forth from its bases at Kiel and Wilhelmshaven. The threat of invasion if the Germans had won a significant victory briefly increased then waned. The naval battle at Jutland on 31 May and 1 June 1916 ended in a stalemate but at least blunted the Kaiser's naval ambitions and probably ended any need to prepare against an invasion of the east coast.

The Londoners had trained hard in Suffolk, formed a coherent military division out of twelve battalions of soldiers from widely different counties and backgrounds. They had marched, showed off their sporting and military prowess to the locals who had supported them in turn and provided recruits, they had dug trenches and defended the east coast from an invasion that was now unlikely.[57] Just a month and a half later, the division moved from Ipswich and on to a real war footing as the troops left Suffolk for final preparations on Salisbury Plain in July 1916[58], remaining for six months training in the area of Heytesbury and Sutton Veny.

Notes

31 Suffolk Record Office, interview with Harry Overton. Item L/40/1/359

32 IWM library, 1915 *John Bull's history of the First Year of the War*

33 Suffolk Record Office, The Evening Star, May 1915

34 Suffolk Record Office The Evening Star, June 15 1915

35 Saunders, A. 1983 *Fortress Britain*, (Liphook) p.211ff

36 Repington, 1920 *The First World War, 1914-1918*, (London) p. 109

37 See Appendix 3

38 56 Division served at Gommecourt in the diversion for the Battle of the Somme, 1916, where it gained its objectives but had to fall back owing to failure on its flanks.

39 National Archives WO95/5466

40 National Archives WO95/2995

41 Arthur Allwood, quoted in 2006 *Shropshire Royal Horse Artillery 1908-1920* edited Derek Harrison with Peter Duckers (Shrewsbury) 2006

42 My sincere thanks to Sarah Poppy of Suffolk Council Archaeology for her help with finding these trench sites.

43 Cuthbert-Keeson *The History and records of the Queen Victoria's Rifles 1792-1922* p279

44 Cuthbert-Keeson *The History and records of the Queen Victoria's Rifles 1792-1922* p279

45 National Archives, WO95/3005

46 Wheeler-Hollohan and Wyatt, *The Ranger's Historical Records*, p. 182-3

47 see Appendices, *The Rangers Historical Records*. Ed Wheeler-Holohan and Wyatt. p.181

48 Suffolk Record Office *The Evening Star*, October 41915

49 Suffolk County Archives The Evening Star, October 4 1915

50 Riddoch and Kemp, *When the Whistle Blows, the story of the Footballers Battalion in the Great War*, (Yeovil) 2008, p 54-55

51 Suffolk Record Office The Evening Star, September – November 1915

52 Suffolk Record Office Evening Star, August 31915

53 IWM library, 1916 *John Bull's Diary of the Second Year of the War*, entry for October 1915

54 Suffolk Record Office Evening Star, October 1915

55 Suffolk Record Office Evening Star, 4 May 1915

56 Suffolk Record Office Evening Star, May 1915

57 The Londoners' place was taken by 72nd Division in 1917 until they were disbanded in 1918

58 Latest research appears to show that it may have been 72nd Division that dug or maintained the trenches at Purdis Farm.

Chapter 3

'When I get back from Hell again'
First Actions: Gallipoli 1915
and Bullecourt May 1917

Two battles defined the early experiences of the men of 58th Division. These were the battles of Gallipoli (1915) and Bullecourt (1917). First London Brigade, a third of the division, was dispatched in December 1914 to Malta to replace regular troops being brought back to the Western Front. The 2/3rd Battalion was to go to Malta, Khartoum and the Dardanelles. The 2/4th Battalion proceeded to Malta and then to Egypt and eventually the Dardanelles (Gallipoli) from 16 October 1915 until the evacuation in January 1916. Two battalions (the 2/3rd and 2/1st Royal Fusiliers) were attached to 29th Division and two to the Royal Naval Division, (the 2/2nd and 2/4th Royal Fusiliers) and took part in the final embarkation from Gallipoli.[59]

The main source for our narrative on the 1 London Brigade, as part of the Mediterranean Expeditionary Force, is Second Lieutenant Howard Hicklenton. He records in depth the move of the 2/4th Battalion, London Regiment (Royal Fusiliers) from Malta to Egypt, The Dardanelles, and back to Egypt. The brigade left its quarters in Maidstone, Kent, in December 1914, before the rest of the division concentrated. From 1 January they were at Malta. Howard Hicklenton arrived on 13 August when they had been in garrison duty for some months.

'The place is altogether very nice indeed, quite quaint of course, the sun is very hot. It is an order that we must wear our helmets between 7.30am and 6pm. There is lovely bathing quite handy and how I wish I could swim. I went down with some of the other officers; I went in and found that I could float on my back after a little persuasion from Williams and the others.'[60]

The battalion was only in Malta for another week before embarking for Alexandria aboard the SS *Southlands*, reaching the city on 25 August 1915 where they were in camp by the beach about three miles out of the city. By early September they were settling into life in Egypt, learning to cope with sunburn, and even Hicklenton was learning to swim, perhaps the extreme heat was the reason as it was one of the only ways to cool down and keep a reasonable level of hygiene. Even so he still ended up suffering from 'Nile belly' and bought the wrong type of camera, for which there was no film available in Egypt. But by the time they embarked for the Dardanelles in November he had sorted himself out with a better camera with film and shows some graduation towards a more military bearing.

The reality of war was dawning on some of the younger, inexperienced officers, and news that the SS *Southlands*[61] had been torpedoed on its way to the Dardanelles was sobering enough for the men, but they of course were somewhat naive in their prospects for trench warfare. Of the military equipment that they took with them those most useless in the trenches were swords, being far too unwieldy and liable to get caught on the barbed wire: 'We have handed in our swords and the Colonel is having a box made and is sending them home for us.'[62] His sole firearm was his pistol, as the army could not decide whether to issue them with rifles. 'I shall in the meantime have to rely on my Webley... I have twelve rounds of ammunition for it, so they can account for one dozen Turks.'[63]

Leaving Alexandria on 9 October on His Majesty's Transport *Karroo* they sailed off into the Mediterranean. After a short voyage to Mudros they transferred to HMT *Sarnia* for the short voyage to 'W' Beach on the Dardanelles by the 16 October where they would get a gentle instruction into the reality of trench warfare.

On reaching the Dardanelles the London Brigade was broken up and the battalions sent to different divisions in the line. Men of the 2/2nd and 2/3rd Battalions were attached to 86 and 88 brigades of 29th Division seeing service at Suvla in September 1915. The Londoners of the 2/1st and 2/4th Battalions were attached to 1 Royal Naval Brigade at Helles. The purpose of these attachments was indoctrination into trench warfare alongside more experienced men. This was swift in coming as even on the march up to the lines on October 19 three men were wounded: Captain Morris, and Privates Housden and Maunder. The 2/4th Battalion were in the Eski Lines and saw the skeletal remains of the Worcester Regiment who had died in droves in the summer battles. They were in trenches which were in places only 15 yards apart and where 'bombing' occurred, that is grenade throwing.

In October much of the work was holding the line and working parties, but in November the weather took a definite turn for the worse, and winter quarters were built with 7,000 sandbags. The men were bombarded uncomfortably close by a Turkish big gun termed affectionately 'Asiatic Annie,' as she fired at them from the Asiatic coast, over the straits and onto the Gallipoli Peninsula. This was uncomfortable, but little damage seems to have been done to the men, although the French guns based near this 'rest camp' barked a reply in the general direction of 'Annie.' The first death in the battalion on the peninsula occurred on 7 November when Private Pfeiffer was shot in the head, dying on the way to hospital. He was buried at Pink Farm Cemetery the next day by the commanding officer, the Adjutant Major Seyd, and the Medical Officer, Lieutenant MacDonell. No one was safe from the harassing effect of artillery. Private Cope, Captain Steven's batman, was killed by a piece of shrapnel when clearing up his officer's dugout. He was hit in a neck artery and bled to death very quickly.[64]

The battalion was in the front line when 52nd Division on their left flank carried out a very successful attack on 5 November, firing mines under the Turkish trenches and assaulting the positions at Krithia Nullah. The 2/4th Battalion's task was to repair trenches and build a strongpoint in the lines. On November 21 a heavy barrage started on the British lines which forced the recall of all working parties to man battle positions in the trenches. A strong Turkish attack developed on the right hand battalion of the Naval Brigade, but this was beaten off easily and no Turks reached the British trenches except prisoners; all was back to normal by 6pm. Many head wounds were suffered by the troops, the head being the most exposed part of the body in trench warfare. Of the wounds suffered many were small but serious enough that an alternative to the cloth cap was searched for. In 1916 this would lead to the production of the steel helmet, but that was months away yet. Lectures on gas were given to the troops and gas masks issued although gas was never used on the peninsula. These were the normal daily routines of trench warfare, but the hot summer and autumn was soon to give way to awful winter weather.

On 26 November 'a storm broke over the Dardanelles which had been threatening for days'.[65] The wind increased during the afternoon, rain came down in torrents and the troops on the ground were caught like rats in a river bank, as their trenches became rivers and the dugouts flooded. The Fusiliers of the 2/3rd at Suvla were worst hit of any of the troops. A day later the wind shifted to the north and an icy wind froze the men and their equipment in the British trenches and several soldiers froze to death while struggling to return to brigade headquarters.[66] This was followed by snow, making the new enemy the weather, and simply to keep from freezing to death increased activity in repairing the trenches and working parties was carried out. The inevitable consequence of the flooding and collapse of many of the trenches was the activity of Turkish snipers accounting for several officers trying to restore the trenches after the storm blew itself out. Soldiers could return to some sort of normality although a large Turkish bombardment on 3 December caused more casualties.

In mid-December the British positions at Suvla Bay and Anzac Cove were evacuated, meaning that more Turkish attention could be lavished on the British positions at Helles, including the Londoners. Further front line duties continued in December for the London Brigades under their respective divisions. The casualty rate increased as the campaign returned to the Helles sector. The machine gun officer of the 2/4th, Lieutenant Dickins, was wounded in the head and Second Lieutenant Hicklenton was put in charge on 21 December. A frightening night followed in his new post, as one of the machine guns was struck by lightning. Even in their rest camp behind the lines they were not safe as 'Asiatic Annie' eventually claimed some victims with two men being killed and five wounded. The last Londoner to be killed on the peninsula was Private L.L. Thompson on 31 December, and he was buried by the officers in Orchard Gully Cemetery on 1 January 1916.[67]

Worsening winter weather and the intervention of Lord Kitchener all played their part in the proposed evacuation of the Dardanelles. The evacuation was carried out in stages and most of the troops were moved out before the final companies pulled out. The evacuation of 88 Brigade from Suvla and Anzac took place on 13 December. Men were being evacuated from Helles from the 31 December in small batches of about company size. Lieutenant Hicklenton was evacuated on 1 January, his machine gunners the following day, this process continuing until 8 January.

The evacuation of the Londoners attached to the Naval Brigade was carried out in complete secrecy. Men were pulled out in groups of about fifty, men staying in the firing lines to maintain a level of activity to give an impression of the normal routines of trench life. Just a few officers remained to erect barricades and set up the massive booby traps that were left for the Turks.

'A hurried roll call, in whispered tones, to find that only two men are missing, and we walk away at a brisk pace for the beach. The three mile journey to the beach is uneventful, and although we are all glad to get away from this detestable land of death and disease, yet one regrets to think of the vain sacrifices which have been made to hold this miserable stretch of territory.'[68]

The men boarded HMS *Grasshopper* via the River Clyde steamer at 'V' beach in a heavy swell:

> 'every man clinging to the nearest support to prevent being washed overboard. The seas get worse, and the destroyer rolls in an alarming manner, but the crew are splendid and in spite of great difficulties, they manage to get hot food and drink to some of our men who are badly injured or exhausted.'[69]

The men saw the booby traps and dumps go up in flames and the whole Turkish artillery opened fire on their former positions on the now abandoned peninsula. They had a grandstand on one of the major events of the campaign. For the moment though, they would return to Mudros and then Egypt to lick their wounds as part of 29th Division before reorganising themselves to serve with 53rd (Welsh) Division before being moved to France. They had been the first men of our division to be treated to the rigours of trench warfare as a cohesive unit. It had been a baptism of fire for them in the final months of a campaign that was doomed from the start; however things in France were hardly better. Once in France the London Battalions would be broken up and sent to the Territorial 47th Division rather than staying in the regular army 29th Division or the Welsh Division.[70]

* * *

A year after the Dardanelles peninsula was evacuated it was the turn of 58th Division to be sent to the front. It would have a further wait, for despite its apparent preparedness it was still months away from action. It moved to the Salisbury Plain area in mid-July 1916, the final preparation area for divisions going to the front and into the hutments vacated by 60th (2/2nd London) Division around Warminster at Sutton Veny and Heytesbury. It was now able to use the long established army training grounds of Salisbury Plain rather than its own sites across Suffolk, the plain affording a landscape and geology that matched that of the front line in France. The final training included brigade and divisional manoeuvres with live firing and artillery barrages. Salisbury Plain was already furnished with miles of trenches alongside both sides of the road over the Larkhill ranges that could be utilised for these manoeuvres.

The division was raising its esprit de corps by this final training. The wellbeing of the troops was very important and battalion and divisional orchestras were a part of this, with such names as the 'Transport Imps' and

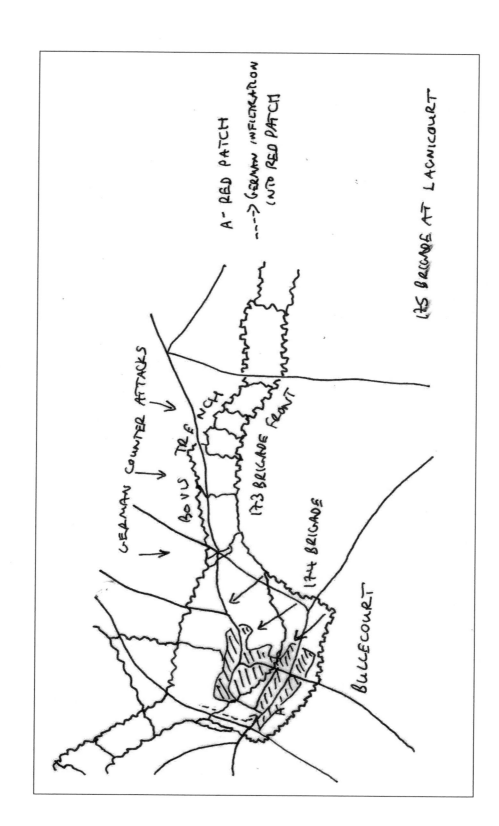

A - RED PATCH

---> GERMAN INFILTRATION INTO RED PATCH

GERMAN COUNTER ATTACKS

BOVIS TRENCH

173 BRIGADE FRONT

174 BRIGADE

BULLECOURT

175 BRIGADE AT LAGNICOURT

'the Goods,' these bands were extremely popular and would sustain the troops in France through hell and back. The soldiers were still employed in November to dig trenches, with the Fifth Battalion digging trenches at Imber on the plain. The division moved to Southampton in late January 1917 and went to a quiet part of the front line for its initiation into trench warfare.

The division moved to France via Le Havre and Rouen. The crossing was generally easily made, however some of the vessels were not ocean-going ships, but Hebridean Island ferries only certified for work close to the shore and some had to pull back into harbour as the sea was very rough. By mid-February the division was in the lines in the north of the old Somme battlefields, between Serre and Ransart, and around Gommecourt. As with the battalions sent to the Dardanelles the division was attached to a battle hardened division, 46th (North Midland) Division. In this period of trench acclimatisation the different London companies were attached to battalions of the Notts and Derby Regiment for several days in the trenches. The period of acclimatisation was gradually extended until the Londoners were able to defend the trench line by themselves. Although a quiet sector of the Somme battlefields was chosen, there were of course casualties. Private W.C. Folkard of the 3rd Battalion was one of the first to be killed on 1 February, and Fusilier Steadman was wounded along with Second Lieutenants Jakeman and Hall.

In this quiet sector the troops became accustomed to trench warfare, the dawn stand-to and night time alerts. The troops were kept busy in and out of the trenches, and the first period in the trenches was followed by a period behind the lines resting and performing labour for the Royal Engineers. A less than quiet period in the trenches was had by the 10th Battalion on 12-13 March 1917. The war diary relates that:

'nine trench mortar bombs dropped in our post number 5. [R.29.a.30.10] between 4.30 and 5pm. Ten rifle grenades [landed] at same spot in the morning, snipers active. Enemy aircraft active between 4 and 6pm. Enemy artillery active against our back areas, several gas shells dropped near Battalion Headquarters at 1.45am and shrapnel was burst against the same place at 10.30am.'[71]

Not only was the enemy fire effective but a sudden change in the weather led to a rapid thaw and some rain caused great dilapidation in the trenches. The division was becoming accustomed to the ways of trench warfare. A nominal number of casualties were expected and the first cases of shell shock occurred, weaker officers and men were sent home on medical grounds due to the weather and conditions. These were the natural wastage, the low level of casualties caused by holding the trenches and not particularly by combat.

The next day British artillery engaged in cutting gaps in the enemy wire. That evening after dark the artillery put down a screen for the officers to reconnoitre for a raid. The enemy were found to be good troops manning strong trenches protected by search lights making no man's land as light as day. The German infantry maintained a heavy and effective fire of rifles and rifle grenades on the Londoner's trenches. The raiding party got back without any casualties but left men wounded in the frontline trench. Casualties for the whole day were two officers and one man killed and two officers and six men wounded.

This experience was not untypical of life in the front line. The Londoners were growing into their role as infantrymen of the trenches; soldiers served in the front line for several days at a time, although in a relatively quiet sector such as Foncquevillers the soldiers were in the front line for up to six days by the end of their acclimatisation period.

It was here that rumours of a German retreat were started, when an order on 25 February stated that:

'indications point to the enemy having retired along front of V Corps. Patrols are being sent out towards Serre, Puisieux and Gommecourt. Be ready to send out patrols and to move on receipt of further orders. Patrols when ordered to be sent out should be platoon strength, with a Lewis Gun, to reconnoitre the German front line.'[72]

A patrol sent out that night found the Germans to be still in possession of their front line and the situation was still the same until 17 March, a fortnight later, when they were seen to have retired back to the newly built Hindenburg Line. Patrols sent out by the division occupied the enemy front lines, but were ordered not to advance forward and this order was completed by other units with more experience. What they found when they did eventually advance was a desolate landscape, the Germans having destroyed every building, uprooted trees and evacuated the majority of the civilian population. The 3rd Battalion advancing on Boiry-Saint-Martin 'pass[ed] through the following villages evacuated by the enemy; Monchy-au-Bois, Adinfer and Boiry-Sainte-Rictrude. These villages have all been demolished by the Germans and in no place was there a whole house standing. The roads have also been blown up at several points.'[73] They found booby traps but there were few casualties resulting as the devices were very crude and easy to spot. One soldier of the 6th Battalion was wounded by a booby trapped trip-wire on 11 April.

The Battle of Bullecourt in April and May 1917 was part of the operations at Arras, after the taking of Vimy Ridge that April. The battle was part of a move designed to penetrate the Hindenburg Line which was the new front line from Arras in the north to Soissons in the south. The British launched an operation with 2nd (Australian) Division, including the British 7th, 11th and 62nd (2nd West Riding) Divisions. This attack was a failure for the Australian and British forces in April but for 58th Division it was their baptism of fire into offensive warfare. The battle saw the village destroyed by the artillery as 'the last remaining houses of Bullecourt were demolished, though many walls still stood a few feet high, while the big cellars, on top of which the rubble acted as a bursting-course, were by no means all destroyed.'[74] Artillery from the London Division was concentrated with batteries from three infantry and one cavalry division to create a unified artillery bombardment. The 173 Brigade was brought into the battle on 12 May in order to relieve the 15th Australian Brigade. The 3rd and 4th London Battalions were in the front line with two companies of the 2nd in reserve.

The 10th Battalion raided Bovis Trench on 13 May. On 17 May the 11th Battalion provided two companies to carry stretcher cases back from the line, sustaining thirty casualties of their own in the process. The 175 Brigade was to come under the orders of 174 Brigade on the same day. This brigade was to attack the infamous 'Red Patch' with the 5th Battalion at 2am on 17 May from near the railway line. The Red Patch was an area of the village near the British lines that was deemed impossible to take and hold due to the German ability to infiltrate troops back in again. Some debate has been made about the role of 58th Division at Bullecourt, with it being accused of merely mopping up the village. Whilst it seems to have made the final attack on the village, the most costly period for the division was in June after the end of the main battle. The initial attack was frontal, made against a defended position, but as J.E. Edmonds, the official historian of the British Army, says 'the enemy was in the midst of preparations, such as the demolition of cellars and dug-outs, for evacuation of the section of which he still held.'[75]

The attack was indeed easily achieved after a hurricane two-minute bombardment and took twenty-three prisoners and five machine guns. The 5th Battalion suffered light casualties with one officer and seven other ranks killed and twenty-one wounded. Almost immediately the 8th Battalion rushed through the 5th Battalion position, took and held the rest of the village taking another thirteen prisoners. The 6th Battalion attacked Bovis Trench on 21 May but the attack did not achieve the objectives due to problems with the flanks and the objective being destroyed by artillery fire. A wounded Second Lieutenant Pickup stated to an officer:

> 'there was no hitch in forming up for attack and the German wire was no obstacle. [I] saw no dug-outs in Bovis Trench. Bovis Trench strongly held. Germans lying just behind it. Heard them call out to our men who were in it to 'dig in'.... [He] believes from various things that Germans were prepared and waiting for our attack.'

He was wounded twice and captured, disarmed and then freed due to his men shooting the Germans, and subsequently crawled back to the British lines. Another survivor Sergeant Garrick 'jumped into a trench almost as soon as barrage lifted off it. [I] was bombed from [the] rear of trench and wounded.' He lay in a shell hole about 20 yards from Bovis Trench until 11pm that night when he had tried to crawl back 'when the Boche barrage and our own started about 9pm. On his way back he nearly crawled into a Boche listening post in a shell hole between Bovis Trench and our lines. '[I] was challenged but they did not fire.'[76]

The initial attack may have been carried with some ease but the German counter-attacks were ferocious.

> 'Really, Alf, I never thought I should come out to tell the tale, it was real hell. Fritz put up a bombardment on our trenches that the boys will never forget. For three hours we laid in the bottom of the trenches awaiting our end. Here and there our trenches were going up and our boys were blown to pieces. I could not have stuck it out much longer. My nerves were starting to give way, officers and men were continually going out with shell shock. It was terrible and I shall never forget the ghastly sights and the stench of the dead was terrible.'[77]

The only consolation was the casualties they wrought on the Germans, lying four deep in front of the trenches.

On a couple of normal days in the line in Bullecourt the 10th Battalion suffered six other ranks killed and twenty-four wounded, another day Second Lieutenant Chapman was sent out with shell shock and three ranks were wounded. The total casualties of the London Division were 32 officers and 680 other ranks (not including those of 175 Brigade at Lagnicourt). Lieutenant V.A. Finlayson of the 5th was unfortunate enough to fall down a well about 90feet deep, but was eventually extracted after six hours without undue physical harm except fatigue; such were the dangers of urban warfare.

The Battle of Bullecourt was over and the division was holding part of the Hindenburg Line proper to the north-east of the village. It was here that they would have a more trying time in defending the position in June 1917. The Germans evacuated the last of Bullecourt by the end of May and retired to the main Hindenburg position to the north-east. The Londoners were moved up to this position and managed to establish a foothold with 173 Brigade plus the 8th Battalion in early June.

A raid was made on the German lines on 14 June at 2.15am. The raid captured two prisoners of the German 119th Reserve-Infanterie-Regiment (RIR), a machine gun, and destroyed two more guns with grenades. The British casualties were Second Lieutenant G.W. Hills and four other ranks killed and two officers and thirty-eight ranks wounded, seven other ranks were posted as missing.

Lieutenant G. Joy of the 10th Battalion won a posthumous Military Cross capturing a hostile machine gun single handed, whilst in charge of a raiding party. He also attacked six of the enemy single handed, killing two of them and although wounded, remained in charge of his party.[78] The result had been hardly worth it but this was part of the give and take of trench warfare. On 15-16 June the Germans launched a large raid to recover the position. One of the 2nd Battalion soldiers who lost his life that night was Tom King who wrote home in a letter on 5 April 'Tell 'Wilkie' I will write her when I get back from Hell again.'[79]

For the rest of the London Division in June there was a last trial operation to give them military training called 'Operation Logeast' which took place in an area of old German trenches behind the lines in the area evacuated by the Germans that spring. Logeast Wood was near Achiet-le-Grand and Miraumont, south of Arras. The aim was to learn the mopping-up of areas taken and especially woods and villages. The devastation of the battlefield meant that a village was much like a wood and vice versa, especially as Logeast Wood had been part of the German lines when they had occupied the area. Here the division was gassed en masse as part of the training; except that the wind changed and the gas was blown away. They also took part in manoeuvres with live artillery barrages to accustom the troops to working with a creeping barrage. The diary of the 11th Battalion refers to one soldier being killed and two wounded in this period, but whether this was due to enemy action, accidents or part of the training is not related.

Part of life away from the front was forming working parties, and for 175 Brigade this involved railway construction at Achiet-le-Grand. The Amiens to Arras railway was being rebuilt after three years in the battlefield with additional light railways from Achiet. One was built to Mory by elements of 58th Division in order to support the fighting at Bullecourt.[80] The men of the infantry brigades were attached to the Royal Engineers as a labour battalion. Another battalion repaired the road from Hamel to Thiepval on the old Somme battlefield. Railway work was under the direction of Brigadier Generals A.C. Joly de Lotbinière, Corps Commander Royal Engineers (attached I Anzac Corps)[81] and A.J. Craven (V Corps) of the Royal Engineers. The men were housed in Nissen hut camps and prefabricated shelters built on the devastated wilderness of the former battlefields. The actual running of the railways was under the Anzac Light Railways detachment. However any available labour was used and in this case the Londoners provided their services as labour gangs. This period of labour lasted throughout May and was continued in June and July.

The division was moved in July to the Havrincourt sector of the Hindenburg Line about 10 miles south-east of their position at Bullecourt. Here the trenches had been dug by the Guards' Division and were generally in tip-top condition. The troops certainly enjoyed being in these trenches as it was generally a quiet sector of the line. The exceptions were trench raids made by the Germans on 12 and 20-21 July. The 9th Battalion raided the German position known as Mow Cop on 21 and Wigan Copse on 23 July. The 10th Battalion was raided as was the adjoining 3rd Division.

The German artillery set up a barrage on the 10th Battalion lines to prevent reinforcements moving forward or runners getting out with information. This occurred between 10.30pm and 11.15pm in various stages by all calibres of guns from trench mortars up to 8inch howitzers. Battalion headquarters received a direct hit, incapacitating a company commander and rendering another unfit to continue his command. The communication with British artillery was bad and the British response to the attack was not regarded as adequate by Colonel Sadlier-Jackson. The raiding party of two officers and 100 men emerged in two parties from Havrincourt Park, moving on Ashton Alley and along the western side of Shropshire Spur. The Spur party never reached the British line and was obviously pinned down. The remaining attack split into three columns with the right column moving up to the British F sap, the centre one up Oxford Valley and the left column towards an abandoned section of British trench.

The attack was defeated and regarded as 'feeble' by the colonel and hardly achieved a foothold in the British lines, leaving one wounded soldier of the 86th Regiment who was brought in from no man's land. The British casualties from the barrage were five other ranks killed and one officer and twenty-nine other ranks wounded. The raid seems to have been defeated by excellent work from a Lewis gunner, and six runners were praised by Colonel Sadlier-Jackson for 'continually running through the barrage and were entirely responsible for keeping me informed with information as to what was happening.'[82] The runners were Privates G. Rose, W. Tyler, T. James, W. Turner, W.J. Johnson and R. Barlow. The German artillery had not been effective and the runners had been very brave and lucky. The emphasis on raids would revisit the division soon when it next moved sector.

Reinforcements would have been greatly welcomed to replace men such as Archie English. Having been wounded in the 1915 battles in France, he was returned to Britain to recover, never to return to the front line.

'Safe in Blighty. We landed at Southampton yesterday morning and as I'm a Londoner they sent me up here: Stockport [near Manchester]. I asked to be sent to London too. But that's the army all over.... Now you shouldn't trouble in the slightest about coming all this way to see me, for it's one deuce of a trip. I really think getting a POSH wound is well worth it. Otherwise I shouldn't have any leave this year, judging by the way they are dishing it out in France. We were talking about it a few weeks ago and far as we could gather the rank and file of the more or less fortunate 1/11th (Finsbury) Battalion will be going on leave somewhere about 1920 - if they're lucky!'[83]

Archie didn't get back to a London hospital, staying at the Stepping Hill Hospital, Hazel Grove, Stockport, and then going to the St John Auxiliary Hospital at Morecombe. The only future enemy action he saw were the dubious attentions of a nurse called Maggie, who was full of forced smiles and unwanted hand holding when no one else could see them. Previously wounded men returned to their units having recovered and replacements came out from the third line units in England. For the division the next move to Belgium was to see it heavily committed. For the moment most of August was spent resting, refitting and training behind the lines for the campaign in Flanders.

Notes

59 Aspinall-Oglander C.F. 1932 *Military Operations*, Gallipoli, Vol II (London) p. 390-391
60 National Army Museum, the papers of Howard Hicklenton, 6th August 1915
61 The SS *Southlands* was saved and steamed to Mudros by the crew of HMS *Racoon*. However the Colonel and 32 men drowned when a life boat capsized.

62 National Army Museum 2001/06/14 letters of 2nd Lieutenant Howard Hicklenton 2/4th Battalion City of London, Royal Fusiliers

63 National Army Museum 2001/06/14 letters of 2nd Lieutenant Howard Hicklenton 2/4th Battalion City of London, Royal Fusiliers

64 Anonymous, 1919 *History of the old 2/4th*, (London) p.61

65 Anonymous, *The History of the old 2/4th Battalion*, (London) 1919, p.58

66 O'Neill, H.C. Royal Fusiliers in the Great War, (Heathfield) p103ff

67 Private L.L. Thompson is buried in Skew Bridge Cemetery, Gallipoli, Turkey.

68 Anonymous, 1919 *The History of the old 2/4th Battalion*, (London) p.70

69 Anonymous, 1919 *The History of the old 2/4th Battalion*, (London) p.70ff

70 29 Division took part in the first day of the Battle of the Somme, sustaining heavy casualties. Their trenches and men are commemorated at the Newfoundland Battlefield Memorial Park at Beaumont Hamel. 47 Division did not take part in the Somme battle until 15 September when it participated in the first tank attack at High Wood where it is also commemorated.

71 National Archives WO95/3009 war diary

72 National Archives, WO95/3005 war diary

73 National Archives WO95/3001 war diary

74 Edmonds, J.E. 1940 *Military Operations* 1917, Vol I (London) p.459

75 Edmonds, J.E. 1940 *Military Operations* 1917, Vol I (London) p.478

76 National Archives WO95/3005 report on 175 Brigade

77 IWM archives 89/7/1 Papers of W.T. King

78 Lt. G Joy died of his wounds (16/7/1917) and is buried at St Sever C.W.G.C. Cemetery, Rouen.

79 IWM archives 89/7/1 papers of W.T. King. Tom King has no known grave and is commemorated on the Arras Memorial.

80 Edmonds, J.E. *Military Operations* 1917, Vol. I (London) 1940 p.457

81 A.C. Joly de Lotbiniere was a Canadian Engineer and forms part of the story in chapter 7

82 National Archives, WO95/3009 report of the Eleventh Battalion

83 IWM, 97/10/1 Papers of Archie English

Chapter 4

St Julien
1–20 September 1917

The initial phase of the Third Battle of Ypres had taken place and was but three weeks old when 58th Division received its orders to entrain for the Ypres Salient on 20 August 1917. The division moved from Arras station, then travelled to Proven, Hopoutre and Godevaersvelde. Two brigades of 58th Division, 174 and 175 were to take over from 48th (South Midland) Division and part of the front of 11th Division with 51st (Highland) Division already fighting to its north at St Julien and Langemarck. The Third Battle of Ypres was a maelstrom and it was into this that 58th Division, as part of the XVIII Corps, was attacking to the north of Ypres from St Julien towards Poelcappelle.

The infamous Ypres Salient was shaped like a sickle around the Belgian town of Ypres, including the Messines Ridge to the south looking like the handle. The salient always remained this shape, just changing in dimensions between 1914 and 1918. The British and French held the high ground in 1914 after the First Battle of Ypres. In May 1915 German gas attacks forced the British back to Ypres as a result of the Second Battle of Ypres, from then until 1917 the Germans held the high ground, the British and French were pushed onto the low ground under constant observation. In 1917 the Anglo-French attack of the Third Battle of Ypres pushed up to the high ground again. In early 1918 the pressure of the German Spring Offensive along the whole front forced a British withdrawal back down to the gates of Ypres in the Fourth Battle of Ypres fought mostly for the Kemmelberg Hills. In the final offensives of 1918 the Belgian army was given the honour of clearing out the salient.

The names that the division would become accustomed to in the landscape of the salient are the British names that were marked on the trench maps. Many are the same as one sees looking at a 1901 Ordnance Survey map of England: Surbiton Villas, The Rectory, Ascot Cottage, all sounding very suburban and Edwardian. There are three types of name though, Flemish names corrupted into English, such as Ypres becoming *Wipers*, and there are descriptive names such as Hellfire Corner, Shrapnel Corner, which would give the average Tommy an idea of their notoriety.[84] Then there were names that regiments gave to sites such as Black Watch Corner, Vancouver Corner, Gallipoli and even La Belle Alliance (from the Battle of Waterloo) and Monument de Hibou in the old French sector. It was easy to find places where certain nationalities had fought, Vancouver Corner, Winnipeg, and Calgary Grange, and from the other side Berlin, Hamburg and Potsdam. Lastly there were the very Edwardian names, a type of jest, names from home such as Sanctuary Wood, Mousetrap Farm, Cheddar Villa. The officers and commanders of the British troops in the area at the time gave these names to features in the landscape. It is the British names that feature in this description of the battles.

The nature of the names attached to the buildings in the landscape was made worse by the fact that the Germans took over existing farm buildings and constructed concrete bunkers inside them. These were referred to by the Germans as *Mannschafts Eisenbeton Unterstände.* (reinforced concrete personnel shelter) or MEBU which was used by the English in lieu, or replaced by farm, the original site function.[85] So when the British attacked, the very industrial name of the farm became a byword for death as an industry, in this case men were mown by the industrial machine guns, thus heightening the horror of the name.[86]

The attacks in August had become stuck in the quagmire and new tactics had to be found to make better progress. In the area taken over by 58th Division north and east of St Julien 48th (South Midland) Division had faltered and stopped just short of the Vancouver Triangle around Springfield. In fact in this area of the battlefield the lines had barely changed since 31 July, the first day of the battle. The village of St Julien fell on 16 August as the 20th (Light) Division took Langemarck. Then 48th Division attacked towards Vancouver Corner, but advanced only slightly in attacks made between 19-31 August in increasingly bad weather. Captain Edwin Campion Vaughan's description of this failed attack in *Some Desperate Glory* is horrific, with the wounded drowning as the shell holes fill with rain water.[87]

The Tank Corps had briefly made good progress but only with enemy strong points that were close to hard road surfaces. The tanks were hindered as they could only use the roads as the fields were too muddy, and the amount of traffic on the roads meant they could not get to the front. A composite company made up of the tanks that made it to the front under Major Broome co-operated with two infantry companies of 11th and 48th

Division in action on 19 August. The attack involved two tanks for each objective and three in reserve. They used the roads both to get to the front and during the action which was targeting several strong points on the front at Cockcroft, Maison de Hibou, the Triangle and Hillock Farm.

According to I Brigade Tank Corps:

'All the strong points except Triangle Farm were cleared of the enemy by the tanks and occupied by the infantry.... Triangle Farm was engaged only by one female tank [equipped only with machine guns] which slipped from the road and became ditched, having had all its Lewis Guns put out of action by the enemy's fire. The crew of this tank got away under cover of darkness at nightfall; the commander of this tank fell into the hands of the enemy, but succeeded in effecting his escape.'[88]

The British were nibbling away at the German front line, but even the most modern weapons were not helping them, and the main result was that the landscape was filling up with broken-down tanks.

The first units of the London Division to see action in the salient were 175 Brigade, with the 12th Battalion followed shortly by the 11th in late August. In order to minimise casualties and to alleviate the obvious overcrowding of the salient the front lines of the division east of St Julien were manned as outpost lines, held by two companies, each with two platoons in the front line and two in support, one company in St Julien, one company around Cheddar Villa. The support battalion was held in readiness on the canal bank 6,000 yards away. This was described as a mixture of German infantry tactics and French artillery methods as the French relied on their Soixante-Quinze, or 75 millimetre guns, to hold the line with artillery fire.[89]

The Germans had developed defence in depth with an outpost line, a defence line and battalions held nearby to counter-attack, a tactic that 58th Division would encounter as they attacked in September 1917. By copying German methods they had countered the German threat to some degree, and by using French artillery methods they became a dynamic force and spared the infantry casualties and hand-to-hand fighting. The Germans were obviously sitting in their defences, with no threat of a large scale counter-attack as the British would not risk losing much of their artillery that was concentrated so close to the front. The only problem of using artillery in such close proximity to the infantry was the amount of casualties it could cause if things went wrong. Liaison and communication were of the highest level, as were training and information for the infantry who had to follow the barrage closely so as not to give the Germans time to man their parapets.

In between the front line and the supporting battalion on the canal bank was all the field artillery of four divisions and a large amount of heavy artillery. This was the area from the canal bank towards Wieltje, an area now including the cemeteries of Divisional Collecting Post, New Irish Farm, La Belle Alliance, Buff's Road, Wieltje Farm, and Track X cemeteries.[90] The area is hidden from the current German front lines at Langemarck and Vancouver Corner, and so was the perfect place to put all the artillery, a fact the Germans saw through aerial reconnaissance resulting in frequent shelling. The area is flat and so perfect for the artillery and railways that were being built there but it would have become quite hemmed in, hence the need to reduce the amount of personnel held there.

The front line battalions were entrusted with the holding of the line in depth and even in the case of a German attack it was more important that the battalions training for the offensive to the west of the canal should carry on their training than that they should be moved up to deal with any local German attacks. Contrary to popular belief the battalions were only in the line for a maximum of four nights of trench holding after which they had to be rested, less if they were in an offensive. No company was to be in the most advanced line, the piquet line, for more than twenty-four hours, otherwise they would be too tired and battle weary to be effective.

British commanders were soon aware that their tactics were not working in the wet conditions prevalent in the salient, and a new way had to be found to press the offensive forward. General Herbert Plumer was leading now at the expense of Gough, and at the same time 58th Division was brought into the line. The division's first task was to settle in but in the first week it was to take part in four planned night time trench raids that were part of the continuing offensive spirit in the salient. This was to harass the Germans and take a series of important points in the German line as a prelude to the next offensive on 20 September. Headquarters ordained that due to the increasing deterioration in the weather large scale operations would be delayed. Their insistence was that the enemy must be continually harassed. There was only so much the artillery was able to do to this end. The divisional commanders were ordered to start a series of trench raids, by surrounding hostile positions by night with platoon sized operations. This was deemed far more likely to produce results than a full-on infantry assault on the whole front by daylight. To this end Maxse, the Corps Commander, ordered active patrolling and that every battalion under his command should undertake 'at least one enterprise during every tour of duty at the Corps front'. Platoons were to be drilled and trained especially for this purpose with artillery support in the offensive.[91] The selected targets were Winnipeg and the Cemetery on the Vancouver to Zonnebeke road and two points near Vancouver Corner in Hubner Trench and Kereselare. The attacks were to be made in the second week of September.

The first raid was to the east of St Julien to Winnipeg and Jury Farm, a MEBU or pill box that jutted out into the British line and could not be captured by frontal assault in the usual way during daylight. The attack was planned for the night of 8-9 September and the attacking troops were B and C companies of the 9th Battalion of 175 Brigade. It is covered in detail in the battalion history. The importance of the raid, that would become a feature of future attacks under Maxse, was the attempt to flank the positions rather than attack them head on.

The aim was to attack and take Spot Farm from the direction of Springfield, take the cemetery from Spot Farm, enable the capture of the crossroads west of Winnipeg from the direction of the cemetery, take a commanding German pill-box at C.d.12.8.8. (army map reference) and finally capture Winnipeg itself. Each of these was to be carried out in a separate operation by stealth raid at night and the object was to surround and capture the garrison. This would facilitate the next offensive by pushing the Germans out of positions that had caused so much harm in the August attacks. The course of the raid was very complicated but the result was a near success.

Patrols were to be sent out to find out the location of posts on the Springfield – Winnipeg road and their strength, the condition of ground between our posts and the Springfield – Winnipeg road and the possibility of working round Spot Farm to the east. A further note was that due to the weather at the time, patrols were to be sent back to the canal bank on completion of their duties to receive hot food and decent accommodation. That meant a further hour's march back to these rest areas, but in compensation hot food and better rest when they got there.

Number 7 and 8 Platoons of 'B' Company were able to take Jury Farm, and found that Spot Farm had been demolished by a 9.5 inch artillery shell with a direct hit and was untenable as a position. Number 8 Platoon pushed onto Winnipeg crossroads and dug in on the east side of it. Unfortunately the Company Commander Captain Walker was wounded having gone up on a personal reconnaissance and it took an hour to get him to a place of safety.

'C' Company was unable to take Springfield and this meant that 'B' Company was unable to hold the remnants of Jury Farm, being under fire from German positions on their flanks and rear. They started with a handicap in that eight men were gassed by the British gas barrage of that evening and reinforcements had to be found, and nine men were lost the previous night, so the reinforcements were a section from another platoon unfamiliar with the ground. The platoons attacking here were under heavy fire from the start and were unable to gain any ground beyond the cemetery. Thus the main German position referred to by its coordinates as C.12.d.8.8 was never taken and with its large garrison of around twenty men was able to prevent the raid achieving its objectives.

The casualties of the raid for the 9th Battalion were Captain Walker, who died of his wounds four days later, Lieutenant Wightwick, one other rank killed and three wounded, and the eight men gassed prior to the raid. German casualties appear to have been thirteen prisoners, some wounded men who were left behind and at least a dozen killed. The battalion was relieved soon afterwards and began its training for the offensive; it was in reserve on 20 September and took part in the attack of 26 September. The raid was reported in London and the Lord Mayor of London wrote to the battalion to congratulate them on their achievements, a view endorsed soon afterwards by Field Marshal Haig. The second raid was meant to continue the work that the first had started, but due to a report by Captain Rose it was postponed indefinitely, due to its being untenable as an operation. Captain Simms wrote:

> 'From information given by Mr Rose I am of the opinion that to carry out the present plan would be an unjustifiable risk of sacrifice of life and I do not think it could possibly succeed. I have an alternate plan but since it entails artillery co-operation it cannot be carried out tonight.'

The third raid was in the area north of the Vancouver Corner–Winnipeg road, at The Promenade, on the southern end of Hubner Trench. This was carried out by the 6th Battalion of 174 Brigade. Two platoons of 'B' Company were detailed for the raid, and they were supported by a hurricane bombardment on the position, a very short and intense bombardment, and protected by a box barrage around it. They lost their commander, Captain Webb, to a 'friendly-fire' shell burst which killed him, the raiders then met severe resistance from the German positions which were well prepared for resistance; so despite some intense exchanges of grenades and rifle fire, nothing much was gained and the raiders retreated with the loss of seven missing including Captain Webb. In fact some sources from the time blame all casualties on the British bombardment whose shells were falling short. This would be a tense time for all as the training for the main offensive on 20 September continued.

The fourth raid on 7-8 September was to attack a MEBU or bunker east of Kereselare which formed the south part of Hubner Trench with the 8th Battalion, also of 174 Brigade. This was just south of the previous raid by the 6th Battalion. The objective was a fortified shell hole at C.6.d.65.95 and was led by Lieutenant Watson and a party of thirty-two riflemen. The party consisted of a covering section who would hold a hedge line in no man's land. It is interesting that a hedge line still existed here, as this part of the front had only recently come into the battle, perhaps it was not as thick as the raiding party would have hoped. Unfortunately the Germans were on their guard and discovered the covering party, so the raiders, under orders to attack if discovered, all attacked at once. The position was taken and it was discovered that the shell hole was linked by a trench to a number of other shell holes and ultimately with a pill box. This pill box was engaged and a considerable amount of machine gun fire was returned. The raiders were then recalled, returning to their positions without further loss. Casualties to the raiding party were two wounded by grenades, one by machine gun fire, and two men escaped wounds with machine gun bullet holes in their helmets.[92] The casualties to the covering party were caused once again by British shelling, killing two other ranks, wounding Second Lieutenant Watson and four other men including an orderly. The British covering barrage prevented fire coming from Hubner Farm.

The partial success of the trench raids was their small scale, which if successful would have advanced the line and taken some of the more troublesome enemy positions in the direct path of 58th Division. By nibbling away at the enemy front they achieved more than a full scale assault by day, as the attacks of 48th Division had shown. The trench raids had shown that success was possible if surprise was used, which was often the problem with Great War attacks, surprise was often not possible. Flanking manoeuvres, taking positions from the flanks was always a possibility. Now the commanders resorted back to artillery to try and destroy particular positions.

On 10 September a heavy artillery shoot was attempted on the MEBU at Jury Farm, but the results were not really worth the effort. Brigadier General H.C. Jackson in command of 175 Brigade reported:

'With regard to the artillery shoot today, it entirely failed in its object; ie. to destroy the Mebus. Everything was in their favour – excellent light, a splendid view of the target from the Observation

Point in St Julien, the most careful observation by a most experienced observer (the Group Commander was observing all day by himself). Two hundred and fifty shells of 6inch and 9.2inch were fired, the ground was ploughed up all round, the garrison, no doubt were frightened, but the net damage done was a chip off one corner. Further to that such barrages entail the withdrawal of such important garrisons as Spot Farm.... There is always the risk that the enemy might slip back there before these posts can be reoccupied by us after dark. Secondly if the shoot succeeds, it removes cover which might be valuable to us when we have captured it.'[93]

This was the problem with the battles; the decision to be made was between too much artillery or not enough. By destroying concrete positions you deny yourself cover; the first trench raid showed that a destroyed bunker led to a withdrawal from an untenable position. The realisation was that some other way to take positions, which were usually concrete bunkers, would have to be found, otherwise this David and Goliath situation between the bunkers, the infantry and the artillery would remain. Command had tried everything, infantry, artillery, tanks, trench raids by night, but with the passing days the emphasis would be on the offensive again, and it was General Plumer who would take the lessons of the trench raids and play it on a larger stage in the Battle of the Menin Road Ridge.

At 3am on 14 September 'A' Company of the 1st Battalion made a company attack on Winnipeg from the direction of Springfield. This attack was a failure in every regard. Of the approximate 120 men who made the attack 87 other ranks were reported missing. The failure of the attack was reported as being due to the strength of the enemy in the positions assaulted.

The Germans counter-attacked at 7.30pm and their attempt was also a failure. After the partial success of the trench raids active patrolling was carried out on the front with the object of gaining contact with the enemy, destroying isolated posts in order to push the enemy line back, disrupt or kill enemy wiring parties. The trench raids meant that the Germans were kept on the defensive, kept under stress and a source of intelligence was maintained. The division's men were seeing more action, although some of these battalions were pulled out of the line and did not take part in the offensive on 20 September.

The key to a successful offensive was the co-operation of different corps of the army, the infantry, Royal Flying Corps, artillery, headquarters, the newly formed Tank Corps and, of course, the Machine Gun Corps. The artillery destroyed enemy positions, morale, and caused casualties, often giving away the exact timing of the offensive (which had happened far too often). The infantry then attacked close behind the barrage, mopping up and taking positions, the Machine Gun Corps laid down a barrage of their own over the heads of the infantry, stopping reinforcements from reaching the enemy front line, and causing casualties behind the enemy front line. The tanks, where they were available, crushed enemy barbed wire, subdued enemy machine gun positions and acted as a general morale crushing factor. The Royal Flying Corps gained aerial superiority, was able to report enemy movements, the fall of artillery, harass the enemy and report infantry gains from pre-arranged signals. It was this cooperation that was being taught prior to the attacks on 20 September, but many factors were in operation both for and against this, including the weather and the ground condition, and if any part of this system broke down it could spell trouble for the infantry on the ground.

The training area for 20 September was at Reigersburg Chateau. This training for the battalions of 58th Division appears to have been overseen by a committee appointed by Maxse, much to the annoyance of the General Officer Commanding, Hew Fanshawe.[94] Maxse may have imposed this training committee as he did not think Fanshawe was a good enough trainer to be left in charge of operations, but Fanshawe must have felt as if he had been undermined. In later correspondence with Maxse he defends his decision to remain quiet on this point, but it was to work against him in the long run.

The key to the coming offensive on the Wurst Farm Ridge was the behaviour of the infantry. They were training to carry out quite a complex manoeuvre, perhaps something more worthy of the parade ground than of battle conditions. The initial attack was to be made by the 8th Battalion, making a direct frontal assault, then each of the 5th Battalion and the 6th Battalion would pass through and the former turn right along the German positions and the latter left along the Stroombeek valley, a very complicated manoeuvre. This involved careful planning and execution with compass bearings to be followed and objectives to be secured. In the vanguard of the attack was 174 Brigade and it was now crucial to get the riflemen ready for the offensive:

'Every minute's training must be concentrated on the particular task in hand in the coming battle. The men in the ranks must be told everything [on] how he is part of an advance all along the line. Now 174 Brigade has the most difficult and therefore the most honourable task, namely that of taking and holding the Wurst Farm heights.'[95]

Maxse was a great trainer and believed thoroughly that the attacks should be rehearsed and the troops fully informed of their role in the battle. Training for the attacks on 20 September was carried out at Reigersburg Chateau, just behind the canal lines, but was later moved into France when German aerial interference caused casualties. There was no doubt where the next attack would fall; it was just a question of tactics as to whether Plumer would succeed where others had failed.

Notes

84 Martin, The *Landscape and Memory of War*, unpublished thesis, The Nottingham Trent University, 1998, p17

85 McCarthy, C. 1995 *The Third Ypres, Passchendaele, the Day by Day Account*. (London) p.7

86 Please refer to the maps for place names in the text

87 Vaughan, E. 2011 *Some Desperate Glory*, Barnsley

88 National Archives WO95/100 Papers relating to I Brigade, Tank Corps

89 National Archives WO95/3003 174 Brigade to Battalion Commanders

90 C.W.G.C. 2004 *Cemeteries and Memorials in Belgium and Northern France*, (Clermont-Ferrand)

91 National Archives WO95/3003 G.S. 66/114 (General Staff XVIII Corps) 28 August 1917

92 National Archives W095/3003

93 National Archives W095/3007

94 see Chapter 7 'Winter'

95 National Archives WO95/3007 175 Infantry Brigade

Chapter 5

'Devils'
The Battle of London Ridge
20–26 September 1917

The infamous Ypres Salient was soon taking its toll on the division and the casualties started to rise. On 1 September one officer and four other ranks were wounded, on 2 September forty other ranks were wounded. In the period to 19 September twenty-one officers and 404 other ranks were wounded including one officer and 109 other ranks gassed.[96] These were partly due to the trench raids which were undertaken and partly to the conditions of trench warfare.

The raids of 7 and 14 September had cleared the way for the attack at Wurst Farm ridge, by moving the line forward and disturbing the Germans' preparations. The term ridge used in context with the attacks here at Vancouver Corner is a misinterpretation; it is not a ridge by any stretch of the imagination. East of the position near Wurst Farm there is a growing ridge that continued all the way round Passchendaele and southwards in the shape of a sickle. At Vancouver this is but a slight rise in the ground. There is, however, enough of a ridge that a windmill was built here by the Belgians before the war. There was a tactical advantage to be gained by attacking and holding this ridge to the south, but not at Vancouver Corner where it is hard to define, as it is so gentle a slope.

Fresh battalions were brought in for the attack; those bloodied in the trench raids were not used in this battle. Lieutenant Colonel Derviche-Jones says in his history of the 8th Battalion that in normal circumstances an attack by a battalion at the strength of 430 men of all ranks on an 800 yard frontage would be doomed to failure. However in this thoroughly rehearsed attack, despite problems with the tanks, the tactic of breaking through and turning really worked. This is proved by the claims by one German officer prisoner who regarded it as 'not fair, as a frontal battle all along the front had been expected, and prepared for'.[97]

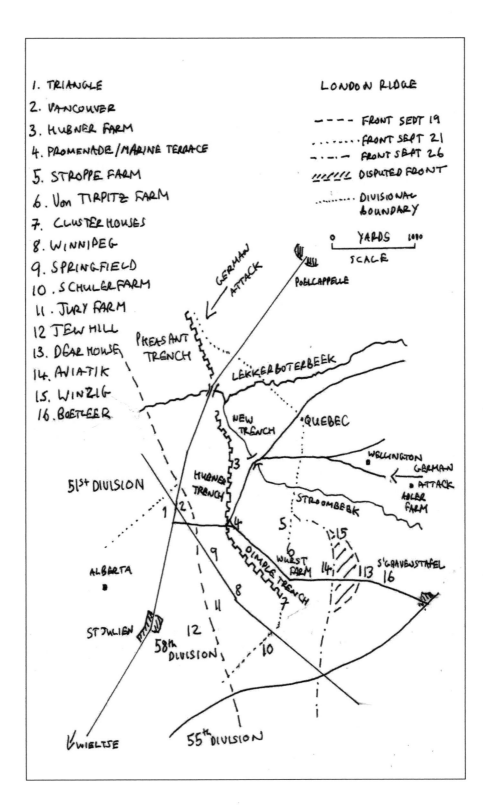

1. TRIANGLE
2. VANCOUVER
3. HUBNER FARM
4. PROMENADE/MARINE TERRACE
5. STROPPE FARM
6. Von TIRPITZ FARM
7. CLUSTER HOUSES
8. WINNIPEG
9. SPRINGFIELD
10. SCHULER FARM
11. JURY FARM
12. JEW HILL
13. DGar HOUSE
14. AVIATIK
15. WINZIG
16. BOETLEER

LONDON RIDGE

- - - - FRONT SEPT 19
. . . . . . FRONT SEPT 21
- . - . - FRONT SEPT 26
/////// DISPUTED FRONT
. . . . . . DIVISIONAL BOUNDARY

0   YARDS   1000
         SCALE

GERMAN ATTACK

POELCAPPELLE

PHEASANT TRENCH

LEKKERBOTERBEEK

NEW TRENCH

QUEBEC

WELLINGTON

GERMAN ATTACK

ADLER FARM

51st DIVISION

HUBNER TRENCH

3

STROOMBEEK

1 2

4

5

6 WURST FARM

DIMPLE TRENCH

9

15

14 113 16

S'GRAVENSTAFEL

ALBERTA

8

7

11

12

10

ST JULIEN

58th DIVISION

WIELTJE

55th DIVISION

The two attacking divisions of Maxse's XVIII Corps were to take the Gravenstafel and Langemarck spurs.[98] The 174 Brigade of 58th Division was to attack whilst 173 Brigade solely mounted a demonstration to divert the attention of the enemy with a 'Chinese attack' made by C Company of the 3rd Battalion. This was to be a feature of Maxse's command and very effective it was too. This shows concern over losses by the High Command and knowledge that huge losses could not be taken without any advance. The 55th (1/West Lancashire) Division to the right was to advance on the Gravenstafel Spur, whilst on the left 51st (Highland) Division attacked towards Poelcappelle.

In 58th Division the 8th Battalion were to attack the Blue Line, followed by the 5th attacking the Brown Line while 6th Battalion passed through and established a new front line. The 8th Battalion attacked and held the line, the 5th Battalion passed through and turned right along the German line and the 6th Battalion passed through and turned left. The attack was in an easterly direction and along the Wurst Farm Ridge, in much the same way that the trench raids were east of St Julien. Part of the line of assembly follows the modern hedge at the rear of the Canadian 1915 memorial. The aim was to break through then roll along the German line rather than attack it head on all the way along, thus minimising casualties. The 8th Battalion were to attack Hubner Farm, Genoa Farm, and Marine View on the right.[99]

This was to be supported by six tanks of 13 Company, E Battalion Tank Corps, of the 1 Tank Brigade. These were to advance with 174 Infantry Brigade, and the number was increased to give added force to the attackers. The tanks involved were E.7 Explosive and E.18 Extirpator with the objective of Cluster House; E.17 Exterminator and E.3 Eclipse with the objective of Wurst Farm; E.19 Eradicator and E.16 Eliminator with the objective of Clifton House. This would certainly have added weight to the attack, but on the day the tanks were unable to reach the front and did not take part, leaving the infantry to go on the offensive themselves.

In preparation for the attack the diary of 58th Trench Mortar Battery for 19 September shows an increasing level of participation. They fired twenty rounds at an enemy MEBU at C.12.d.7.8. with five effective hits, and on the burst of the seventh round eight of the enemy were seen to leave the pill box and disappear over the ridge; one prisoner was brought in. Two other targets, a strong trench to the east of the cemetery and suspected earthworks near Jury Farm, were harassed with five rounds each. For Trench Mortar Battery V58 the attack on 20 September was a bitter sweet affair, they fired on two targets and fired only five rounds owing to the lack of light to see their target and the burst of the bombs. After firing three rounds at the second target a German 5.9 inch shell burst directly on the positions destroying all the ammunition and the guns, which were blown 20 yards, but amazingly there were no casualties to the crew.[100]

For those who thought that the lot of the infantry or the tank crews was bad, spare a thought for the commanders. Even the battalion headquarters could be a shocking, unhealthy place to be: Hibou Farm, the bunker where the commanders directing the forthcoming attack were, was described as 'disgusting, a concrete shelter with the floor consisting of corrugated iron sheets on cross timbers, and with water (with two dead Boche in) underneath'.[101]

They were sitting ducks for the German artillery who knew exactly where all the bunkers were and often treated them to a dose of their own medicine. The Germans were also shelling key points, such as St Julien, where they knew headquarters and observation posts would be located. An early but very significant casualty was the commander of 173 Brigade, Brigadier General B.C. Freyburg VC DSO, who was hit by a high explosive shell at 8pm on 19 September, near to the headquarters of the 4th Battalion. Yet, despite his ten wounds he continued to command his brigade from a stretcher until 11am on the morning of the attack, he 'inspired everyone with his own cheerful courage and example, until a medical officer ordered his evacuation'.[102] He handed over to Lieutenant Colonel W.R.H. Dann, the commander of 4th Battalion, this was not the last command in a crisis for Colonel Dann. But a significant casualty like General Freyburg would have some effect on the decisions being made and on the way the battle played out.

The starting line was not a trench, but rather a shell hole line. This was due to the lack of trenches and the fact that occupying a trench gave the enemy a target to fire at, whereas if the line was forward of this then the attackers would be at an advantage and nearer to the objective when the attack started.[103] This was a difficult tactic to employ and mistakes were made as it relied on the artillery keeping the enemy in their dugouts. The taping party under Captain Heaton was crucial with his team of Second Lieutenants Tregelles, Chancellor, and Hitch, two NCOs and ten platoon guides. Captain Heaton was responsible for the taping of the line and assembly of the battalion. In this instance the taping of the line was easily accomplished with only one casualty.[104]

The German line was a fortified trench line, Hubner Trench, or what was left of it. The trench was protected in front with fortified shell holes, barbed wire entanglements, machine gun posts and trench mortars, with concrete bunkers behind the trenches. Further back were fortified strong points, such as Hubner Farm and Genoa, which were pre-war farm buildings, turned into a veritable fortress. These were virtually indestructible unless receiving a direct hit by the heaviest artillery. German soldiers tended to use the bunkers just as accommodation, and by the end of the battles of Passchendaele they did not shelter in the bunkers, taking their chances in the shell holes due to the effect of concussion on the bunkers.

The 8th Battalion left the camp at Reigersburg at 10pm on 19 September, marching by platoons with 200 yards in between. Considerable delay was caused by a heavily laden machine gun section in front, by rain which made the duckboards slippery and by gaps in the track caused by hostile shelling. Of more inconvenience the battalion had to get round a derelict tank and climb over an ammunition train showing that the organisation of the lines of communication was not always effective. This meant that the battalion was one and a half hours late at the assembly point. When it did reach the assembly point it was quickly and easily moved to the taped line, and the companies were in position by 3.45am, after a night without any sleep.

The strength of the battalion at zero hour was seventeen officers and 433 other ranks, (there were thirty-seven in the headquarters' section), so 401 men attacked in four companies with C Company being the strongest at 110 men. The company objectives were as follows from south to north, A Company to take Marine View, C Company the Promenade and Genoa Farm, B Company two groups of 10 pillboxes, and D Company to take Hubner Farm.

The attack of A Company went according to plan. The attack started at 5.40am and the whole line of skirmishers advanced on a 700 yard front, following the creeping barrage closely. For the first 50 yards no opposition was met, and then they were met with machine gun fire and rifle fire. Second lieutenant Sloan was killed and 4 Platoon was almost wiped out. The line advanced to Hubner Trench where a brief stand off ensued, but the Germans were engaged with Lewis guns and rifle grenades, whilst some Post Office Rifles worked round their flanks, at which time most of the Germans fled or surrendered, the remainder who offered resistance being killed. A group of Germans on the right flank also fled when their flanks were turned. From this point no further organised resistance was met and the advance continued, with the mopping up of dug outs and pillboxes. Dimple Trench was captured and Marine View, despite continued machine gun fire from

Genoa Farm. A Company was now being commanded by Sergeant Harris, since all the officers had become casualties. The consolidation work was organised by Harris, his flanks secure by keeping in contact with the 4th Battalion, who gave the company some reinforcements since 4 Platoon had been almost wiped out in the attack.

C Company met with no fire until 100 yards from the Promenade (windmill) when it came under heavy machine gun and rifle fire, with stick bombs and also liquid fire bombs. Once again the enemy posts were engaged with grenades and Lewis guns. Fifty Germans surrendered once their position at the left of the Promenade was outflanked. The company was reorganised by a wounded Second Lieutenant Richardson, and Genoa Farm was captured with the help of the 5th Battalion who then moved through the 8th Battalion and took over the advance. Sergeant Francis assumed command of the company when the officers became casualties.

B Company advanced with the creeping barrage and stayed within 30 yards of it until their final objective. The enemy wire was crossed easily and Hubner Trench taken without any major difficulty. Most of the trench had been demolished by shell fire and the remaining shell holes were taken by bayoneting or shooting the Germans manning them. It was in this company that Sergeant Alfred Knight won the Victoria Cross for rushing through the barrage, attacking the Germans and disabling their machine guns.[105] Most of the machine gun fire came from the flanks and from a way behind but the advance never wavered and was continued in the original formation. German shell fire was light, even the enfilading machine gun fire from Genoa Farm was slight and not maintained.

The 5th Battalion moved off from camp at Reigersburg at 10.45pm. The battalion passed across the area between the canal and the front line, noting 'the terrible din and noise of our gun positions, where the massed artillery was belching forth death and destruction all night without ceasing. The ground quaked with the incessant shock of discharge, while the flash was so dazzling that to keep a sense of direction was nearly impossible in the darkness and the rain.'[106]

This was the result of massing all the artillery in one flat area between English Farm and Irish Farm. Casualties to this battalion on the march to the front were also light, being four on the way up and two whilst massed on the jumping off line. In all this din most of the men were so exhausted that they fell asleep on the taped line, only relieved by eating a sandwich with which they had been provided. The assault at 5.45am was preceded by a machine gun barrage just before zero hour, where elevated machine guns would pour fire on the enemy lines and the area to its rear to stop any movement and cause maximum casualties to any reinforcements trying to reach the front line.

As with the 8th Battalion, all the officers except one became casualties early on. This affected the advance and caused much confusion in the direction of the attack. The Germans called down a barrage, which grew worse till 6.45am, especially around Hubner Farm and Arbre. Hostile machine gun fire was accurate and well maintained. At Hubner Farm the 5th Battalion came to the aid of the Post Office Rifles and helped them capture it. The 5th Battalion claimed that some Highlanders from the adjoining Highland Division participated in the attack on Hubner Farm as they believed it to be Quebec Farm. Hubner Farm and the MEBU to the west of it were both sites of considerable resistance to the attackers, making the actions of Sergeant Knight all the more remarkable. It was here, at Hubner, that A and D Companies went forward under heavy machine gun fire and suffered considerable casualties.

It appears that Hubner farm was taken by an assault coordinated by Captain Kelly, who, marshalling elements of the 9th Royal Scots, 5th Battalion and the depleted remnants of his own D Company, 'finally captured the farm with only thirteen men, taking over one hundred unwounded men, and thirty wounded men, prisoner'.[107] The German position at Hubner Farm was engaged frontally by a Lewis gun, and attacked by a corporal and four men of D Company, whilst the party of Royal Scots and men of the London Rifle Brigade attacked on the left flank. This small victory at Hubner Farm appears to be the crucial engagement of the whole attack of 58th Division and the source of most of the medals awarded.

The advance of the 5th Battalion was met with harassing fire, until they passed through the 8th Battalion, and took on their own part of the attack. The method used to maintain their direction was by advancing on a compass bearing. Since once again most of the company officers were killed or wounded in the advance, it was up to the NCOs to continue the advance. However Tirpitz Farm was distinguishable by the hedge lines and ditches around it so the attackers could focus on that for direction. On the other hand Stroppe Farm and Genoa were not distinguishable from the landscape as particular locations and were not found. When it came to consolidating the line a shell hole line on the line of Stroppe and Tirpitz was established until they were relieved by B Company of the 7th Battalion.[108]

The infantry were often cut off from their headquarters and lines of communication, when telephone lines were destroyed by artillery, flares and visual signals were used, but in the case of mist or conditions of bad light these were not much use. One method used was messenger dogs.

'On four separate occasions, when owing to the mist or smoke of the barrage, visual signalling was not possible; dogs came through a heavy barrage from Wurst farm to Alberta with important messages. On one occasion a dog covered this distance in seven minutes.'

This was a better solution in bad conditions but,

'as the dogs vary in their reliability, I would strongly recommend that they be permanently attached to brigade signal sections so that absolute confidence in them may be gained by battalions. In future I intend to send dogs forward with the rear attacking wave. Owing to their closeness to the ground their chances of getting through a hostile barrage and of escaping machine gun fire are infinitely greater than the chances of [human] runners so doing.'

On this occasion the dogs may have proved their worth, but human runners could also perform acts of bravery. Frederick Edwards won his Military Medal as he had shown 'exceptional bravery in the delivery of important despatches, had on all occasions to pass through the enemy barrage, his cool confidence was entirely responsible for the good cooperation of the barrage guns, and enabled them to switch to enemy concentrations in the shortest possible time. In addition he carried messages to the forward guns, the location of which was uncertain, and brought back valuable information.'[109]

So 174 Brigade had met with some considerable success, but it was on the right flank that problems occurred for 173 Brigade had a wounded commander, General Freyburg, and that really sums up their luck in this attack. As with the rest of the division the tanks failed to make any progress in the mud, not even being able to advance up what was left of the road. The advance continued well, the dummy attack of C Company of the 3rd Battalion having some success as a diversion.

The 4th Battalion attack took Winnipeg crossroads, and then the Blue Line, the first objective. A report was then received at 6.15am that the Schuler Galleries, a line of bunkers, had been taken, and four hours later Schuler Farm had been confirmed taken by the division, who were facing a counter-attack. 'A smoke barrage was put down by the enemy at 9am and had become intense by 10.40am at which hour 164 Brigade reported a counter-attack in progress.'[110] An SOS flare by 164 Brigade indicated a counter-attack there at 12.13pm that was beaten off by 12.56pm. The Germans were prepared for the attack and were countering it by 10am with considerable preparation and additional forces being brought up by the afternoon.

It was not until 3.32pm that it was queried whether the Schuler Galleries had been overrun and properly mopped up, a battle patrol having been sent out to investigate at 2pm. The patrol subsequently reported that an attack by a platoon of the 4th Battalion had not succeeded owing firstly to the failure of their tank support and secondly a strong point in front of Schuler Farm which had decimated the attacking platoon. Only a sergeant and six men survived the devastating fire that was laid down by the Germans here. The creeping barrage had of course passed on long before and offered no support. One platoon of the 2nd Battalion was sent to reinforce the stricken 4th Battalion, to put out posts between Winnipeg and the top of the ridge, and a company of the 3rd to reinforce their own forward companies to the south of their flank. There were still quite a number of Germans in the area around Schuler Farm and the valley of the Hannebeek. It was not until 4pm on 20 September that Schuler Farm was confirmed as taken. It took an attack by 164 Brigade and a personal reconnaissance by Lieutenant Middlemiss (during which he was sniped at and wounded by fire from another post) to establish the position here.[111] The Germans could sense the British were massing around them and surrendered to 164 Brigade in daylight on 21 September.

The Germans were now concentrating forces. Counter-attacks had started that morning but these were reactive attacks by local forces. Stronger forces were brought up by the afternoon. At about 3pm a German force of over a thousand advancing along the Adler Farm to Wellington Road south of Varlet Farm was destroyed by the British artillery.

> 'Our fire was very effective, and they came on in excellent order until they extended [into attack formation]. From the moment of extension, the morale, which had till then been of the highest praise, went to pieces, and they disappeared into shell holes with the utmost speed. Only a few came on and these melted away under the heavy fire.'[112]

This was the advantage gained by the British holding the higher ground at Hubner Farm.

Now that the British had struck it was time for the Germans to counter-attack, which they did that evening in strength. General Haig wrote that the 'enemy attacks were numerous and determined. Fifth Army reported that three heavy counter-attacks were achieved against XVIII Corps between 6 and 6.30pm. They were all destroyed and the enemy suffered very heavy losses… about twenty thousand' against the whole Corps.[113] The area around

Pheasant Trench was particularly littered with enemy dead. One of these attacks was directed against 58th Division, with the failed attack at Pheasant Trench directed against 51st Division to the north. Another attempt was made on 21 September against 55th Division at Hill 37 to the south.

One of the main factors in the disruption and destruction of these German counter-attacks was the use of artillery and indeed machine gun barrages to saturate German rear areas with bullets and especially known concentrations of enemy troops. Temporary Second Lieutenant Reginald W. Kemp won his Military Medal:

> 'when in charge of a battery of machine guns, [he] had to advance through a heavy enemy barrage to engage his targets. By his skill and judgement he accomplished this without casualties. His gun positions were heavily shelled but his coolness and example inspired his men to keep all their guns firing. He carried out exceptionally difficult orders under harassing conditions. It was largely due to his grasping the situation so quickly that the enemy counter-attacks were disorganised before they materialised.'[114]

Opposite 58th Division 'rifle fire was opened when the Germans, estimated at two thousand opposite this division alone, arrived at 650 yards range, by which time their numbers were already thinned out by casualties.' The artillery was quickly organised to throw down a barrage on the collecting German counter-attack units that had an effect 'beyond description, and the enemy stampeded'. [115]

In response to the German counter-attacks which failed, Maxse wrote on 21 September:

> 'Just think of the second line Post Office Rifles standing up to the flower of the German Army and mowing them down with machine guns and rifles after they themselves being subjected to one half-hour of the most furious enemy shelling which has ever been borne! As evidence of the Post Office valour is entirely derived from the Highlanders on their immediate left I feel I can accept it as absolutely correct.'[116]

The second line Territorials had proved their mettle both in the offensive and defensive.

> 'Yesterday [I] went out to greet my second line Post Office Rifles on the way out of the trenches and you never saw such faces, never! They had all killed Huns themselves.'[117]

Colonel Green of the Tenth Battalion asked some soldiers of the adjoining Highland Division how his men had fought to which they replied 'They are not ordinary soldiers, but devils.'[118]

The attack not only won Sergeant Knight his Victoria Cross but in all forty medals to the Post Office Rifles and twenty medals for the London Rifle Brigade. This is proof of the excellence of the division's attack, as those on their flanks were unable to fulfil their objectives. Plumer deemed the attack generally a success, but it was a very limited bite and hold offensive, no break-out was achieved, the tanks broke down and were not able to support the infantry, so once again it was an infantry and artillery battle. As we saw in the previous chapter the support systems that were being constructed further back could not advance whilst the Germans held the high ground. But artillery held sway in this battle and it would not be until the generals realized how the tanks could help that the artillery would be lessened and the tanks fulfil expectations.

About this time an order appears that was intended to strengthen this resolve. High Command was determined to advance, at whatever cost, the word was passed down: 'the word retire will not be used on any account. Anyone heard using the word will be treated as an enemy and shot. This is to be explained to all ranks.' The first time this order appears in the archive is on 24 September 1917. This shows the absolute resolution of the High Command to advance and push the Germans back.[119] There were stragglers posts where errant riflemen would be gathered up, and if found lacking a reason to be there, unwounded or absent without leave, were returned to duty in the front line. On 26 September these were men provided by the 10th Battalion formed of one NCO and three Riflemen. Posts were set up at the cross-roads at Triangle Farm and the cross-roads in St Julien, 'it will be the duty of these posts to examine all stragglers; to direct wounded men to the nearest Regimental Aid Post and all unwounded men to their units in the front line'. The men were allowed the benefit of the doubt as to why they were there and returned to duty.

On 26 September it was decided that an advance along the rest of Wurst Farm Ridge should be undertaken as part of the Battle of Polygon Wood. The assault was to be made by the 9th and 12th Battalions. They were to attack in cooperation with the Sherwood Foresters of 59th (2 North Midland) Division on their right. The Corps Cyclist Battalion would carry out a diversion with dummies in a Chinese attack with the intention of drawing fire off the main assault. In this use of Chinese attacks the dummy soldiers would be operated rather like the targets in a disappearing rifle range, which seen through an artillery barrage would give the impression of an attack in progress, thus diverting attention from the real attack. The 9th Battalion history states that this took place on the left flank of the attack, which is on the flank opposite to the Sherwood Forester's attack. The 9th Battalion had been in the line after the previous attack but this was their first attack since the raids two weeks earlier; the Rangers were facing their first combat since their trench raid had been called off.[120]

From the start things went wrong for the attackers; fate was not on their side. The approach march to the front was made under a heavy barrage, both explosive and gas shell being used, the guides were not very good and finally the weather spoiled the attack. The morning was misty and the smoke from the barrage further reduced visibility so the dummy attack was no use in such conditions. The conditions being like this meant that confusion was maximised but the scale of the attack was hidden from the German defenders, some of whom were apparently sent scarpering away when attempting to form up for an assault on Wurst Farm.

The attack started before dawn and only had any cohesion when dawn broke and the mist cleared. The attack on Winzig on the left flank, one of the key objectives, was not successful with a platoon of D Company being almost wiped out in the attempt.[121] Reinforcements, including parts of the 10th and 12th Battalions, later raised the numbers of the depleted 9th Battalion to a force able to hold the territory gained against German counter-attacks that afternoon. The only choice left to the Brigadier was to put them all under the command of Colonel Barham to give the defence some sort of cohesion. The attack was designed to ease pressure on the left flank of 59th Division who made good advances and took their objectives at an angle to the attack of 58th Division.[122] The Rangers and 9th Battalion's attack was not as good as that of either their Notts and Derby partners or the previous attack on 20 September, and not for the first time in the battle the ground taken was hardly worth the casualties and the failure of the diversion had meant that the full fire of the German machine guns had concentrated on the Londoners.

In this attack Lieutenants Rose and Hooper were lost. Rose, who had done much to reconnoitre and postpone the earlier trench raid, had lost his life just less than three weeks later. Rifleman Dunstone performed a notable action: 'When finding that he was among the remnants of 10 Platoon, being among four survivors, he found a Colour Sergeant Major, a Sergeant and Lewis gun section, he took command over these NCOs and held the position with a captured German machine gun.' Dunstone was promoted to Corporal and awarded the Military Medal. This was once again the theme of the attack that most officers were killed or wounded and it was up to the NCOs and Riflemen to form them into a cohesive unit and hold the line.

The official verdict of the attack of 175 Brigade was that it lost cohesion, and did not take most of the final objective. This was caused by the use of a protective barrage on the left to cover the unguarded flank, which was mistaken by the infantry for the creeping barrage and led to them losing direction in the mist.[123] An attack that should have been able to take the ground relatively easily due to the pressure of the main offensive was unable to achieve this through weather conditions and mistakes by the infantry. But on a brighter note the Wurst Farm Ridge was renamed London Ridge in the division's honour, for the sacrifice and resolve that it had shown.

Unfortunately the limited bite and hold attack by both 58th and 59th divisions left the high ground at s'Gravenstafel in German hands, and the British only occupied half of the ridge here which now had to be taken by frontal assault. The divisions' objective had been Boetleer Farm, and it had only reached Aviatik Farm, not quite within striking distance of the high point of the ridge at s'Gravenstafel. In *The Times History of the War* it states that later the Germans concentrated all their artillery in that region on the Londoners and drove them back. But our men returned to the charge and recovered the positions they had evacuated. In honour of their achievements the Western end of the s'Gravenstafel Ridge was thenceforth called London Ridge.

According to the Official History it would have 'been courting defeat to have pushed in the direction of s'Gravenstafel beyond Aviatik Farm and the hamlet of Boetleer'.[124] It was the New Zealand Division who had the task of taking the Gravenstafel ridge, and it is their memorial that stands at the crossroads there.

The medical condition of the troops after the attack of 20 September is interesting. The division took over for a time the Advanced Dressing Stations at Essex Farm and Duhallow. At this stage they would have operated from the post 1916 concrete structure that exists today at Essex Farm.[125] The casualties increased on 20 September from one officer and two other ranks (until 12 midday) to twelve officers and 118 other ranks for the twenty-four hours to 21 September, and then nine officers and ninety-five other ranks on 22 September, down to two officers and thirty-eight other ranks on 23 September. We can tell from this that it took at least two to three hours for the wounded to be transported from the battlefield to the canal bank, despite its being only several miles.

The brigades of the division now licked their wounds, they had showed resolve and won through with mostly high praise, but whether the men were 'devils' or not they had achieved most of their objectives, although for considerable losses. They had lost 499 men that day, but had not had the losses of the adjoining divisions, 1,110 for 59th Division and 15,375 total for the British forces attacking that day. Since 20 September the London Division had had 1,236 casualties. Of these casualties, nineteen officers and 237 other ranks had been killed; thirty-six officers and 827 men wounded and 171 other ranks missing.[126] The division had suffered enormous casualties, like the rest of the British Army around Ypres. The Germans had massed their artillery against them in response and the Londoners had succeeded against the odds. It was the British response to the problems faced that was most revealing.

Notes

96 National Archives, WO95/2997

97 B.P.M.A., Derviche-Jones, *History of the 8th Battalion Post Office Rifles*, 1914-1918, p.22

98 Edmonds, J, *Military Operations*, 1917 Vol II, (London) p268 ff

99 Marine View is better known as the Windmill the Germans called De Tothenmulle and is associated with Erich Maria Remarque, the writer of *All Quiet on the Western Front*, who was stationed here in 1915.

100 National Archives, WO95/2995

101 British Postal Museum and archive, Derviche-Jones, *History of the Post Office Rifles*, p.23

102 National Archives, WO95/3001 Report on operations

103 The area was forward of and near Springfield which forms part of the macabre descriptions by Edwin Vaughan in his diaries in *'Some Desperate Glory'* which describes the attacks of 48 Midland Division in August 1917

104 National Archives, WO95/3006

105 See Appendix for full citation

106 Maurice, F. 1921 *The History of the London Rifle Brigade*, 1859-1919 (London) p.296

107 British Postal Museum and Archive, Derviche-Jones, *History of the Post Office Rifles*, 1914-1918, p.24

108 National Archives W095/3005

109 National Archives WO95/2996

110 National Archives WO95/3001

111 National Archives WO95/3001 report on actions

112 National Archives WO95/3001 report on actions

113 Haig Diaries, courtesy of the National Library of Scotland

114 National Archives WO95/2996

115 Edmunds, *Official History of Military Operations*, 1917 Vol III, p.275

116 quoted Baynes, *Far From a Donkey*. p.178

117 quoted Baynes, *Far From a Donkey*. p.178

118 quote from 51st (Highland) Division, to Colonel Green September 1917 in Fenton-Jones *The Story of the 10th Battalion London Regiment* Dec 1917 p. 23 courtesy of Hackney Archives

119 Marix Evans, M. *Passchendaele, The Hollow Victory*, (Barnsley) 2005 p.88. Gives some clue as to the potential cause, in the reported rout of 124 Brigade.

120 Cuthbert-Keeson, 1923 *The History and Records of Queen Victoria's Rifles*, (London) p.351

121 Wheeler-Holohan, 1921 *The Ranger's Historical Record*, p.205 ff

122 Edmunds J.E. *Military Operations*, 1917 Vol III p.288-9

123 National Archives WO95/3007

124 Cuthbert-Keeson, 1923 *The History and Records of Queen Victoria's Rifles* (London) p.351

125 This is most famous as being the site where John McCrae wrote his 1915 poem 'In Flanders Fields'

126 Edmonds, 1947 *Military Operations*, 1917 Vol. II p. 279

Chapter 6

The Road to Poelcappelle
August–December 1917

The initial attack of 20 September could not have succeeded without the full co-operation of the units supporting it from its base at Reigersburg Camp, west of the canal line, and the infrastructure that was built to support the attack. Each British Corps had its own corridor of communication from the rear to the front line maintained by that unit for its own offensive operations. This was a system in its simplest terms from army level down to corps, division and brigade level. All routes led from the Channel ports; Le Havre, Rouen, Boulogne and Calais, and to some degree Dunkerque.

On the front line defence was the first action to be considered on the newly won territory, as the Germans were sure to counter-attack in strength. After the ground had been won, the terrain would be consolidated and then cleared up, bodies buried and the area reorganised. With the general lack of trenches on the newly won ground shell holes usually formed the line, and these would be consolidated with sandbag revetments; often these shell holes were joined up to from the new line. To avoid wastage and loss of morale it was of great importance that the minimum of fatigue and exposure was caused to the troops holding the zone of offense and defence. Thus the Corps Commander, Lieutenant General Sir Ivor Maxse, visited the battle area and complained at the 'unsanitary condition of the dugouts and shelters occupied by the officers and men of 58th Division in the forward area'.[127]

On 21 September the work undertaken involved clearing up the dead at the entrance to the bunker at Hubner Farm, scene of Sergeant Knight's medal winning attack. Whether this always happened was not obvious although human decency would dictate that all bodies be given a decent burial, although this was not always possible in the front lines.

The work of consolidation led to the need for better access to the front line areas, as the attacks on 20 September had captured the higher ground of the Wurst Farm Ridge, all the ground that was under observation before was now in dead ground and this allowed the British to work with alacrity in building their system of communication. The High Command dictated the strategy and Lieutenant-Colonel MacDonald, the Army chief of

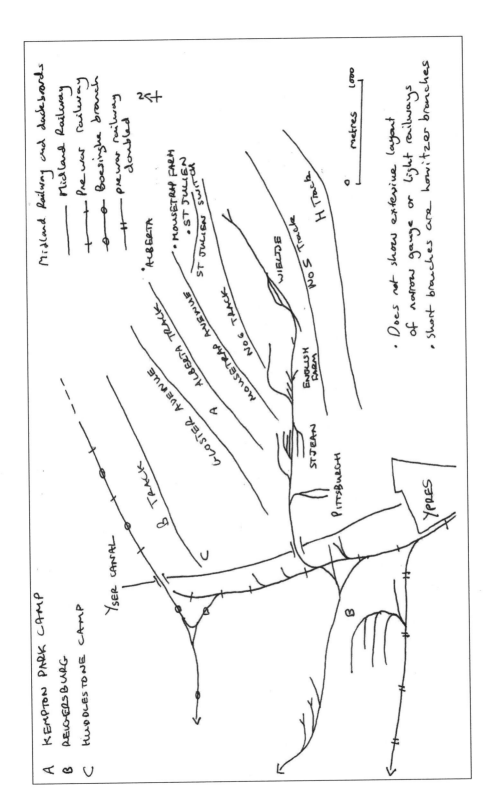

tramways, suggested that 'over soft or muddy ground the employment of longitudinal sills made of beech or other rough forest planks two to three inches thick is strongly advocated'.[128]

At the highest level army supplies and transport were being organised, and this involved a huge force behind the lines. As the Londoners had found earlier that year a great deal of time was required to perform service as labour for the Royal Engineers. As many as 20,000 men would be required as labour in the area covered by British headquarters, and 8,000 men in labour units on the Western Front, during active operations at the front. This pool of labour would prepare roads for field artillery and other light horse and vehicle traffic, construct roads for heavy artillery drawn by tractors as well as the completion of roads for normal motor transport.

As the advance continued it became necessary to advance the lines of communication to reinforce the soldiers fighting. The Battle of the Somme in 1916 had shown that advancing over muddy ground was problematic but the first mention of offensive use of duckboard tracks is in the aftermath of the German retreat to the Hindenburg Line to the south in January 1917 when a subsequently cancelled order stated that instructions in the case of the enemy withdrawal were that on each brigade front 'communication trenches should be opened without delay on at least two of the sites already reconnoitred in conjunction with the Corps of Royal Engineers, these will subsequently be increased to four on each brigade front. Foot tracks over the open will be prepared simultaneously with the communication trenches'.[129]

It was obvious that to build communication trenches all the way to the Hindenburg Line would have been impossible, but after two and a half years of trench warfare they were so indoctrinated with this idea that this was an obvious reaction.[130] The order also included foot tracks over the top. This was a defining moment in the history of the Great War; the deadlock of trench warfare was changing towards what was termed semi-open warfare, although it would take most of 1917 to become apparent. The first idea of a longer distance communication track with duckboards was born when it was decided that 'the first thing to make is a foot track, properly duck boarded, so that men can walk easily and carry up loads of material, food, water, ammunition and so on'. That was on the Somme battlefields, but it was in the Ypres Salient that the duck-board track would be most utilised.

The Fifth Army Chief Engineer Major-General P.G. Grant instructed that laying trench boards across the shell torn zone up to the new fighting line must be stressed, and that there should be at least two up and two down trench board tracks on a division front. This was to be accomplished by deciding beforehand on the alignment and marking out the route with screw pickets or posts, or indeed tape on the ground which would be followed by the parties laying the track. The XVIII Corps' Commander of Royal Engineers A.C. Joly de Lotbinière wrote after the attack of 20 September 'This will enable us to push forward our roads 1,000 yards east of the Steenbeek and will enable us to work by day to the Steenbeek'.[131]

The 511 Field Company spent 27 September constructing a duckboard track from the Ypres-Boesinghe Road to divisional headquarters, and repairing a track from Hurst Park to Gloster Farm. Across the divisional front thousands of yards of pre-fabricated duckboard tracks were laid out across the terrain, made by the Labour Corps at depots at Eperlecques in France, a heavily wooded area. The construction of the duckboard tracks did not go unnoticed by the Germans and the maintenance of the tracks was a costly affair.[132] The casualties of the company between 1-11 November were five killed, (Sappers L.N. Edwards, A.L. Carter, W.G. Raw, Corporal Smith and one other) seven wounded and two gassed. To protect the troops using the tracks the British had in place a plan to deceive the Germans of the location of the duckboard tracks, this was that not all tracks constructed were used. Also dummy tracks and positions were made and the routes used were changed frequently. One report suggests that different tracks may have been used depending on the weather, with northern, central and southern routes within the divisional line of communications. The papers of Major Morris show wet weather and dry weather routes. One was the wet weather Bath Road from Bridge number two on the canal to Hugel Hollow on the Steenbeek, passing Fish Farm, Hill Top Farm and Oblong Farm. The Queen's Road was a dry weather route and followed pre war roads. In reality this meant that dirt tracks could be used in dry weather, duckboard tracks in wet weather and taped tracks by night.[133] The plan involved doubling the number of tracks existing and used; dummy machine gun positions and shelters were constructed, and the use of camouflage disrupting movement wherever possible, especially on the flat plateau around Poelcappelle. The result of this was to split the effect of German artillery barrages and reduce casualties, although considerable delay could still be caused for troops moving up to the front. Dry weather was essential for rapid movement and the other options were only second best, as can be imagined.

On the night of 19-20 September the 8th Battalion were delayed in their movement to the front by a heavily laden machine gun section that was slow moving, greasy duckboards, by gaps in the track caused by shelling and by more substantial objects, such as an ammunition train that must have caused a nervous moment for the troops to cross, and a derelict tank. This caused a delay of one and a half hours in getting to the assembly positions but seems to have caused more discomfort than the German shelling around the areas of Admirals Road, Kitchener's Wood, Alberta and Hibou. Only one casualty was suffered by intermittent German machine gun fire during this long approach march and no name is recorded as having been a fatality at this stage.[134] The battalion's strength on entering the line was 450 officers and men, a figure that was going to be halved later that morning. The duckboard tracks had played their part with deception and ruse under the cover of night meaning that casualties were avoided and the attack could be made at full battle strength. Of course this was very lucky, other battalions did not share the 8th Battalion's luck, and traversing the muddy wasteland in full kit, at night under shellfire, in the rain must have been terrifying. Major Morris and his machine gun crews had a hot reception on Jew Hill:

At 06.45 The battery moved up to forward position on Jews Hill [sic] under moderate shell fire. On arrival at Jews Hill the enemy concentrated with 5.9 inch [shells] on the position and as I saw it was unadvisable to [remain?] I moved forward to the forward slop of the Jew Hill where the shelling was a little less and proceeded to dig in and prepare fresh cover.'

The attack was a success due to the closeness of the following infantry to the barrage, and in order to achieve this aim the guns moved forward as the infantry advanced. Once again the terrain was a shell blasted muddy wasteland, so the infrastructure had to be built from scratch. The basic system of advancing the guns was to make roads for the light artillery and mule tracks and railways to feed them ammunition and move in the heavy guns and howitzers. The army had standard gauge (often called broad gauge as opposed to narrow gauge) railways that moved troops towards the front and took out wounded and brought in supplies, which in turn fed light railways and in turn narrow gauge railways and tractor tracks.

East of Poperinghe the British maintained three railway lines that supplied the northern and central part of the salient. The original line to Ypres was doubled, a line was constructed north to Proven and towards the Channel ports with two additional west-east lines parallel to it. This was the Midland Railway and an additional one to the north. The northern one connected at Boesinghe with the original pre-war line to Langemarck. The Midland Railway was extended over the canal and became known as the Midland Railway Extension, the whole also known by some as the Great

Midland Railway. Thus British railway construction in 1917 was systematic and vast in order to supply the coming offensive. These triple lines were an obvious sign to the Germans of the Allies' intentions.

The system was originally based on the theory of having a loop within each corps area, with tramways for each division so they could operate independently and congestion would not be a problem between divisions. The broad gauge, light railways and tramways ran parallel to each other but are quite hard to explain as a system. The loop was meant to be constructed with spurs so that if an advance was made another loop could be constructed by pulling up one to the rear and placing it in front of the current one, this way there was no effect on supplies or the position of artillery during the battles. In reality the loop system was abandoned due to time and lack of manpower, and branch lines were created that supplied a corps. One was built to the south of Ypres, one to the north at Wieltje, and one at Boesinghe. The Wieltje branch, called The Midland Railway, was the most advanced, largest, and not built on a pre-war line unlike the Boesinghe and Hellfire Corner branches.

Huge quantities of stone were moved to the front line sidings at Wieltje, beside the main road, where 400 tons per day were brought in at the start of operations. Lieutenant-Colonel Macdonald, the 5th Army Chief of Tramways suggested that in an active area of operations 8,000 men were required in labour units and 20,000 men across the army area just to maintain the offensive operations at the front. This was for road mending of the St Julien road, for new roads and corduroy tracks that avoided the main road and also for ballast for the railway system.

On 2 October Brigadier-General A.C. Joly de Lotbinière regretted having to give up a battalion of labour lent to him by 9th Division to advance the light railway system. Three days later he received the Hood and Hawke battalions from 63 Royal Naval Division to help with labour in his sector.[135] So even with the considerable amount of manpower available for the advance, the engineers felt under pressure of manpower, and now with the success of Plumer's offensives and the need to continue the attack before the weather changed, all possible manpower was being used to advance the rail and track heads to the front. Whilst the advances at the Passchendaele end seemed slow, to the rear echelons moving with the advance a 1,000 yard advance seemed a very big undertaking which was reflected in the numbers of casualties to the attacking battalions.

The Battle of Messines Ridge, the preliminary to Third Ypres, had been the first battle in which ammunition and supplies were delivered by rail straight to the front.[136] At Third Ypres each battery was meant to have its own feeder line but the reality was that the ground was often too bad and the guns ended up being placed next to the main railways, with manpower being used to push the ammunition wagons. This meant that the guns could not operate at full capacity in supporting the attacks at the front.

Major General P.G. Grant was able to report that in the August attacks of the Fifth Army it had constructed 18 miles of railway and carried 20,000 tons of ammunition. There was a lack of manpower and the delivery rate to the guns was not good, with the result that Ford Model F tractors were ordered to pull the wagons on the tramlines. Some of these tractors were built in Ireland under the Fordson contract, but in 1916 the Ministry of Munitions placed an order for 6,000 from the USA, 254 of which were supplied by late 1917 and may have been used at Ypres.[137] Some were no doubt used for agriculture, but it seems that some were destined for the front. The Ford tractors that supplied the guns would have produced no smoke to betray the positions of the guns, and certainly no sparks which could have endangered the ammunition.

The field artillery was further forward than the heavy artillery and had a system of push feeder lines, operated by the soldiers, that led from the tractor lines. The use of railways to supply all the artillery meant that there was a very high level of infrastructure to be built by the Royal Engineers, but that once built they could supply the guns with the amount of shells that they needed to create the heavy artillery barrages that were a feature of the campaign.

Lieutenant Colonel Neil Fraser–Tytler[138] wrote: 'There is a great improvement of the roads as compared with that of the roads in the October Somme fighting of last year. Now they are being made by experts instead of being tinkered at by battalions in reserve, also last year there were no duckboard walks to get around on.'[139]

Colonel Lees recalled, just to the north of 58th Division:

'The work of the Pioneers in connection with these duck walks [sic] is deserving of the highest praise. Very great assistance was also received from the brigade in the line, who had small parties working continuously throughout the day carrying [duckboards] to the track heads.... the right hand duckboard track reached a point 150 yards beyond Vee Bend, one portion being laid three times over, owing to damage by shell fire. The left hand track reached Louvois Farm, this represents almost exactly 5,000 yards run of duckboard laid.'[140]

By March 1918 there were twenty different tracks in the British zone of the salient between Boesinghe and Hooge, with names ranging from A Track, B

Track, H Track (a rare double track), Grouse Avenue, Alberta Track, Peter Pan Track, Bellevue Track, Helles Track and Jabber Track,[141] reflecting the diversity of the British forces in the salient. In 58th Division's area Mouse Trap Track, Bath Track and Alberta Track were some of the names used. Few of these names have survived with the exception of X Track cemetery, which is misleading as it was not on track X, that was further away, but because it was near Cross Roads Farm. It is here that some of the men of the 8th Battalion are buried, mostly casualties from their first week in the salient. Under the pressure and fatigue of the front the reality of the duckboard tracks could be somewhat different from the theory. Beyond Poelcappelle the experience of the 7th Battalion was that 'the track had been hurriedly laid under difficulties, the duckboards had been placed on top of the mud and consequently tipped at various angles and time after time men slithered off the slippery boards into the adjacent mud and had to be pulled out.'[142]

Central to the advance in the area of 58th Division was the railway to Wieltje that became known as The Midland Railway after the Army Controller of the Railway Operating Division, Colonel Paget, formerly superintendent of the Midland Railway in England.[143] This was to become the major artery in the north of the salient. The plan involved making new bridges across the Ypres canal to take the transport, railways and soldiers across into the salient. The ruins of the village of Wieltje were cleared and probably used as infill for new railway sidings on top of or beside the village. A junction at Reigersburg North led to the way over the canal and new howitzer spurs, sidings and ammunition dumps were built here and also at Saint Jean, English Farm, and Wieltje. This was roughly on the line of the present N38 northern Ypres bypass, but then swinging south past English Farm and to the site of the overpass of the A19 motorway at Wieltje so no traces exist of this railway today. In the photo IWM Q46622 there is an intake pipe and presumably a pump from the canal to supply the water tank for the locomotives at St Jean. The whole thing, including the bridge looks like something from the Wild West, and indeed Joly de Lotbinière was a Canadian engineer.

The advance of the railway system meant that the troops of 58th Division could be brought forward closer to the line by train, and on 26 October the 9th and 12th Battalions were brought up to Irish Farm in advance of the 10th and 11th Battalions at Reigersburg camp west of the canal line. This meant that the battalions would be spaced out along the communication corridor and the move to the front would be much easier. The 8th Battalion was in reserve to this formation and so was brought up later.

This image of trainloads of troops being brought up by standard gauge steam trains relatively close to the front is one that has largely been lost from modern images of the war. Likewise the idea of troops being taken back after a battle this way, such as the 6th on relief after their attack, by light railway from Kitchener's Wood area has been lost. This relief by light railway on 22 September, so soon after the advance, although from a point behind the lines, is a testament to the effort placed on the railways.[144]

A personnel train was made up of the following stock on 26 September when 58th Division was relieved: two brake vans, forty-four third-class coaches (forty men each, notice these are not the horse wagons so often referred to as 'Homme forty, cheval eight' unless the 'third-class coaches' is an attempt at humour), two first class coaches for the officers and two covered goods wagons for the Lewis guns and other heavy equipment. An omnibus train on the other hand was one passenger coach, thirty covered wagons, seventeen flat cars for general stores and two brake vans for railwaymen only.[145] It is reckoned that to move an entire division by train required a minimum of twelve trains such as those listed above.

The railway was handed over to the 264 Railway Company (Royal Engineers) in June 1917; by 26 June they were constructing Howitzer Spurs at Trois Tours, presumably to support the start of offensive operations on 31 July.[146] On 10 July they were widening a bridge over the Ieper Leie canal, and building supply sidings at Reigersburg Chateau on 17 July. The work of the 'Great Midland Railway' was started on the first day of the Third Battle of Ypres, the first inkling that the push would be in a north-east direction, and therefore supplies would be able to avoid passing though Ypres altogether.[147]

An idea of the progress of the railway, built from scratch over boggy and devastated ground, can be gleaned from the war diary of 268 Company Royal Engineers who progressed with earthworks, whilst 264 Company Royal Engineers constructed track, culverts, bridges etc with the aid of the Australian Rail Operating Division. By 18 August they had reached St Jean and were building a stone siding there, by 26 August the stone siding at Zouave, by 1 September the main line track was laid as far as English Farm with four Howitzer spurs, A, B, C and D at the same spot. On 6 September track was being laid at St Jean for a station and loop, by 2 November a coal siding was being built at Wieltje, and by the time they handed over to 113 Railway Construction Company on 27 November the sidings at Merrythought, visible in the photo Q46629 were constructed.[148] This gives an idea of the rapid construction that went on behind the front all through the summer and autumn of 1917.

The XVIII Corps Light Railway was to be brought into use by 26 December 1917. The failure to advance along London Ridge had meant a delay in the building of the Midland Railway, as the Germans had observation over the area from the ridge. Again this was too late for the battles of the autumn of 1917, but they saved carrying parties and mules from doing this work. General Haig wanted to continue the offensive in the spring of 1918, and this seems to be the reason the railway was continued during the winter.[149] The Midland Railway line was photographed in late February 1918, by which time it was complete, but too late for the offensive that officially ended in November 1917, see photo.

The heavy infrastructure that was being constructed could easily be seen by the Germans and would have been heavily shelled. Many of the men who died under bombardment were buried nearby in cemeteries such as Wieltje Farm. This Commonwealth War Graves Commission cemetery gives an interesting insight into the dynamics of the advance of the Midland Railway and its associated sidings and heavy artillery batteries. The site was behind the lines before the battle and was not created until the battle began. The first casualties are mostly infantry and machine gunners in July and August 1917, as the initial attacks were made then, they handed over to the Royal Field Artillery in mid-August, then it must have become a dressing station as the graves are mostly Royal Army Medical Corps, a few Royal Engineers in September as the railway advanced and the roads were repaired, the first Royal Garrison Artillery (heavy artillery) on 10 September and finally a New Zealander and a Canadian Engineer in October. There are infantry buried here from throughout the autumn of 1917 as either the soldiers were barracked in this area which was under sporadic shellfire and suffered occasional bombing or they were employed on working parties on the communications network highlighted in this chapter. There are 105 known graves in the cemetery.[150]

Notice that construction of the Midland Railway did not start until the first day of the offensive despite only going as far as the old German second line. Of the existing railways in the Ypres Salient two go in a north-easterly direction, towards Roulers, and the Midland was heading in this direction as well. In the case of a breakout of the salient towards Ostend and the coast this was the expected direction of the axis of advance. The anticipated advance was to be made on three railway lines, with the Midland as the main strategic railway, a new railway being preferred to rebuilding two others. Due to the failure to break out and the switch to campaigns such as Cambrai and then on to the defensive in the early spring of 1918, the Midland Railway never reached its potential.

Pictures of the railway are mostly quite empty of traffic, with few trains featuring in the sidings, a relic of the artillery battle that had been fought and the weight of armaments operating in the salient in late 1917. It had been a passing moment in military history, with the emphasis in 1918 being defensive; this line was evacuated in April 1918 during the German Spring Offensive. In fact the front line fell back to St Jean. Aerial photos show the line cratered and abandoned. Parts of the line that ran parallel to the Ypres-Poperinghe line and supplied the Midland Railway remained in the 1920s and they are shown on the Ypres League map. Some track was no doubt salvaged for the reconstruction of the pre-war lines to aid the advances of September 1918. In the post war period the Midland Railway was removed, but the tramways that co-existed with it remain in part as the reconstruction of the former battlefields started.

The three types of communication built towards the front line were separate but depended heavily upon each other. The duckboard tracks were built independently across the landscape, but the roads and railways were often built side by side to allow the carrying out of maintenance for each other. Thus the road could repair railways and the railway could carry stone for the roads, and interchange between the two was easy if one was knocked out. This was fine when dealing with humans but the mules preferred to use the roads rather than the mule tracks and so barbed wire strands were erected to keep the animals off the motor transport routes. Immediately to the north of Ypres there were lorry parks with 170 lorries available to take supplies to the front, and hundreds more further back.[151] The picture is somewhat different to Verdun where there was one road only and it was crammed with lorries, here a broader salient was reached by a multitude of roads, tracks and routes, with diversions round bottlenecks and bridges over canals and rivers.[152] The main bottleneck was Ypres itself and the canal but the XVIII Corps routes, including the Midland Railway, avoided this. Lorries could take supplies from the railways or in addition to them and therefore much increase the supply chain to the front line, with everything that the 58th Division needed to advance, from ammunition supplies to barrack buildings that were erected around Irish Farm and Kempton Park and corrugated iron shelters for the front line.

At the front there was always a gap between the road head and the front, and in the case of the Battle of Passchendaele beyond this was the mire of no man's land. Since the ground was so chewed up and wet, trenches did not exist in many places, the front was a line of shell holes, sometimes connected, more often not. By the time the 8th Battalion came to attack beyond Poelcappelle on 28 October the front was just like this.

'After a great difficulty in traversing the waterlogged ground we arrived at a point where a white tape had been laid for us to assemble on. As we were in a very exposed position we had to get down despite the mud and water. Several others and I lay on our backs on the inside of a shell hole and were soon soaking wet. At 6am exactly our barrage started and unfortunately opened up right on top of us knocking out many of our men. However in the dim light we attempted to advance but were caught in machine gun fire and we became literally stuck in the mud.'[153]

The battalion report does not record that the British barrage opened up on British troops but records the German barrage as causing these fatalities.[154]

The success of the units at the front depended on the provision of duckboard tracks, road and rail infrastructure behind the lines. When the infrastructure was broken or congested then, as always with supply in battle, the forces at the front could not operate efficiently. The successes of the attacks in the Battle of the Menin Road were partly a result of good tactics, but partly of course the result of a good supply network and moderate weather. When this network broke down due to the weather or the sheer distance between the camps at the rear and the front line then the attacks at the front would suffer. The service offered to the wounded troops going back to base was not always very good: 'the mules and drivers had been waiting for hours and just went like mad regardless of the state of the road.'[154]

In the later stages of the Battle of Passchendaele, Canadian forces only built roads across the shattered morass, as only stone built roads would be of any use in the terrible conditions on the ground. The duckboard tracks were used where possible, but the roads could cross the terrain across the shell holes. It is not surprising that the advance slowed down when the infrastructure could not be built due to the state of the ground. The engineers had given the attack impetus which meant that the middle stages of the battle achieved some success. The delays in attacking were partly to rest the troops but partly to give the supply system and the engineers some chance to advance and bring up the supplies needed for the next attack. The delay caused by the continual problem of supplies and the advance of the logistics and infrastructure gave the Germans time to dig in, re-supply and anticipate the next attack.

The reason that General Haig gave for continuing the battle until 10 November was to protect his forces from observation from the highest part of the ridge, yet even at the end of the battle, a retreat back down to the starting line seemed a better option, an idea that would be pursued when the Germans attacked in the spring of 1918. When they did attack, they would have advanced towards a landscape now populated with roads, tracks, railways and new encampments that had sprung up in the previous six months.

The infrastructure that XVIII Corps created for the northern flank of Third Ypres in the region of Wieltje became the main artery for supplies in the northern part of the salient and probably the most successful, due to the level ground and the formation of the Midland Railway system here. This entire infrastructure could advance the supply system, which allowed the attacks to continue right to Passchendaele itself. We may doubt the reasons for continuing the battle until 10 November 1917 but it is sure that the effort put in to supplying the troops at the front was as modern for the time as possible and no effort was spared to reinforce and assist them. It is unfortunate that this has not come to be the popular view of the battle in modern perceptions of Third Ypres.

Notes

127 National Archives WO95/3003

128 National Archives WO158/171

129 National Archives WO 95/2779

130 National Archives WO 95/2779

131 National Archives WO 95/956 XVIII Corps Chief Engineer

132 Lance Corporal W.J. Fussell was amongst casualties of 503 Field Company killed whilst undertaking maintenance on the tracks on 20 September and is buried at Buffs Road Cemetery.

133 IWM MISC 74/27/1 papers of Major C.J.Morris

134 National Archives W095/3006 H.Q. 174 Brigade

135 National Archives WO95/2996

136 Edmunds J.E. *Official History of Military Operations* 1917, Vol II p.39

137 The Shirehampton Tractor Museum near Bristol has a 1920 version of this model F tractor in its collection. Perhaps these tractors, like the horses, were also shipped to Avonmouth.

138 149 Royal Horse Artillery Brigade, 35 Division

139 Fraser-Tytler, *Field Guns in France*, (London) 1922, p. 215

140 National Archives, WO 95/1202 Guards Division

141 From The Imperial War Museum Trench Map Archive NMP, DVD

142 Planck, 1946 *The History of the Seventh Battalion in the Great War* (London) p.180

143 Cecil Paget (1874-1936) worked for the Midland Railway at Derby before the war and designed a revolutionary but temperamental new locomotive. He served as Commander of the Railway Operating Department 1915-1918 commanding 25,000 men. From *The Paget locomotive*, Clayton, reprint of Railway Gazette No. 2 (1945)

144 Godfrey, The Cast Iron Sixth, p.150ff

145 National Archives WO95/3003

146 National Archives WO95/4054

147 National Archives WO95/4054

148 IWM Transport series Q46629 (Q46620-46631 Midland Railway Extension shows the full extent of this railway in the non-digitised collection and see map)

149 Prior and Wilson, 1996 *Passchendaele, The Untold Story* (Yale) p.146

150 Commonwealth War Graves can be found on the cwgc.org website

151 Henniker, A.M. 1937 Official History, *Transportation on the Western Front* (London) map

152 Horne, Alistair, 1962 *The Price of Glory; Verdun 1916*, (London) page 147-8

153 Messenger, 1982 *Terriers in the Trenches*, (Chippenham) p.92

154

Chapter 7

Poelcappelle
October 1917

The 58th Division was now hardened to the fight and those battalions which had had to be improved were away from the line preparing for their next role in the battle. The division had taken London Ridge advancing in a south-eastwards direction, across the line of advance. The battle now swung back to the north-east, and Plumer and Gough could address the question of taking the village of Poelcappelle. This northern flank of the Third Battle of Ypres has not received much attention from the historian. The official historian, Brigadier Edmonds, does not cover the important operations in the northern flank of the battle in any great detail after 13 October. Instead he chooses to concentrate on the battle for Passchendaele where the Anzacs and Canadians suffered such high losses for gaining the high ground around the village.

In order to understand better the participation of 58th Division in the attacks of late October it is necessary to look in some detail at the battles for the village of Poelcappelle. They preceded the attacks of 58th Division in the area, for which Poelcappelle is not a battle honour. The successes of 18th (Eastern) Division, of which their historian is very energetic in portraying, are summed up in the phrase: '53 Brigade's victory at Poelcappelle on 22 October came after bitter and repeated disappointments, like a beam of light in a dark place.'[155]

This was Maxse's old division, which had, despite the failure of initial attacks, achieved its objectives. The battle of Poelcappelle was as important on the northern flank as the attacks on Passchendaele village and really defined the battles for the northern flank of the Third Battle of Ypres. It is important to the history of 58th Division to understand what preceded their attacks in late October 1917 and realize the importance of the village on this part of the battlefield.

Poelcappelle sits on a slight plateau above this part of the Salient with slopes leading down to the Lekkerboterbeek. As the line advanced north-eastwards the village came into the area of battle. This was a small village, but like every other in the Salient, had become heavily fortified and was taken only after considerable losses. Poelcappelle military cemetery covers a large area and within its walls eighty-four per cent of its 7,442 graves are marked as unknown soldiers. It is a reminder of the savage fighting in this sector of the salient, and the awful conditions of the ground that meant that few bodies were identifiable after the war. It is no stretch of the imagination to see this cemetery as another Tyne Cot, although one third smaller and hidden behind a large wall. It is easily ignored but is one of the most poignant large British cemeteries in the salient and a true indicator of the conditions of the northern flank of the attacks. Those unknown Riflemen of the London Division buried here are recorded by name on the wall on the Tyne Cot Memorial.[156]

On 23 September General Gough had felt 'disinclined to take all of Poelcappelle village because it would form a pronounced salient'. General Haig's opinion was that 'we should be able to accomplish things after the next offensive. So Kiggell visited him [Gough] this afternoon and asked him to make preparation to take the whole village if all goes well during the next attack'.[157]

The result of the attacks on 20 and 26 September was that success seemed more likely in the northern part of the Salient where the attacks of the XVIII Corps had taken the newly won London Ridge and given impetus to the attacks in that area. The next attacks were to be on 4 October (the Battle of Broodseinde), where the Australian and New Zealand Army Corps would press up to the flanks of Passchendaele Ridge. British forces also advanced towards Poelcappelle, with Brigades of 11th (Northern) Division, 48th (South Midland) and I Brigade Tank Corps which supplied for support ten tanks which made a great difference to the advance of the infantry both in their armoured role and as a morale boosting weapon for the infantry. Tanks were able to chase the Germans out of Poelcappelle and were only stopped by a developing German counter-attack that afternoon.

Maxse wrote of 4 October that it was 'very successful and the care and time spent during the preliminary training were well repaid'. Later he wrote that:

'the tanks, especially those carrying 6-pounders co-operating with 11th Division during 4 [October attack] were of the greatest assistance especially near Poelcappelle church where they demoralised the enemy. They were also useful in carrying up SAA [small arms ammunition] before returning, all SAA was handed over to the infantry, also their Lewis guns. This practically solved all the problems of SAA supply. Some wounded were also evacuated on tanks. Could this system be developed more and on the night before a battle could not tanks bring up water, rations and SAA, Stokes [mortar] shells etc to front companies and save carrying parties?'[158]

The tanks may have proved themselves at St Julien, but their days in the salient were numbered. As much as Maxse may have wanted further tank support the presence of wrecks on the St Julien to Poelcappelle road, the only firm going to get the tanks into action, meant that tank operations were suspended by I Brigade Tank Corps on 13 October, with one being successfully blown up as an experiment at Springfield with 260lb of guncotton on 21 October to prove how they could be cleared from roads. On 24 October all tanks were moved back to their railhead at Oosthoek Wood to re-equip and move south for other operations in November.[159] The history of 1 Tank Brigade's actions in the Ypres Salient is described as 'an immense amount of labour and movement, in comparison with which it must be admitted that the results achieved were disproportionately small'. But it does go on to say that 'the practical value of the new arm in making possible the capture of positions which could defy the most spirited attacks was the major positive result of the actions in the Salient.'

The tide was turning against the German defences for 'attacks on concrete strong points and consolidated shell holes, as regards the former, it was quickly found that they were quickly reduced by a combination of fire and enveloping movements. As regards consolidated shell holes they were very deep.... And proved traps for the enemy as once they were occupied troops could not get out of them again.'[160] Now the infantry would have to continue the fight with help from decreasing amounts of artillery and in increasingly wet and boggy conditions. To the north of Poelcappelle 29th Division and 4th Division of XIV Corps attacked and made some progress. Their casualties of 1,338 and 310 respectively showed the way the battle was turning into a grim battle of attrition, with 4,283 casualties in the Fifth Army in just the next two days around Poelcappelle.

The next attack on 9 October was termed the Battle of Poelcappelle and good progress was made by the XIV Corps towards Houthulst in cooperation with the French First Army. The French had good artillery support and made 4,000 yards progress; 29th Division and the Guards Division made ample progress northwards but progress everywhere else that day was slim and casualties high.

October 12 brought the first of the actions termed the First Battle of Passchendaele; the XVIII Corps at Poelcappelle was not well supported by artillery and suffered accordingly, with better progress being made by XIV

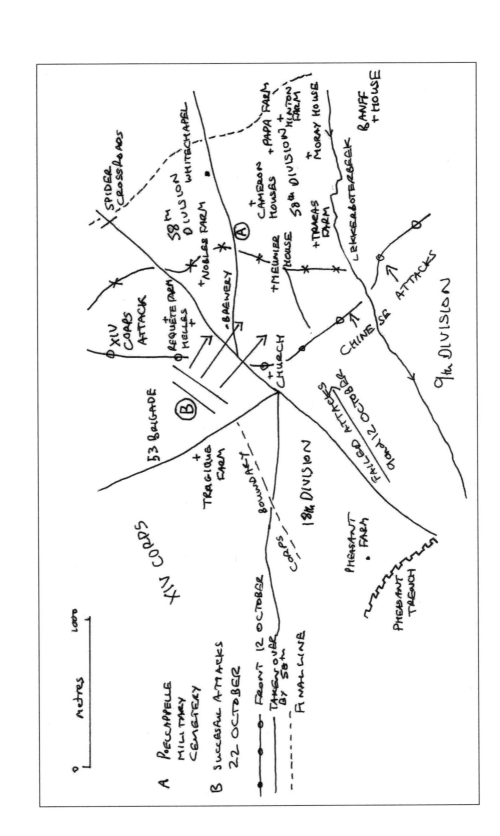

Corps to the north. Casualties for the Fifth Army on the northern flank were almost 11,000 between the 9 and 14 October, 1,669 of those being from 18th Division. Only the Guards' Division, on the fringes of Houthulst forest had higher casualties in Fifth Army. On 22 October Maxse attacked again.

The northern part of the village of Poelcappelle, the Brewery, Helles House, Meunier House, Nobles Farm and Tracas Farm all contained concrete structures and crater positions of great strength and most of them had been unsuccessfully attacked on the 9 and 12 October. Since that date however they had been treated to four days intensive bombardment by the heavy artillery of XIV Corps. Indeed it was realized by both corps that Helles House and Meunier House must be captured and held if any successful advance was to be achieved north or south of it by either corps. The XIV Corps salient enabled them to form up in it and protect the left flank during attacks.[161]

Frontal attacks on the village of Poelcappelle had failed to achieve their objectives. The Official History states that on 8 October the XVIII Corps was to advance another 1,200 yards up to the Poelcappelle spur and towards the main ridge around Westroosebeek. 'The assaulting battalions of 11 and 48 Divisions, found by 32 Brigade and 144 Brigade were however raked by machine gun fire at the outset.'[162] Already exhausted by the march up on the previous night, lasting fourteen and a half hours, they were not in a fit state to meet this opposition. This meant 4th Division on the right was unable to reach its objectives, but a front line was achieved east of the Poelcappelle to Houthulst Road. Clearly a better way of attacking this village, which was far from the canal bank and the assembled artillery, had to be found.

Maxse had a solution and moved in his old command 18th Division, attacking on 22 October. They used a mixture of subterfuge and deception by the infantry which had triumphed during the trench raids and offensive of September. The attack was described in an official army circular to three Corps in the Fifth Army as an anonymous attack in the Fifth Army area, since they did not want the location to be leaked to the Germans. The attack was supported by an artillery barrage on the whole Second and Fifth Army front, to give the impression of a larger attack and supported also by the French Army to the north. Once again the Official History, written after the war, barely mentions Maxse's victory that day. But the original army circular reported:

> 'A salient in our line [Poelcappelle] afforded an opportunity to form
> up the attacking infantry obliquely to the enemy's defences. From
> this salient the assaulting companies were launched, each against a

specified area, and they captured their objective by surprise rather than by weight of numbers. In fact, two battalions attacking from the salient accomplished on this day that which a fresh brigade had failed to achieve in a frontal attack on two previous occasions.

'A simultaneous Chinese frontal attack was undertaken by the Corps Cyclist Battalion on a front of 1,200 yards, this time the weather and light were right for this diversion. This battalion had during four months been trained to execute sham attacks with dummy figures, and on this occasion they attracted the attention of the enemy to the wrong direction, and drew a good deal of fire which would otherwise have been directed to the assaulting battalions.'

The two battalions of 53 Brigade from 18th Division had dug themselves in before the attack in slit trenches, rather than shell holes or trenches, thus affording some protection to its riflemen, and the oblique attack had surprised the Germans. The effect of the Chinese attack, as seen through an artillery barrage, was to draw fire off the main attackers. It is interesting, though, that the Corps Cyclists' sham attack had been being prepared for four months, that is since July 1917. It had taken this long to prove Maxse right again; true this tactic had been used to some extent on 20 September with good effect, but Maxse still blew his own trumpet.

'The XVIII are again "blue eyed boys" in consequence of being the only ones to capture all their objectives on 22 October and to hold them definitely.'[163]

With hindsight this all seems very straightforward. Any attack though was the result of a great deal of staff work at headquarters. Once the attack started the outcome was not always certain and the period of the attack was one of furrowed brows and sweat for the commanders. The confusion of command in any headquarters can be seen in the way that messages reached the commanders in their forward headquarters. Messages were received out of sequence and some are rather confusing.[164]

The first message is reported at 7.25am, that 'small parties of our troops now visible. Line taken forward of Pheasant Farm at 7.32am'. [from a Forward Observation Post].

At 7.40am Division phoned in a report that 'Aeroplane reports red flares and Fans [ground signals] at Brewery and Helles. Enemy holding pill box at [army coordinate] V.14.d.4.9. [message timed 6.50am may have come by runner].

At 8.25am an infantry unit with the call sign CIDER reported 'Brewery in our hands. A and D Companies in touch [sic] Posts believed to be established about V.20.a.7.8 [army coordinate], message timed at 7.25am.'

At 8.30am it was recorded that 'Royal Artillery observer reports 7.55am our troops can be seen at the top of Meunier House Hill'.

This shows the way that information reached the commanders on the ground, various messages are quite old and arrive out of sequence. It was up to the staff to interpret the information from their commanders on the ground, but it was not the only way that this might be accomplished. At 10.05am a message was received by carrier pigeon from A Company, Essex Regiment that stated: 'All objectives captured including Meunier House. Very weak and done up.' This presumably means that the soldiers are very weak in numbers and suffered heavy casualties in the fighting. This gives an idea of how the day proceeded for the staff at headquarters and each unit sending bits of information by various means, including telephone, runner, carrier pigeon, and even by rocket but not it seems on this occasion, by dog.

The history of 18th Division clearly states the victory as that of General Higginson, the Brigade Commander, and goes on to salute him.

'The final capture of the cluster of tree stumps, pill-boxes, and bits of brick that stuck sufficiently far out of the mud to be recognisable as Poelcappelle, and also of Meunier House and Tracas Farm, was affected by a brilliant operation in which General Higginson bluffed and outmanoeuvred the Germans. A Chinese attack to the south of the village, where dummy figures on poles drew the enemy fire, masked a move in which the weight was thrown to the north, and two battalions of 53 Brigade, the 8th Norfolks and the 10th Essex, won strong points whose conquest had defied all previous attempts.'[165]

This was all very good but the reality of the battle of Poelcappelle was that it was a long way from the lines of communication, being about 41/2 miles from Ypres, a little over two from the most advanced railheads at St Jan, 2 to 3 miles of greasy, half submerged, and often shell damaged duckboard track. The artillery just could not amass the guns it needed to support the attack due to the guns and limbers being stuck in the mud, so they had to rely on the heavy artillery to pulverise the enemy positions, and this further destroyed everything so much that the whole landscape descended into a muddy bog. It was into this blasted landscape that 58th Division was brought after the victories of the previous week at the end of October. They were not moving towards Passchendaele village but parallel and 3 miles from it. Still the order of High Command was to push forward. General Gough wrote on 22 October that 'the Fifth Army attack[ed] with three Divisions;

Poelcappelle and the Brewery east of the village being finally cleared, and generally speaking all objectives gained, several counter-attacks were repulsed with heavy loss to the enemy.'[166]

The casualties for the day for Fifth Army were 2 officers killed and 21 wounded, 58 other ranks killed, 377 wounded and 21 missing, with about 125 German prisoners taken and an unknown amount killed and wounded.[167]

The 18th Division had taken the village and now it was the turn of 58th Division to relieve them. It was just the time to bring in a fresh division as the Germans were massing for a counter-attack that would start at 7.10am on 24 October. The 2nd and the 3rd Battalions were in the front line now with the 4th Battalion in support while 174 Brigade was in reserve at Siege Camp and 175 Brigade was in training at Saint Jansterbiezen, near Poperinghe.

The next day:

'At 7.10am the enemy counter-attacked in great strength on our left flank and on Cameron House. The right attack [against] 57 Division on our left failed to advance, causing our flank on the Spider Cross Roads to be very exposed and unfortunately the enemy succeeded in getting round it and driving his counter-attack home, completely cutting off the advanced posts, and rolling up our attack along the northern portion of the advance.'

The strategic advantage of continuing the advance at Poelcappelle was to relieve the pressure on the attacks at Passchendaele village, Haig's last gasp attempt to crest the high ground of the salient. Hence perhaps the reiteration of the order: 'The word retire will not be used on any account. Anyone heard using the word will be treated as an enemy and shot. This is to be explained to all ranks.' In this case it was Captain Pullar of 206 Machine Gun Company who recorded the order. In this phrase is to be seen the importance of the village of Poelcappelle and its capture.

The role given to the divisions involved on the left hand flank of the British attack was to support the Canadian assault on Passchendaele. The 58th Division was right in this and the actions on 26 and 30 October were made to directly support those attacks – this was London's sacrifice for the objective that Field Marshall Haig demanded.

The actions on 26 October by Fifth Army cost 5,402 casualties, the Canadian losses between 26 October and 10 November 1917 were 12,403, and the British losses between 4 October and 12 November were 138,787. The attacks on 30 October by 63rd and 58th Divisions cost 2,000 casualties,

1,349 of these to 58th Division. They were really not advancing at all, just slithering around in the mud. But with a choice of being shot by the Germans, taking their chances in no man's land, being shot for cowardice by their own side or possibly facing a court martial, the men chose no man's land with the possibility of surviving. If any men ran and were shot out of hand we would not know, as no one would have recorded or admitted that it happened.

It was reported at this stage by 63rd Division, on the flank of 58th Division, near Wallenmollen, that 'in the majority of cases the enemy uses his pillboxes as a barrack, and defends from neighbouring shell holes or from a small trench just in rear. Pill boxes must therefore be approached from the flanks.'[168]

The attack on 26 October was launched by 173 Brigade, the 2nd and 3rd battalions with the 1st in support. The attack of A Company, 2nd Battalion, managed to clear four pillboxes at Cameron House and sent back seventeen prisoners. D Company stormed a pillbox and sent back thirty-two prisoners. The German counter-attack was met fiercely, but A Company had to withdraw under pressure, D Company were able to hold onto their position, but C Company were unable to take Moray House, though they tried all day. Casualties were high for this battalion, at 11 officers and 386 other ranks, killed, missing and wounded.[169]

The 3rd Battalion advanced to Spider Crossroads, and came to a halt, mired in mud. They managed to some extent to keep up with the 2nd Battalion, but the German tactics of wearing down attacking troops at their flanks and then counter-attacking with heavy forces worked in the awful conditions. The German counter-attack drove them back to their original line. The 4th Battalion counter-attacked, but lost 11 officers and 368 other ranks.[170] On this day a Machine Gun Corps battery fired 70,000 rounds in support of attacks.[171] The 3rd Battalion at the end of the day could only muster two officers and seventeen men, not even including their Commander, Lieutenant-Colonel P.W. Beresford, who was killed that day.

The attrition and the conditions meant that brigades were changed over regularly and so it was the turn of 174 Brigade to relieve 173.

'The Brigade will move on 28 October in accordance with detailed orders to be issued later. Probably the Ninth and Twelfth Battalions fighting portion will march out of camp at about 7am and proceed from Railhoek by train to Irish Farm:' [along the Midland Railway] 'The Tenth and Eleventh will proceed by train to Reigersburg;'[172]

The attacking battalions would be in column formation when they moved off to the front and no (or few) hindrances would be met. There was some delay to the attack as it was initially postponed for a few days until the weather improved.

On 30 October 174 Brigade attacked with the 8th Battalion and a company of the 6th Battalion, the advance was about 100 yards. Nobles Farm was occupied by the 6th Battalion. In the personal recollections of Arthur Borseberry we find a very harrowing tale of the march up of the battalion, at what I am convinced is this time, although the evidence as to which attack is difficult to place.

> 'The ground over which we had to pass was a quagmire, men were falling and slipping off the duckboards into the mire and sinking. The order was "keep moving, don't stop. 'ow about our comrades sinking in the mud Sergeant?" the call would go out, "so and so has fallen in." He would be shot before he suffocated in the liquefied ooze. I cried a lot on that journey.'

So the British were shooting their own soldiers, out of mercy, rather than letting them drown in the mud or even attempt to rescue them.[173] Were these men shot out of mercy, or were they seen as deserting their post, and therefore shot for failing to do their duty and advance? This truly was the grimmest of battles.

The attack was planned at short notice and therefore the reconnaissance could only be made the night before, however this was overcome with more guides acting as route markers and three coloured lights put out facing the rear, so the battalion coming from the rear could tell where to go. The report on the attack records:

> 'In spite of hostile shelling with shrapnel, 5.9inch and gas shells, the battalion was formed up on the taped lines with less than twenty casualties within six hours of leaving camp at Kempton Park.'

Kempton Park was a spot on the old German lines a mile north of Wieltje, so the approach march was about 3 miles over duckboard tracks. Were the troops lost or shot on the march up to attack also recorded as these twenty casualties? The attack was to take place at 5.50am, but the troops were in place by 1.45am, so had a four hour wait, with a barrage and machine gun fire opening up on them, causing 20 casualties. The Germans had detected their presence due to the bright moonlight under which they assembled. The German barrage which had taken place between 3am and 4.30am was renewed when they attacked.[174]

The way the attack proceeded was that two companies were in the van, D and B, with C and A behind them. The assaulting companies had one section each extended as skirmishers, the remaining sections of leading battalions in sections in file, rear platoons in two lines of section in file. The reserves were Lewis gun sections, one in the assault and three in support and four at Battalion HQ with eight more in Pheasant Trench. The strength of attack was three officers and one hundred men for D Company, three officers and eighty-six men for B Company, with three officers and ninety-five men for C Company and three officers and ninety-three men for A Company, so four hundred and eight men in all, including the HQ section.

The objectives were Moray House and part of Track Trench for D Company and Papa Farm and Hinton Farm for C Company on the right. On the left B Company was to attack Cameron Houses and A Company part of Track Trench.

The attack of D Company was met with fierce opposition in the form of rifle fire from Track Trench, with machine gun fire from the flanks wiping out two sections under Second Lieutenant R. Tweddle before they got within 100 yards of Moray House, the officer being the only man returning unwounded from the initial attack. Other sections were unable to make headway due to the state of the ground, becoming stuck in the mud and then becoming casualties. The covering barrage was not heavy enough to keep the Germans' heads down and so significant opposition was met.

C Company was faced with very deep mud after 30 yards, with their Lewis gun being lost in the mud; most rifles could not be fired due to being covered in mud. They were fired on from across the Lekkerboterbeek, with two machine guns and rifle fire also coming from Track Trench. Six men and the company commander, Captain Gunning, managed to get within 100 yards of Track Trench but on trying to find a way forward five out of the six men became casualties; the enemy could be clearly seen in Track Trench being carefully supervised by an officer with nine machine guns directed at the Post Office Rifles. The British forces found it impossible to gain any initiative and had to set up whatever posts they could until relieved.

B Company followed D Company after a two minute pause and immediately became stuck in the mud, at the same time as being hit by the enemy barrage which came behind them and pushed them forward, at the same time heavy enemy machine gun fire opened up on them at once causing considerable casualties to groups of riflemen. Second Lieutenant Booth and nine or ten men managed to get within 150 yards of their objective, Cameron House. Some return fire was put down by these men and then they managed to set up posts while Second Lieutenant Booth managed to get back to Meunier House to report.

A Company advanced with the barrage but became stuck in the mud in which 'men sank to their knees or thighs'. Sergeant Fisher managed to be one of the few to advance further under protective rapid fire to try to reach men of B Company, due to an enemy machine gun post. Very heavy casualties were caused to the company and all officers became casualties or were missing.

All in all it had been a terrible day, and the casualties to the Battalion were crippling. The casualties of the 8th Battalion were five officers killed and five wounded and thirty-four Riflemen and forty-two wounded with 173 missing.[175] Communications had broken down entirely with all signal equipment lost in the attacking companies, only five company signallers returning, and all pigeoniers killed, wounded or missing. The company runners mostly were killed or missing, whilst others took six to seven hours to return owing to the nature of the ground. Second Lieutenant Booth managed to return to a signal centre which was set up at Meunier House.

This is the official version from the Colonel of the Battalion, Colonel De Vesian. Of course most of the Riflemen did not see the picture in the same way, however much they had been trained. One rifleman gave his version of events:

> 'We were able to get a little cover on the edge of some shell holes and here we were pinned down as the slightest movement brought enemy fire. The day seemed endless. All day there was intermittent shell fire and we were showered with water and mud when one exploded near. Several of our chaps who moved were picked off by snipers.'

An enemy sniper was also reported up a tree, so he could look down on the battlefield, and the attackers were unable to fire back. However at one point a truce seems to have occurred and parties under a Red Cross flag were able to try to help the wounded; the same reporter noted 'I remember being surprised that they were not fired upon by the Germans'.[176] Eventually dusk brought relief for those who were left and the bedraggled, hungry and cold survivors managed to crawl back to their own lines. Any ground that had been taken was largely lost as the battalion were too weak to hold it. This was the last attack at Poelcappelle, and it is obvious it should not have been made at all. The bigger picture meant that these attacks had to be made in the face of overwhelming odds. The attacks did have the result of forming a perimeter to Poelcappelle village, although it is unlikely that the cost was worth the ground gained.

One soldier remembered the colonel giving a pep talk after the failed attack, 'telling the lads not to be disappointed at apparently achieving nothing. We had in fact succeeded, as the object had been to draw fire, while the Canadians had made a surprise flank attack and captured Passchendaele.'[177] Whether the Canadian attack at Passchendaele was a surprise we can only surmise but the fact was that they had captured the village and the end was in sight.

Even while the operations were over for any large scale infantry attack, the men of the 5th Battalion were ordered to undertake one last operation, effectively mopping up. A pillbox had been identified as a snipers' nest and it was to this that a small party of the 5th was sent. A platoon from D Company, under Second Lieutenant Stokes, was sent forward. Their progress was impeded by the mud and awful conditions of the ground, which gave the enemy time to reinforce and artillery fire was started against them.

'Before the party was within striking distance, fierce machine gun fire and rifle fire was started on them, and the officer fell mortally wounded, and several of his men with him. One section, however, under the platoon sergeant, Sergeant Graton, got to close quarters and had the satisfaction of killing some of the enemy with their bayonets, but the party was too small to hold the position, and was compelled to withdraw in the face of greater numbers.'[178]

The raid was considered a failure, but some relief was taken in the fact that the enemy continued shelling and firing for some considerable time and the wasteful expenditure of ammunition was considered ample compensation. The 5th's casualties in three days in the line were 1 officer killed and 1 wounded, 38 other ranks killed and 36 wounded. They were relieved by the 9th Battalion.

These unsuccessful attacks reaped a high casualty list and were the price that the officers and riflemen of 58th Division paid at Poelcappelle so the pressure could be maintained on the Germans in the Salient. Canadian patrols made it into the village of Passchendaele on the days that 58th Division attacked at Poelcappelle, and the Germans were evacuating the village, but it was not held until the attacks of 6 November. The German forces were still able to offer strong and effective resistance in these awful conditions. It was not just the infantry that were mired by the conditions, we have seen that the artillery was becoming unsuccessful, mostly weak in supporting attacks, as they were unable to move their guns easily, and the distance from the lines of communication made matters worse, so what had worked in September and October was now definitely not working by November.

There were other pressing concerns further afield for Field Marshall Haig, the collapse on the Italian front necessitated moving several divisions to that theatre of operations. The Russian Revolution meant concerns were growing over their part in the war at all. Of the French Army mutinies Haig was kept somewhat in the dark, but they were mostly over but general concern over the French Army's ability to continue would have been considerable. That was why he had tied down so many divisions to press the advance at Ypres.

It was now obvious that no further advances or attacks could or should be made. Haig pressed on at Passchendaele with Canadian forces and wanted to give the impression of continuing to attack. The last surge at Passchendaele was not really intended to break through, but to win the high ground marked by the church there. His main objective was now to concentrate on the attack approaching at Cambrai on 20 November, an attack that was, for once, made under conditions of the highest secrecy. It was there that the Division's first line Territorial counterpart, 47th Division, would become involved at Bourlon Wood.[179]

As for 58th Division it was kept in place at Poelcappelle, where so many of its men lay, to hold the line, now frozen and featureless, in the November and December nights.

Notes

155 Nichols, 1922 *The 18th Division in the Great War* (Blackwood) p.232 ff
156 The Menin Gate Memorial records 55,000 men posted as missing between 1914 and August 1917, therefore our Riflemen are recorded on the Tyne Cot Memorial to the missing which records a further 35,000. Poelcappelle Military Cemetery was designed by Charles Holden.
157 Liddell-Hart archive at King's College London, The Haig Diaries MF874
158 IWM Archives, The Papers of Sir Ivor Maxse, 18 Division
159 National Archives W095/100 Papers of I Brigade Tank Corps
160 IWM archive The Papers of Sir Ivor Maxse, 18 Division
161 IWM archive The Papers of Sir Ivor Maxse, 18 Division,
162 Edmonds, J.E. Military Operations, France and Belgium 1917 Vol II, p. 332
163 Baynes, John 1995 *Far From a Donkey, The Life of Sir Ivor Maxse* (London) p.180
164 National Archives WO95/2016 General Staff, 18 Division
165 Nichols, 1922 *The 18th Division in the Great War* (Blackwood) p.232
166 Gough, 1931 *The Fifth Army*, (London) p. 213
167 Edmonds, *Military Operations* 1917 Vol II, p.348
168 IWM Archive, The Papers of Sir Ivor Maxse,

169 H. C O'Neill, *The Royal Fusiliers in the Great War* (Heathfield) p.200ff

170 McCarthy, Chris, 1995 *The Third Ypres, Passchendaele* (London) p.129ff

171 National Archives WO95/3006

172 National Archives WO95/3003

173 IWM Archives MISC 139/2165 Arthur Borseberry

174 National Archives W095/3007

175 Messenger, 1982 *Terriers in the Trenches* (Chippenham) p.92

176 Messenger, 1982 *Terriers in the Trenches* (Chippenham) p.91

177 IWM archives MISC 139/ 2165 F35 the papers of C.W. Wagner

178 Maurice, *History of the London Rifle Brigade* (London) 1921 p.302

179 Maude, Alan, 1922 *The History of the 47th (London) Division 1914-1919* (London)

Chapter 8

Winter
November 1917–January 1918

A shift of emphasis now took place and it was not only in the shell holes of the front that the change reverberated as a seismic change also occurred in the British command. On the front this meant a change to the defensive at Poelcappelle, in the command structure of the British Army changes were occurring that would shake it from bottom to top.

For the soldiers in the front line the trek to their positions was still dangerous. Rifleman W. Young remembered:

> 'our destination was a pill box known as the Brewery, Poelcappelle, and as we neared it the shells were still falling in dangerous proximity. We should do well to arrive safely. But just as we arrived a shell came screaming into our midst and men were flung in all directions. As far as I can remember there were eight or nine casualties from that one shell. However the front did calm down and a few days before Christmas some fairly heavy falls of snow occurred and the whole landscape was transformed. We looked down on a vast panorama of white over the German lines; it was strangely quiet for this sector, perhaps partly due to the snow.'[180]

On the evening of 7 November 1917 a patrol was made of the new front by Lieutenant Henderson, Corporal Britten and nineteen other ranks 'to ascertain the position and strength of the enemy.' The first 500 yards was virtually impassable, but beyond that the road to Spider Crossroads was hard but covered in six to nine inches of mud.

> 'When near Spider Cross [roads] the patrol noticed on the left of the crossroads a ruined building with a wall about eight feet high on the nearside with a cluster of shelters, dugouts and cellars around it and in the debris voices were heard, entrances to the dug outs were seen amongst the debris, also a Boche sentry, he was shot and his screams aroused the garrison.'

The Lewis gunners were sent a few yards down the road to the right to cover and saw a few Boche to the left running away, they were fired at. Meanwhile the remainder of the patrol dealt with the occupants of the dug-outs and shelters. The patrol was satisfied that at least twenty were killed or seriously wounded by bayonet or rifle fire at a distance of a few feet. The prisoners were sent back in small groups. The Germans were now certainly alerted to the presence of the British and ominously a party of the enemy was seen in the distance. The British rearguard prepared to fire, but their guns jammed with the mud. They withdrew towards Helles which they reached at about 1.30am. After a moment of intense nerves the rearguard were not fired on, and it appears that the party of Germans were unaware of the patrol. During the withdrawal Lance Corporal Chapman noticed another German off to the flank 'the man ran off to a shelter in which were three others, Lance Corporal Chapman killed three and the fourth ran off'.

The haul from the raid was twenty-three prisoners and the British had two casualties; Corporal Britten was wounded and Private Menzies received a head wound. The patrol was praised by General Jackson in his covering letter attached to the report and forwarded to the Army Commander, 'although the operation started as a patrol, it was a 'model raid' for the British Army.' The reward was a full battalion parade with the new General Officer in Command, Major General A.B.E. Cator, buglers and band in attendance on 10 November 1917. All the men were decorated for the patrol.[181] Second Lieutenant Henderson received the Distinguished Service Order, Corporal Britten and Lance Corporal Chapman, the Distinguished Conduct Medal and the rest of the men, the Military Medal.

It had been a briefly glorious moment for the Hackney men at the end of a ruthless campaign. 'The Corps Commander wishes to emphasise the importance of incessant patrolling under the existing conditions of semi-open warfare, especially with a view to ascertaining whether there are any enemy posts or other removable obstacles between the forming up lines and the line of barrage.' This was the spirit in which the Hackney men had undertaken their patrol.

With the ground at Poelcappelle won it was now time to consolidate the defences there. 'The garrison of Poelcappelle are still too much concentrated at the Brewery end. It must be clearly understood that the importance of Poelcappelle is to bring flanking fire to bear on the north and south as well as to the east.'[182] This was to make the most of the defensive position of the village which stood on a slight plateau. The men of the 5th battalion involved in the small raid on 31 October were back in the line on 10 November after a week's rest. This was the day that the offensive ended and the change in emphasis meant a quieter, but by no means safer time in the front line.

The defence of the Poelcappelle sector was complex, as the ground taken at such cost was not to be easily given up. The streams of the Lekkerboterbeek and the Brombeek were to be held by the brigades of 58th Division through Christmas. Active patrolling was carried on, although with the offensive at an end and operations closing down for the winter there was not much to do. The patrols became very ordinary and followed maintained tracks and bridges built by the Royal Engineers. On the right flank these were from Gloster Farm south-eastwards to Burns House and from Tracas MEBU due south to Shaft. On the left flank from Taube Farm to army coordinate V.7.a.4.4.[183] These routes were on well established paths either with tape to guide the riflemen or luminous discs; at streams duckboards or bridges were used and camouflaged with mud, a local resource available in good quantity.

The line held and the defences available at Poelcappelle were redefined over the winter. As the boggy ground froze attacks were somewhat more of a threat although unlikely with the recently offensive at Cambrai being the centre of attention. The right sub sector with its headquarters at Norfolk House was to be held by a platoon at all costs; the riflemen here were expendable. Supporting platoons at Gloster Farm and the Brewery were to also hold their ground, and not to be used for reinforcement of the front line. The two supporting platoons of the centre company accommodated in Poelcappelle were at the disposal of the company commander for either reinforcing or counter-attacking Meunier Hill, which also was to be held at all costs. The company in battalion reserve in Pheasant Farm was available for immediate counter-attack duties. There were eight Vickers machine guns available in the sector; two at Tracas Farm, the Brewery, and one each at Nobles Farm and Helles, with a further two at Gloster Farm.

This defence was repeated on the left sub sector, with headquarters at Louis Farm, with posts at String Houses, Compromise Farm, Water House, Senegal Farm and Taube were once again to be held at all costs, with a company at Tragique Farm and Miller's Houses for counter-attack. Eight Vickers machine guns were available spread between Requete Farm, String, Waterhouses, Senegal, and Taube in the same distribution. The second line was on the line of Flora Cott, New Houses, Pheasant trench, Schreiboom and the railway line with a support battalion back at Pheasant trench. Deep dugouts were in the process of being constructed in the Pheasant Trench area by the Royal Engineers, with the intention of giving the soldiers some warmth and protection over the coming winter. Some sporadic counter-attacks were made by the Germans in December 1917, notably a gas attack on 12 December. But given the Official History's predisposition to cover other events then what are we to surmise from its silence?

The daily rituals of warfare were quite normalised after the close down of the Passchendaele campaign. Most of the heavy artillery was moved to the Cambrai front for the operations there on 20 November. The Tank Corps had finally come of age and it was the operations at Poelcappelle that had given them their chance for glory and a tank-led attack at Cambrai that showed to some extent what could be achieved if the artillery would let up. Third Ypres had been the last pure artillery battle, now it would be part of an all arms battle and not the lead arm. That is not to say that there would not be great artillery barrages, but from now on the British would be led by the need to break through with cavalry, both armoured and horse bound, and the infantry in unison.

Keeping morale and discipline was seen as a major problem, as on Christmas Day 1917, an order was issued in case of an attack, but more likely to control a possible collapse of discipline on the festive day. Stragglers posts were once again set up at Pheasant Trench and Eagle Trench for any riflemen who thought a trip home would be preferable. It was on this day that a new system of defence was initiated around Poelcappelle, after all it was probably better to keep the troops occupied and warm by working them when the surmised attack did not materialise. At least for the 9th Battalion a celebration was held for Christmas Day on 5 January behind the lines in a rest camp to make up for holding the line over Christmas.

Discipline was kept in true military style by inspections and endless rounds of cleaning and re-inspection. The new commander of the Division, General Cator, visited the horse teams in the transport lines during the first week of December and was pleased by their 'whole turn out [which] was excellent, one or two minor points in the harness and fitting still want working up, but I was delighted to see how hard they were working at it and they are setting up a splendid example to the whole division. It is bound to raise the whole standard.'[184]

Praise was the officers' way of keeping morale and standards, and therefore discipline, at a high standard, and the men of the 1st Battalion, attached to the Field Ambulance on stretcher bearing duties were no exception. Colonel Houghton, the Acting Divisional Medical Surgeon of the London Division expressed his praise:

'With little opportunity for preliminary instruction this party very quickly learned their duties, and by their courage and endurance under shell and rifle fire, were the means of saving many wounded and transporting them to the Dressing Station. I would particularly mention the able manner in which Captain John Venning, 2/1 London Regiment, organised the party into squads, and supervised Relay posts on the lines of Evacuation. Second Lieutenant W.L.T. Webb rendered very valuable service, particularly on the night of 30-31 October, at Meunier House when in charge of a detachment clearing the battlefield. Corporal H.J. Baldwin showed splendid courage and organising ability under similar circumstances. J.C. Clarke showed great courage and endurance whilst carrying stretchers under heavy fire through mud and shell holes.'[185]

So it was not just offensive action that the men of the division were chosen to perform, but unarmed roles as well, in the worst conditions. There had been some sort of truce, but this was only temporary, and the rifle fire would be desultory like the shellfire. The courage of these men, whilst not bearing arms, was steady and the resolve to help their comrades steadfast.

The new defensive system was to be based around defended localities such as minor hills or pillboxes, the many captured MEBUs. Already by the end of the offensive in 1917 selected German pill boxes were being blown up to stop them being re-used should the Germans reoccupy the salient, and as the likelihood of a spring offensive increased with the Russian capitulation at the Treaty of Brest-Litovsk, then even more were destroyed. Those that would serve a useful purpose were turned, that is re-used with a fortified weaker side reinforced with a breastwork of sandbags or any other debris that could be used. At Gourmier Farm near Langemarck an example can be found of concrete being used to fortify the weak side of a German MEBU. This is a very large bunker, but most bunkers were of the sort to be seen in Langemarck German Cemetery rather than those in Tyne Cot British cemetery which are machine-gun posts.

The role of Sir Ivor Maxse as XVIII Corps Commander was important and Maxse had always been a great reformer and trainer of the troops under his command. He was described by Sir Basil Liddell Hart as 'looking like a Tartar Chief, whose appearance aptly fitted his manner in dealing with lazy or inefficient seniors or subordinates'.[186] The role of corps commander obviously required men of the greatest aptitude and resources, and with competent staffs.

The success at Poelcappelle by 18th Division on 22 October, although at a heavy price, had come about because of Maxse's command, and the use of the Chinese attack by dummy soldiers had no doubt drawn fire away from the main attack in the north. The use of tanks which were able to get into the village as it offered a hard surface for them to operate on, showed the way for future operations. Without operations of note like St Julien and Poelcappelle, the tank might have been dropped from army operations, the Battle of Cambrai might not have occurred and military history might have been different.[187]

The fate of Major General Hew Fanshawe, the former General Officer Commanding 58th Division was that he found himself fighting for his command against Maxse, who, acting under orders from army headquarters, had to make a short report on all his divisional commanders.[188] Maxse rated him as indecisive and unknowledgeable. 'He lacks capacity to command. In the planning stage he plays a minor part and appears to have little influence over his subordinates.' The division fought well on 20 and 26 September but Maxse thought that it did not get much assistance from its commander before the battle.

The divisional commander was sacked when he achieved his objectives and the GOC of 55th Division was not. Maxse may have done this in order to take the credit for the success of the attack on the Wurst Farm Ridge. Fanshawe may not have been an able commander or trainer which was why the pre-offensive training was led by a committee of officers from his evidently excellent staff. Fanshawe was relieved of his command on 9 October, having obviously failed to impress Maxse, Plumer and Haig as to his abilities.

However, his assault on the Wurst Farm positions was a success and it was 55th Division on his right that was not able to take its objectives, failed to clear the Schuler Galleries successfully and was unable to make as much headway, whilst Fanshawe's division gained many medals, including a Victoria Cross, for its advance carried out with one wounded brigadier. The attack had been followed to the letter as a limited bite and hold operation, with no mandate to advance further. In Chapter Five I showed how it was meticulously planned and how it was brilliantly executed, but Fanshawe was replaced by Cator from the Scots Guards due to his inability to reply to criticism, both aimed at his lack of skills as a trainer and as to the character of the officers under his command. As for the officers and men 1,236 more were now dead, missing or wounded in five days.[189]

'Fanshawe is not a good trainer having little knowledge of the subject.' But if he had been, Maxse doubted he could either teach or enforce his views. 'I see no signs of grip or drive and think his division would be a very valuable one if placed in stronger hands. Throughout the operations Major

General Fanshawe has done his very best and has been most willing to carry out all instructions given to him, but one cannot help wishing that he possessed more decision of character for this sort of fighting.'[190]

Fanshawe replied at length that he regretted the adverse opinion that had been formed of his command and asked for the judicial intervention of the commander-in-chief. He claimed that Brigadier Holland had come to see him and told him the general plan of offensive operations for the division. Maxse himself had come to the headquarters on 13 September and personally asked him for his proposed plan of attack with which he had agreed, saying it was better. Secondly he stated that the division had fought well and achieved a success. Also he had stayed quiet after the order to place the brigade training in the hands of a committee to avoid undermining Maxse. Lastly he stated that Maxse's 'disparaging remarks about his officers being teachers at a girl's school' had been resented. Fanshawe had commanded the division for a year and wanted to take responsibility and credit for the division's performance in battle.

An officer who was there at the time reported Maxse as saying:

'Gentlemen, you lead your men credibly, but you are too polite. The spirit of the attack I have just witnessed savours more of the Sunday school than of the sanguinary battle. Far too gentle and kind. Your commands should be short and sharp: less "if you please" about them, more calculated to exact instant automatic obedience from the soldier's brain, half paralysed by noise and shock. Swear, gentlemen, swear; the men like it so long as you don't repeat yourself, cultivate a vocabulary.'

The observing officer then stated 'a vivid imagination is very necessary to stimulate much enthusiasm or language over a tree stump labelled X Farm, representing a pillbox full of treacherous Boches'.[191] History does not reveal what swear word he had in mind, but the experience of battle would no doubt have some bearing on this. This is a worthwhile anecdote on the nature of the London Territorials, not being soldiers by profession, but professionals in the city, called up to military service, who before the war had partaken in military training outside of their professional careers.

There were changes at the top, but at a lower level the attacks had not gone that well either. After their failed attack on 26 September the men of the 9th Battalion of the Queen Victoria's Rifles were brought before an enquiry at which officers and men of the battalion were asked to state how the advance went, the nature of the attack and what went wrong. This was undertaken at the lowest, platoon level. One can imagine red faces all round at what should have been a relatively easy advance, although hindered by the weather, an unhelpful artillery barrage and an impossible landscape of ruins. The London Division was subsequently replaced in the line by 48th (South Midland) Division.

One Rifleman stated:

> 'We found nothing that resembled Vale House but went well beyond where I thought it would be. Then I told them [the men] to drop into shell holes and tried to find out where we were when it got lighter. I saw someone in front with our hats on [British tin hats]. It turned out to be Mr Marshall with 14 platoon. He asked me what I thought the direction was as he had thought he was wrong and I thought I was wrong, and thought we had come too far.'

Of the men in his platoon two were killed, six wounded, one missing and thirteen returned, but it had not been a success by any means. Casualties for the 9th had been heavy, at 180 out of the 400 engaged, so it is not surprising that cohesion was lost, with seven of the fourteen officers also casualties.

Fanshawe had previously been sacked after the attacks on Saint-Eloi in 1916, where it was deemed that Canadian troops had not succeeded, but it was not considered politically correct to sack a Canadian commander, so Fanshawe was sacked instead. It seems that High Command had it in for Hew Fanshawe and he was made a scapegoat.

The report and rebuttal did not save Fanshawe's reputation as he was relieved of command on 6 October 1917 and replaced by Major General Cator from the Guards Division.[192] Of all the general officers in the Passchendaele battles Fanshawe was the only one to be replaced who wasn't wounded or killed. In fact he had been replaced before the battle even started, as soon as his divisional training was run by the committee of junior officers. This shows little regard for the triumphs of the division in such conditions, and also that seismic pressures in the command structure were real and would continue to shift in the coming months and eventually lead to both Gough and Maxse being replaced in the shuffle that would follow the German attacks of March 1918. This was an attack in which 58th Division would play a considerable part. No doubt Fanshawe's inability to train his battalions had led to some of the failures in the attacks of 26 September that had led to his dismissal. Maxse had seen this problem in the period prior to the attack, most problems had been addressed and the division had succeeded well beyond expectations on 20 September, but had come acropper on 26 September. Hard training had once again been forced on the division behind the lines.

Now that the Passchendaele campaign was over and the front was being held, another problem was the change from offensive to defensive action as the evidence pointed to a likely German spring offensive as armies were released from the Eastern Front.

What was the condition of the British soldier after Passchendaele? The Official History of casualties and medical statistics gives figures for 1917 for the whole British Army in France and Flanders. For the whole year 131,761 were killed, 49,832 died of wounds, 30,956 were missing, and 23,227 became prisoners of war. For admissions to hospital, for anything from meningitis to diphtheria, dysentery, pneumonia, venereal disease to frostbite there were plenty of men in hospital. The usual round of disease and sickness was accelerated by the awful conditions, cold, lack of basic sanitation, cramped living conditions and constant fear that attended the troops on a daily basis.

There were 1,050 different diseases, conditions, injuries, wounds or illnesses that the British soldier suffered from in the Great War.[193] Officers and other ranks were far more likely to have an injury or disease than a wound. The chance of being wounded, rather than being killed or dying of the wound, was high. The death rate amongst junior officers was sometimes as high as one in five of those who served.[194] The strain of battle was a continuing issue and the tightening of the leash in the 'no retreat order' was proof of this. It was also trying for commanders. As Fanshawe got his marching orders the commander of the 9th Battalion, Lieutenant-Colonel P.E. Langworthy-Parry, left after a short leave:

> 'I suppose the strain of the campaign which lately had been rather great, was beginning to tell upon me, and although I was prepared to carry on it was decided that a job less strenuous than commanding a battalion in the field under the conditions then existing should be found for me. I was accordingly recommended for the command of a battalion at home.'[195]

How many of the infantry had this kind of choice? Those that were mentally strained were accused of cowardice, ended up with neurasthenia (shell-shock) or worse in mental hospitals. The colonel spent the rest of the war commanding the reserve 3/8th (Post Office Rifles) at Blackdown in England.[196] The campaign had taken its toll not only on the riflemen of the division but also its commanders, Fanshawe and Langworthy-Parry. Maxse the Corps Commander was moved to become head of the Inspectorate of Training in April 1918.[197] There were several categories that affected the soldier: military, physical, mental and disease. The greatest of these was in fact disease, the mental factors were least understood, and the military need was to keep the man in the line as long as he was physically fit. Only officers above the rank of colonel seem to have been affected by political considerations.

The Daily Sketch of 3 January 1918 contains a typical example of how the battles at Passchendaele affected the troops, especially the officers. An anonymous captain of an unnamed regiment was found shot in a second class railway carriage at Woking station. Unfortunately the man had missed killing himself, but he was fatally wounded and died in hospital that evening – another victim of the battles, not killed by the enemy directly, but still a casualty of the war.

For the wounded there was the slow recovery from wounds made worse by the lengthy time of treatment, gas gangrene and every other wretched condition made worse by the war. Even for those lucky enough to get a Blighty wound, ending up at the casualty clearing stations and base hospitals on the Channel coast, there was the perilous trip back to England. Bertram Ralph only spent two weeks in the battalion before being wounded in his first attack, then en-route to England his ship, the SS *Warida*, was torpedoed and he had a lucky escape.

'Over 100 men perished. I came to as a wounded Tommy was trying to pull me up the stairs onto the deck, and with alternate periods of consciousness saw the less wounded getting over the side. Being unable to do this a sailor picked me up and dropped me over the rail of the listing ship and [I] was caught by a sailor on a destroyer alongside.'[198]

For those who survived the front and returned safely across the Channel, there was a chance to recover and start putting their lives back together. Returning wounded to England Captain W. Maile had to fight to get back to London:

'on arrival at Dover stretcher cases were dumped on the quay and sorted as to their destination by a red tabbed staff officer; Birmingham, London, or the West Country. He informed me I was going to Birmingham. Not much good as I lived near London. A heated argument ensued...I was put on a London train. More trouble on arrival at Charing Cross at 2am. Here another red tabbed chap informed me I was going to a temporary hospital in Park Lane. A further argument ensued, but I won in the end and was duly put on an ambulance all to myself and taken to my old hospital. Outside Charing Cross there was an extraordinary scene. Although it was then 3am there were literally hundreds of people waiting to greet us, cheering and throwing cigarettes and flowers into the ambulance as they made their way through the jam packed crowds.'[199] See Photo.

They were being welcomed back to London, even in the dead of night.

London had a whole system of Territorial Force hospitals which expanded during the war. These were divided into districts under five main hospitals which were Camberwell, Chelsea, Wandsworth, Denmark Hill and Lambeth. The buildings taken over for hospitals ranged from London City Council schools to lunatic asylums, workhouses and poor law infirmaries, hutted camps, colleges and civil hospitals. By 1917 London had a capacity of 36,664 beds, 20,000 of which were under War Office auspices.[200]

For those that made it safely back to Blighty, whether wounded or on short periods of leave, of course seeing their family was of most concern to them. P.G. Ackrell lived in the country and sets a most picturesque scene of his homecoming. This could have been a poster about what they were fighting for:

'To get from my home I would either have to walk or hire a conveyance. I had no desire to walk four miles, although I had walked miles in France... I hired a wagonette with a driver to take me home. The horse cantered at a steady trot after ascending the long hill out of town. On approaching the village it was downhill. My sister Grace knew I was coming and spotted me coming down the hill and went to inform my dear old mother... It was home sweet home for a fortnight. I hugged and kissed my sister and mother. I saw my father later.'

But leave never lasted long and soon the day of return to the war came:

'On the day of my departure I hired a pony and trap to take me to the station....My two sisters who took turns holding the reins....The shrill note of the whistle sounded and we were off, I waved my handkerchief to my sisters who waved back.'[201]

This was a rosy picture of the soldier on leave. An anonymous soldier wrote a more realistic picture:

'I told my mother don't touch or come near me as I am covered with lice. This was true as I had dodged having a bath at Boulogne. I went into the bathroom and stripped off all my clothes and threw them out of the window into the garden. The khaki uniform I buried in the garden and burnt the underclothing. I wore civilian dress for the whole of my leave, digging up my uniform a day or so before I had to return to France.'

Any leave was sorely needed in 1918 as the division was to meet some of its greatest challenges in the months ahead. The first necessity to get through was the disbandment of many of the battalions that had served since 1915 to meet the changing needs of the front line. Many were disbanded or amalgamated from 47th Division into 58th Division. Manpower shortages and the arrival of the Americans meant that British forces had to be reorganised to meet the growing German threat of a spring offensive. As the French persuaded the British to take over more of the line, the British Third Army was moved south, adjoining the French in the St Quentin area. It was to this sector that the London Division was now sent.

Notes

180 B.P.M.A. Young, *With the Post Office Rifles in France and Flanders*, 1915-1918.
181 Hackney Archives, Wardrop, *Tenth County of London Regiment* p. 9-10 see Appendix IV
182 National Archives WO95/3003 HQ 175 Infantry Brigade
183 National Archives WO95/3007 Papers relating to 175 Brigade
184 National Archives WO95/3001 letter
185 National Archives WO95/3001 letter
186 IWM The Papers of Sir Ivor Maxse, GOC XVIII Corps 1917-18, IWM introduction
187 IWM The Papers of Sir Ivor Maxse, GOC XVIII Corps 1917-18
188 There were three Fanshawe brothers who all served in High Command in the Great War, Robert, Edward and Hew Fanshawe. Hew Fanshawe had previously been a cavalry Corps commander and commanded V Corps and had been made a scapegoat after a disaster at St Eloi in 1916. He went on to command the 18th Indian Division in Mesopotamia.
189 Edmonds, *Military Operations*, 1917 Vol II, p. 279
190 IWM 69/53/3 The papers of Sir Ivor Maxse
191 Maurice, F. 1921 *The History of the London Rifle Brigade*, (London) p.295
192 Cator was in turn relieved by General Ramsay in 1918
193 Mitchell and Smith, 1931 *Medical Services* (London) p.274
194 Cuthbert-Keeson, 1923 *History and Records of the Queen Victoria's Rifles* p.357ff
195 The 3/8th Battalion took part in the filming of the film 'The Great Love,' now lost
196 Maxse was vilified for his part in the somewhat questionable retreat of the Fifth Army in the German March Offensives.
197 IWM Archive MISC 139/2165 F27 the papers of Bertram Ralph
198 IWM Archive 76/65/1 the papers of Captain W.C.D. Maile
199 Winter and Robert, 1997 *Capital Cities at War*, (Cambridge) p.94f
200 IWM Archive 11955 papers of P.G. Ackrell
201 IWM Archive MISC 2165/139 FA 9 ibid

Chapter 9

Pour la France!
January–April 1918

The 58th Division left the salient for ever on the 7-8 January 1918 where so many of its men lay in the fields around St Julien and Poelcappelle. It was now assigned to III Corps on the Somme front to take over the line from a French division, whose trenches the British were now occupying. The town of St Quentin lay 11 kilometres to the north. The makeup of III Corps was as follows from south to north; 58th and 18th (Eastern), 14th (Light), and 2nd and 3rd Cavalry Divisions as the mobile arm. Just as the division had moved into a defensive role in the Salient, now it was in a defensive role near St Quentin. It sat astride the Oise river, 173 Brigade to the north and 175 and 174 Brigades in that order to the south. This order of battle was to have consequences for the brigades in the coming battle.

The divisional front that 173 Brigade held lay on the high ground above the Oise River, mostly on bluffs above the marshes, from the boundary of the Londoners at Vendeuil, through Travecy, down to the banks of the river opposite La Fère. The towns behind the front are industrial with the marshalling yards of Tergnier in the valley of the St. Quentin canal to the west. Behind this is a charming French town, Chauny, an important and bustling place in the regional economy.

Brigadier General Cox, Sir Douglas Haig's Intelligence chief, believed twenty German divisions, not identified on the Western Front for more than a month, were training for an offensive, whilst another officer on the staff, Birch, 'does not think that the enemy intends to attack in force on the Western Front'.[202] He was to find out soon how wrong he had been in this deduction. The generals worried that the three divisions of III Corps held a front 30,200 yards long, a front that the Corps Commander Lieutenant General Butler said was too long for his infantry and especially for the artillery, but he was happy with the battle zone,[203] for the front was not now just a system of trenches, but an outpost line, the forward-most line, behind which was a series of an area of redoubts and keeps. Two of the defensive structures in the area were the Fort de Liez and the Fort de Vendeuil,

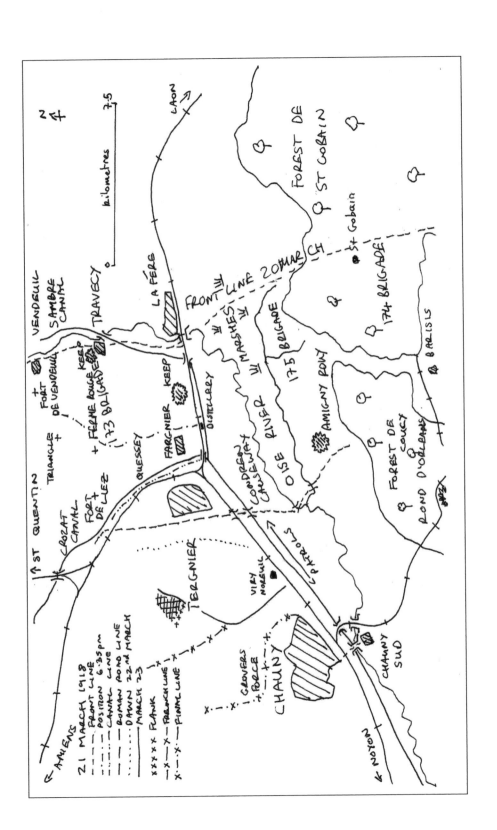

nineteenth century defensive forts, which no doubt the Germans had blown up in their 1917 retreat, but seem to have been still available as defensive structures, although not included in the German Hindenburg lines. The Fort de Liez was in 58th Division lines but the Fort de Vendeuil was within those of 18th Division. These would play an important but not crucial role in the days ahead.

The area defended by 58th Division was a long one for undermanned battalions, but was safer due to the canals fronting the position – at least that was the theory. North of the Oise River, west of the Sambre canal, and with the St Quentin canal at its back was 173 Brigade holding the villages of Vendeuil and Travecy adjoining 18th Division south of St Quentin. The ancient fortified town of La Fère was in its front and the forest of Courcy on the right in the area of 175 and 174 brigades. This landscape offered prospects for both attacker and defender, as the canals formed natural, and straight, defensive lines.

On 18 March General Haig wrote in his diary 'there are no signs of an immediate attack on the French front, but the enemy has the forces necessary to make one at short notice'. On 19 March he wrote that Brigadier Cox says 'the movement of troops from Germany into France continues. We don't yet know what the trains are carrying, but troops are not coming to Flanders but are going to Valenciennes'.[204]

The 173 Brigade diary notes ominously that 19-20 March were remarkably quiet days.

For the Londoners the move south brought a change from the devastation of Ypres, reinforcements arrived to bring the battalions some way to full strength, but never to their previous manpower. Many of these men came from disbanded battalions in 47th Division, men with a heavy heart at being moved, but they soon settled in. Each brigade in the line now would have only three battalions instead of four, many of these now being under strength to start with. Reinforcements were 9 officers and 201 other ranks to the 6th Battalion, 12 officers and 190 other ranks to the 7th Battalion, and 6 officers and 152 other ranks to the 8th Battalion. Those battalions that were disbanded in 47th Division lost their 1/- standing, and the 2/- battalion became the (for example) 8th Battalion, ie. a first line unit of that battalion.

The 1st, 5th and 11th battalions of 58th Division were also disbanded, the London Rifle Brigade becoming part of the 2/28 (Artists' Rifles) Battalion London Regiment, attached to 63rd (Royal Naval) Division and fighting under that name until the end of the war. This was not a popular move and many felt that those who had died were being let down by amalgamation of units. Many felt it was a demotion to move to 58th Division. Rifleman Holt felt this disappointment, 'It is now 08.20 and I have already had a bath, been shaved, had my boots cleaned and had breakfast, so I have 'been busy.' Slept last night four in a first class compartment from 8 o'clock till 6 this morning – beautifully comfortable. We cooked ourselves a five course dinner last night before turning in and the sleeping bag is a great success at present.' However his comfortable surroundings were to be slightly insulted when he was posted to the 58th Division. On 9 November (1917) he wrote, 'I am still at the corps rest camp waiting to go up to the battalion, but am not particularly looking forward to it as things do not seem to be nearly as well run as in the 47th; there is not the same confidence.'[205]

As early as the end of February the British had found the positions on the Oise to be less than secure against attack. In February daily patrols reported the River Oise frozen hard and not a serious obstacle against an enemy attack. On 26 February the 174th Brigade had noted 'a patrol of 6th Battalion London Regiment under Second Lieutenant Sampson had penetrated the enemy lines on the previous night.'[206] The thaw that followed made patrolling increasingly difficult, and alerted the enemy to their presence who now inflicted casualties on these patrols.

The position of the division behind the Sambre canal should have been a good one. It was the Germans who gained though by managing the river levels. In the days before the attack the River Oise water level dropped by six inches in twenty-four hours. The Germans were clearly manipulating it and the previously good positions behind this natural moat deteriorated as the marshes dried up. The problem with the position was that the battle zone was too far forward, being within artillery range of the Germans. Had it been made further back and out of range of German artillery then the troops could have been accommodated on site, and worked longer, thus providing quicker results and a more solid line.

The British were realising late in the day that their line was not strong enough, and trying to do something about it. In February and March Royal Engineers set about creating a line further back, behind Barisis, and this meant cutting down hundreds of trees, creating new defensive keeps at the Rond D'Epinois, the Clos des Vignes, and the Rond D'Orleans. In the sector north of the Oise the areas of Ferme Rouge, the Fort de Liez and the Sambre canal formed the defensive zone.

The Royal Engineers knew they were trying to buy time and any troops available were thrown into wiring the strong points for the expected attack. III Corps troops were brought in to help the Divisional Engineers as all available manpower was needed. At the Rond D'Orleans the 180 men of the 1/1st Northumberland Hussars were busy in wiring parties, meanwhile the newly formed 16th and 18th Entrenching Battalions dug trenches on the reserve Green Line, the field companies of the Royal Engineers were busy, as were the 1/4th Suffolk Pioneers.[207] The Tunnelling Companies were employed in digging dugouts at the rate of ten a fortnight. Even Italian workmen were brought to the front to help with the work. The front was therefore organised in 'strong points, mutually supporting each other by fire and with plenty of wire between'. Another of these strong points was the school at Fargniers, often referred to as a barracks. It was a telegraph station, military post and school. Now heavily fortified it was a front line strong point.[208] 'On 21 March the defences of the battle zone were undoubtedly strong as a whole, but incomplete.'[209]

At the last minute the British changed their defensive strategy in Operational Order number 80. Now the villages in the Bois De Courcy, La Fortelle and the keep at Amigny, would form the front line of the battle zone. The way the infantry occupied this zone was that one battalion would be in the forward zone with four companies, two in the line, one in the local keep or strongpoint and one in reserve. This meant that the companies could fall back on the keeps if heavily attacked, whilst as the Germans would filter round the strong points they would soon be surrounded.

The artillery bombardment started around 4.40am at 21 March and all parts of 58th Division's front were heavily bombarded. This 'drumfire' worked its way from front line to rear lines and back again. Telephone communications were destroyed by hits on headquarters and very quickly runners were the only communication available due to the heavy fog. In the sector of 175 and 174 brigades south of the Oise it was soon obvious though that the main battle was occurring to the north, as the artillery fire was much heavier there. Around St Quentin the shelling was intense and the frontline soldiers suffered accordingly. The shelling of La Fortelle and La Butte de Rouy continued, and cross-roads and battery positions were shelled all day. British guns were destroyed at these positions leading to the batteries being withdrawn out of danger that evening. Casualties were surprisingly light in this sector with the 9th Battalion suffering two wounded men, the 10th one man killed and five wounded and the 12th no casualties at all.

In this southern sector the main German thrust seems to have come at Vendeuil at around 6am against 18th Division, but south of here the 2nd Battalion were soon engaged also. The lack of visibility suited the attackers and they made easy progress around the flanks of the strong points. West of

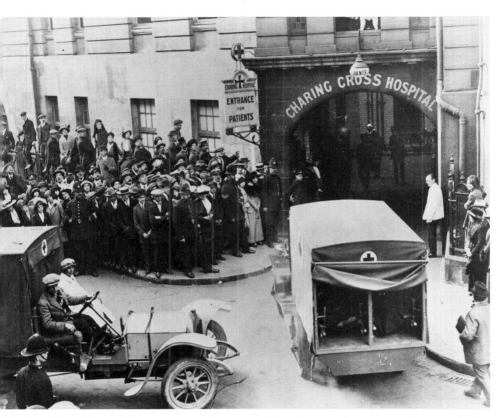

Charing Cross Hospital, wounded arriving watched by crowds, a scene that would be replicated throughout the war. *(10272227 Mary Evans Picture Library)*

Sergeant Knight VC and his wife Mabel, with his comrades. *(Image provided by British Postal Museum and Archive, copyright of Mrs Anne Walsh)*

Palace Road, Dalston, visited by Queen Mary, showing loyalty and scrolls. *(10731815 Illustrated London New/Mary Evans)*

Aerial picture of the trenches at Purdis Farm, Suffolk, 1943. *(EH/NMR)*

Midland Railway Extension (1) The sidings at St Jan, busy in early 1918. *(Q_046625 Imperial War Museum)*

Midland Railway Extension (2) The station at Wieltje, empty in early 1918, the road crossing and stone siding on right. *(Q_46629 Imperial War Museum)*

Duckboard Tracks in the Salient, the Alberta track (double) and the bunker visible in the devastated landscape. *(Q 046147 Imperial War Museum)*

Great War trenches survive at Purdis Farm, Ipswich, Suffolk. *(Author)*

The site of the Wieltje station today, with motorway overpass, the road crossing in the foreground is discernable in the original picture. *(Author)*

A soldier of the 58th in the trenches at Barisis with a French comrade. The Divisional crest is visible on the British soldier's helmet. *(Q_008700 Imperial War Museum)*

203. LA FÈRE dévastée (Aisne) — Les Ponts sur le Canal à Beautor

The canal at La Fère, empty of water, showing how little an obstacle it presented, with later bridges. *(FRAD00226_02811 Aisne Archives)*

Destroyed bridge at La Fère, showing how it would allow soldiers to cross, and later replacement bridge. *(Q_037205 Imperial War Museum)*

Chipilly Memorial by Henri Gauquié, owned by the Reserve Forces and Cadets Association for Greater London. *(Courtesy of Joanne Legg, www.greatwar.co.uk)*

La Fère the ruined school was defended stoutly but soon overcome by trench mortar fire and two German tanks. Survivors of the garrison broke out and rejoined their battalion to the west, the fog no doubt suiting the flight of the defenders this time. To the north the 7th Buffs (East Kent) of 18th Division held on at Vendeuil until 22 March. The forward zone battalions were standing their ground and slowing the advance of the Germans. It was no walkover for the attackers here. The soldiers of the 2nd Battalion at Travecy were soon under attack. They had been informed that positions in the forward zone would not be reinforced in the event of an enemy attack. The soldiers had fortified the remains of the village and engaged the enemy attack from this position. Travecy stands on the banks of the Sambre canal and beside the St Quentin to La Fère road, and so was at a crucial point for the Germans spilling forward.

Captain Harper was in command of the keep at Travecy and reported that there were no attacks on 21 March until late in the morning when:

> 'the enemy tried to bomb us out at 12pm, but was repulsed. At 7.40pm, just before dark the enemy attacked us from all sides, under cover of many machine guns. There was hot fighting for about an hour after which the enemy withdrew. Mr Roberts (left flank platoon) had meanwhile withdrawn to the keep, as he had been surrounded. I had with me now Mr Clapham, Mr Gibson, Mr Roberts and about fifty of my men and ten trench mortar men. That Friday dawned in another thick mist. We heard no sound of firing, other than our own, and no artillery fire up to this time. On the 22 March the enemy again attacked at dawn, but was repulsed with heavy losses.'[210]

Realising they were completely cut off they brewed up some tea and awaited the next attack, now down to fifty men through casualties. Later the mist cleared and they saw German transport on the road from La Fère to St Quentin, upon which they opened fire, the Germans bombed them with aircraft, but the final straw was when a British aeroplane bombed them. In the evening the Germans massed to attack again and in response they opened fire but the Germans replied with heavy machine gun fire. The British then surrendered having made a great account of themselves for two days. [211]

At Vendeuil and Ferme Rouge the Londoners fought hard. Everywhere on the front British troops were heavily engaged against the storm troopers. But on 174 and 175 brigades' front all remained calm. Patrols confirmed that the enemy were not attacking on their front. General Cator needed to secure the flank along the Oise valley to the north where his troops were heavily pressed. An attack south across the Oise was a possibility with the lowered water level. The flank of 175 Brigade was opening up and it was soon necessary to move reserves in order to hold it. Patrols were put out by the brigade to maintain contact with 173 Brigade. These included men of the 10th Battalion and went out along the Condren causeway and the marshes west of Servais.

By mid-morning on 21 March the mist and fog were clearing slightly, and the forts at Vendeuil and Liez were able to communicate by light signals. The commander of the Fort de Liez, Captain Fine, reported that Fort Vendeuil was requesting counter-attacks as essential.[212] At 1.30pm the Germans were seen massing to the south and south-west to attack. The fort held out until 6pm after a particularly heavy German bombardment was directed upon it, when the fort went quiet and presumably surrendered or was overcome.

In 173 Brigade sector the Germans were advancing on the hard pressed Londoners. At Ferme Rouge on the high ground the fog cleared and the enemy were seen in large numbers and engaged. Meanwhile the Royal Field Artillery fired on the river crossings used by the Germans. The British had been stirred to the fight and reserves were sent up to support their comrades in the battle zone. The 3rd Battalion sent two companies to support the 4th Battalion at Fargniers and Ferme Rouge, whilst the remainder patrolled and tried to keep contact with the 2nd Battalion. A first suggestion of counter-attack was refused; it was all about holding the ground and inflicting casualties where possible. A second counter-attack was made on the distillery east of Fargniers, though, and it was recaptured. Ferme Rouge was captured by the Germans at 3.45pm. The 4th Battalion reported that the enemy were in the eastern end of Fargniers and large numbers were in front of Quessy and threatening to break through near the copse and shrubbery at T.15.a. At 3.23pm two machine guns were sent to the 4th Battalion to bolster their defence. Local reserves were sent up by the 1/4th Suffolks at Ferme Rouge to participate in a counter-attack which failed and the 3rd Battalion went to Fargniers. By 6.50pm the fighting was coming to a close and essentially the forward zone had fallen although the battle zone had held except some local penetrations at the distillery, Ferme Rouge and in Fargnier.

The infantry could at least retreat with their rifles, the artillery was not always so lucky. The men of the Trench Mortar Batteries were unable to save their guns, and although their casualties were light, they lost one man killed, this being Gunner A.O. Davies, and one wounded. The mortars were close support weapons and were dug in near the front.[213] The brigade had faced a day of assault with its own troops but now the pressure was starting to tell and reinforcements had to be brought up from somewhere. So 175 Brigade now brought the 8th Battalion into the battle and the troops previously engaged as entrenching battalions and engineers, all were brought up to the front to hold on as long as possible.

To the north 18th Division was sorely pressed and it was here that a gap a mile wide started to appear in the British front line. The locality of The Triangle north-east of Ferme Rouge was the critical point between divisions and it was here that help was needed. Two platoons of the 3rd Battalion only reached the farm, and made an unsuccessful counter-attack. The line from here to the Crozat canal and from there to the St Quentin canal was to be held at all costs.[214]

As for the heavily depleted battalions of 173 Brigade, they were reformed with any men available and had ceased to function independently but became a force under various colonels. Grover's Force, north of the Oise and Shepherd's Force to the south were born. Grover's Force comprised the 503rd Field Company Royal Engineers and men of the 3rd Battalion City of London. Shepherd's Force comprised the 18th Entrenching Battalion, 6th (dismounted) Cavalry Brigade, C Company 1/4th Suffolk Regiment, and later a detachment of the divisional signal school. To the south 174 Brigade sent reasonably fresh and complete battalions in to the battle. The 8th Battalion was already dispatched to hold the Crozat canal at Tergnier. At 8pm a further measure was implemented: all troops in the battle zone were placed under the control of the commander of the 4th Battalion, Colonel Grover.

All that day the Royal Engineers had been preparing the bridges for demolition, a plan that had been in operation for about a month. A rapid response plan now ensured that bridges were blown as soon as they were threatened with capture. The likelihood of the future retirement of 173 Brigade to west of the St Quentin canal at Tergnier meant that more bridges were to be blown up. To the rear of 58th Division the 2nd Cavalry were at the behest of III Corps and, quickly dismounted, were brought up to the Crozat canal line as infantry. Counter-attacks were planned and then stopped against the Fort de Liez on the high ground just outside the village of Liez. The dismounted cavalry formed a line on the Liez to Vendeuil road to cover retreating infantry. The enemy had crossed the Crozat canal at Quessy to the south and were advancing on Voel. They were now established in Fargniers and had a bridgehead in Tergnier.

The morning of 22 March also dawned foggy. The 8th Battalion was now entrenched behind the Crozat canal at Tergnier, the 3rd and 4th Battalions having been relieved in the line. The war diary states that all the fighting in this sector was borne by the 8th Battalion and a motor machine gun unit with 182 Tunnelling Company at the railway bridge. The Germans managed to cross the canal at 1.15pm at bridge 21. The bridges had been blown by the Royal Engineers, but there is a difference between blowing up a bridge and rendering it unusable to a single line of infantry who can still cross on the damaged girders, and this would be a theme of the day as the Army Commander General Gough and his commander of Royal Engineers disputed how the bridges were blown. It was very hard to blow a bridge so entirely that the girders were not still useable to enemy infantry. Answering this general criticism Colonel Savage, the Divisional Commander of Royal Engineers wrote that:

> 'while the preparations begun beforehand aimed at destroying bridges as road bridges, brigade and battalion commanders were not satisfied and did not consider demolition complete until the bridges had been rendered unusable to the enemy infantry. The impression gathered was that infantry commanders thought that demolition would vaporise the bridges into thin air and leave practically nothing behind.'[215] See Photo.

On the front at this point it was not only the bridges that formed a passage for the German storm troopers but also the canal locks. As stated by British command, these were sufficiently narrow that with planks or small bridges are easily crossed by infantry, or within a few hours engineers could use the footings as the basis for a heavier bridge. However the report of the last stand at Travecy states that they caught enemy traffic using the St Quentin to La Fère road, in a southerly direction on 22 March, so it seems that the majority of German forces were coming south from St Quentin rather than across from La Fère, which was somewhat hemmed in by the canals.

The enemy, on crossing the canal westwards with three battalions tried to extend his flank south along the bank to clear them of enfilading fire. These attacks were met with heavy and sustained resistance by the 8th Battalion who drove off all enemy attacks during the day. In the fog the confusion was heightened by not knowing who was friend or foe. The 8th Battalion reported that 'about midday the enemy adopted the ruse of clothing parties of their men in uniforms of captured or killed men'.[216] The companies on the left, A and B on the north side were overrun by this deception, but C and D companies held on, despite being surrounded, broke out on the afternoon of 23 March, and retired to Chauny.[217] Rifleman Walter Young, being an unarmed stretcher bearer 'could not believe they were German soldiers, for only about five minutes before we had come almost past the spot where they now were'.[218] He was forced to surrender. The 8th Battalion had left behind 300 men of all ranks, killed, missing or wounded.

This gave other forces time to dig in on the ground behind Tergnier, roughly following the line of a Roman road north to south. The 18th Entrenching Battalion was in the Green Line behind the 8th Battalion and now took charge of the brigade headquarters 'the line was held all through the day, and at dawn a counter-attack was launched by some French troops, although not very successful'.[219]

That morning at 8am the French had brought up reinforcements to the heavily pressed British forces. They launched a counter-attack but failed to make any headway as they had not arrived in strength and their artillery was not yet deployed sufficiently for the quick firing French Soixante-Quinze guns to provide effective artillery support.

As the serious attacks north of the Oise continued and the situation of most of the British Army as far north as Arras was severely at risk, 174 Brigade south of the Oise were largely untroubled by the attacks. An attempted raid by the Germans on the left flank of the brigade was easily repulsed. The right flank was bombarded by trench mortars from 8pm to 9.30pm, but otherwise only the 8th Battalion, sent north to bolster 173 Brigade, was heavily engaged holding the canal line. In fact the main events south of the Oise were the readiness of Germans to surrender or desert, before or during the offensive. A Lieutenant Becker, of the 18th Infantry, Third Bavarian Regiment, was captured and interviewed. The 9th Battalion captured five men of the 60th Landwehr Regiment who had taken part in the successful attack on La Frette but had retreated in disorder due to the British artillery barrage. They had fallen back on the marshes and lost their way.[220]

Patrols put out to maintain contact with 173 brigade failed to find out much information, but it was eventually discovered at 9pm that the enemy had advanced as far as Condren. The serious issue now was the 6,000 yard gap between British forces north and south of the Oise River. This led to much pressure to form a flank of 174 Brigade and withdraw from the Barisis front, and therefore to bow to the pressure north of the river and form some sort of northern flank, perhaps even fall back to the Sambre-Aisne canal.

On 23 March at 7am a French attack was counter productive, as they retired in disorder due to lack of ammunition, and carried with them men of 18th Division who lost heart, or took advantage of the French retreat, to retire also. The retreat here opened a gap between 58th Division, French forces, and 18th Division to the north. Grover's Force formed a northern flank and held the gap. But the threat by German cavalry to the Roman road line was still that it might be surrounded. A Fusilier Brigade was formed out of elements of the 2nd, 3rd and 4th Battalions under Colonel W.R.H. Dann to protect this flank on 26 March. The survivors were two companies of the 4th at 205, all ranks, one company of the 2nd at 179, all ranks, and one company of the 3rd at 189 all ranks.

The Germans were still controlling the water levels of the Oise and now released a torrent of water to stop British reinforcements crossing the river, almost catching some men of the Condren garrison trying to retreat south of the river under pressure from German attacks, who did not know the way but who made their way through up to 5 feet of water whilst under fire from German machine guns on the north bank. The Condren garrison was joined by two companies of French infantry who used the Condren causeway and foot bridges until they too were blown up. The Germans were now protecting their flank and possibly trying to hamper the work of engineers trying to blow the bridges, but it was mostly too late. This meant the two brigades south of the Oise were safe from attack from the north bank of the Oise. Also there were no London Division soldiers north of the river.

The situation was such on 24 March that the French forces reinforcing the British Divisions in the III Corps area at the hinge between the British and French armies were put into the position of being in command. Thus the British forces north of the Oise now came under command of the French General Pellé,[221] of the V French Corps, a wise move by the Allies to ensure that the two armies kept together, and did not retreat in opposite directions. The 58th Division came under the command of the First French Cavalry Corps, VI French Army. The stand of 173 Brigade had certainly delayed the enemy attacks and more importantly they had held the join between the British and French armies. But now the headlong retreat of the rest of the British Army meant that their position should be handed back to the French Army.

The fighting died down for the exhausted survivors of 173 Brigade and 8th Battalion. The war diary records that morale was good but they needed new clothes and rest. In the period from 21-24 March the casualties to the 3rd Battalion were 18 officers and 341 other ranks, out of a strength of 47 officers and 909 other ranks on 20 March.

To the south the remainder of the division was largely untouched by the battle, although artillery still caused casualties. Various alarms were spread as 174 Brigade suspected German attacks that were about to be launched but never materialised. The Germans were trying now trying to establish a bridgehead south of the Oise and attacked Chauny Sud (south). The enemy launched this by putting planks across the blown sections of the bridges and footbridges, using a boat or pontoons, and infiltrating across the river. Defending this position was 16th Entrenching Battalion under Colonel W.H. Micholls.

On 27 March this battalion relieved 246 French Infantry Regiment. The sector presented only one weak point at Chauny Sud. Two bridges crossing the river had only been partly destroyed and could still be crossed in single file. The first three days were quiet. But on 31 March at 5.30am the Germans tried to cross in strength. They advanced on two fronts, slipping past British posts in the dark. This advance was made against little opposition as a vital Lewis gun jammed at the crucial moment and the Germans spilled across in some numbers. An immediate counter-attack by the support company of the 16th Entrenching Battalion 'failed to dislodge the snipers and machine guns which the enemy quickly established among the walls of the ruins'.[222]

A British artillery barrage was thrown down on the SOS Line, a pre-arranged line to aid the British defenders. The British counter-attacked at 11am, pushing most of the attackers back to the river but failed to dislodge again the enemy positions in the ruins. Twenty-three prisoners and one machine gun were taken. These men were found to be storm troopers, and were to be backed up by a mass of German infantry. Further German attacks by the infantry were repulsed in the afternoon at 5.45pm. A British barrage by heavy guns and mortars was established and in the evening an advance was made to flush out the remaining enemy troops. The attack had failed, despite using their storm troopers and many Germans now surrendered, with around 60 dead and 51 captured. The German PoWs, mostly of 251 Infantry Regiment, stated that it was the British artillery that had smashed the attack, as 58th Division artillery was mostly intact in the brigades south of the river and could therefore contribute to the battle with the French with overwhelming and decisive force. British casualties were light with one officer and seven other ranks killed, twenty-four wounded and three missing.

This was really the last decisive move against 58th Division and its associated units in the German Spring Offensive, except for a German raid on the Amigny Keep in 175 Brigade's sector. This seems to have become possible due to the French taking over a position which protected the flank of the keep, and in particular controlled a sunken road at the front of it. The resultant infiltration by the Germans meant that the British were taken unawares.[223] The German activity on this front was increasing and the amount of observation balloons and aircraft activity pointed to a likely offensive here. It was at this point that the remaining sector was handed back to the French, and the new redoubts and keeps here were taken over by their forces. The Germans did attack here between 6 and 9 April 1918 under Operation Archangel, but the attack only advanced as far as the Aillette canal.

As they came under French control the division received the communiqué put out by Marshall Petain which was passed on to brigades of the division:

'The enemy has flung himself on us in a supreme effort. His aim is to separate us from the British to open the road to Paris. Cost what it may we must stop him. Stick to your ground. Stand Fast. Other troops are at hand, together with them, fling yourselves on the invader. This is the battle of the war! Soldiers of the Marne, of the Yser, of Verdun, to you I make my appeal. The fate of France hangs in the balance. Petain.'

To this was added the Brigadier's translation and appeal:

'We are with the French and it is therefore doubly our duty to show them what sort of fighters their Allies are. The French commander speaks of the soldiers of the Marne, Yser, and Verdun. What he says applies equally to the men of Bullecourt, Ypres, and Cambrai.'[224]

The other troops at hand were reserves and of course the Americans who were soon arriving in numbers.

This appeal calls on the troops to continue to show some British pluck while the reference to the men of Cambrai shows the proportion of men who had been transferred to 58th Division from 47th Division before the March offensive. What this battle made clear was that 58th Division, and indeed the British III Corps, had learned the lessons of Passchendaele. With stout hearts and even under duress they had formed up however they could under Grover's and Shepherd's Forces, and stood their ground. The division had only been on the edge of the German attack but had resisted, the hinge between the French and British Armies had held, they had not broken and truly they had come of age as a fighting force. Maxse had been right when he longed for the presence of the London Division. Edmonds, in his Official History is unusually ecstatic in writing, 'it is astonishing that a force containing such a variety of units, and un-used to co-operate, should have held up the enemy so long; the truth is that his [the German] artillery gave him little assistance'.[225]

But it was the British soldiers' ability to adapt to circumstances that won the day and 58th Division had nobly played its part. As the reinforcements formed of the disbanded battalions of 47th Division had strengthened the division, the resolve to win the war was mounting. The commanders of 58th Division were under temporary French command and were saved by French intervention in the grey zone between the two armies.

To the north of 58th Division the Fifth Army took the brunt of the German attack. The official Australian war historian Charles Bean says that General Gough 'was receiving alarming reports of [Fifth Army's] exhaustion and disorganisation. According to these not merely did it fail to exhibit the bulldog tenacity expected from British infantry in defence but its organisation and system of communication was so shattered that it was incapable of serious resistance.'

Nevertheless casualties to 173 Brigade between 21 March and 5 April were 2,234 for 58th Division out of a total of 13,995 for III Corps. These were mostly accounted for by the 87 officers and 1,606 soldiers missing, a proportion of whom were captured by the Germans. Most casualties had occurred in 173 Brigade, which had been severely mauled. The 4th Battalion now comprised only 40 men, the colonel and a colour sergeant major, having suffered 21 officer casualties and 650 other ranks in eight days fighting.[226] The 58th Division was now listed as an exhausted division by Field Marshal Sir Douglas Haig.[227] Although this was somewhat misleading, as only part of the division had been engaged, this brigade had certainly been engaged in the fighting. The division was handed back to British control after ten days under French command. This international system of command and control had worked and following the Doullens Conference on 26 March Haig had handed control of the entire British Army to French control under Marshal Foch to enable an overall command in the emergency. It is interesting to see how the London Division had pre-empted this hand over of command by several days.

Notes

202 Courtesy of the National Library of Scotland
203 Papers of Field Marshal Sir John Creer Dill courtesy of the Trustees of the Liddell Hart Centre for Military Archives

204 IWM Archive, MISC 1988/09/13 The papers of Holt

205 National Archives WO95/3004

206 National Archives WO95/697 III Corps R.E.

207 Today this has been rebuilt and forms a complex, open to the public, as home to the Musée de la Resistance et de la Deportation de Picardie of the Second World War.

208 National Archives WO95/534

209 IWM Archive 74/76/1 The papers of Captain Harper MC

210 IWM Archive 74/76/1 The papers of Captain Harper, diary of his service and captivity

211 National Archives WO95/2049

212 Harrison and Duckers (ed) *Shropshire R.H.A. 1908-1920,*

213 National Archives, WO95/3000

214 National Archives, WO95/2994 58 Division C.R.E.

215 Derviche-Jones, *History of the Post Office Rifles* (Aldershot) 1919, p.28 courtesy of B.P.M.A.

216 Messenger, *History of the Post Office Rifles* (London) 1988 p. 111ff

217 IWM 88/57/1 the papers of Rifleman Walter Young

218 National Archives, WO 95/700, 18 Entrenching Battalion

219 National Archives WO 95/3008

220 Edmunds, *Military Operations* 1918 Vol 1 p. 402

221 National Archives, WO 95/700, Lt-Colonel W.H. Micholls

222 National Archives, WO95/3008

223 National Archives, WO95/3004

224 Edmonds, J.E. *Military Operations,* 1918 Vol. 1 p.337

225 National Archives, WO95/3001 war diary

226 Edmonds J.E. *Military Operations* 1918 Vol II p 113

227 Wheeler-Holohan and Wyatt (ed.) 1921 *The Rangers Historical Record* (London) p.224

Chapter 10

Infantry and Cavalry
The Battle of the Avre
4–6 April 1918

The units of the London Division pulling out were hampered by the weight and numbers of French infantry at the canal bridges; they reached the rail head tired but with good morale. The crucial thing was that even though the division had had one of its brigades mauled, the remaining units were mostly unchanged and had survived intact to fight another day. A good deal of the fighting had fallen on corps and army troops, such as the entrenching battalions, whilst the French reinforcements had arrived in time to help 173 Brigade.

The 58th Division was pulled back to Amiens, via a long seven hour train journey, during which they slipped past the closest part of the German line, only 3 miles away, but were largely unhindered in their progress. The train in which the Rangers Battalion was moved back came under shell fire at Boves.[228] The train carrying the 9th Battalion heard strange noises:

> 'After a while the noises got more pronounced, one which seemed to come from somewhere close at hand reproducing all the several noises of a shell. We then discovered that the said noises were not fog signals but French guns in action. The train was running along in front of the French batteries and the Germans were shelling the railway. It was not many seconds before all lights were out and not a sound could be heard along the length of the train.'[229]

A narrow escape, luck was with the division that night as a direct hit on any train would have caused havoc.

The division now detrained at Longeau, a railway junction just outside Amiens, and a small part was brought almost immediately into the battles at Villers-Bretonneux. In just nine days the German advance had crossed the old Somme battlefields and now threatened Amiens, a major city and railway junction, vital to the Allied war machine. The town of Villers-

Bretonneux lay just 6 miles away from Amiens and overlooked it from the edge of the chalk escarpment. The battle had reached here on 30 March, whilst 58th Division were still fighting in the south of the vast swathe of territory re-captured by the Germans between Arras and St Quentin.

Villers-Bretonneux was a prosperous manufacturing town of over 5,000 inhabitants and 1,101 houses on a level site. It contained nine cotton mills, three brick works, a hat factory and a beet preparation works. It lay on the railway from Amiens to Noye and St Quentin, astride the old Roman road due east to Peronne, and so was at a vital crossroads.[230] The town lay mostly south of the Roman road, between it and the railway, with the Roman road on the highest ridge. The railway to the east sits mostly in a deep cutting with road bridges over it, although at some points to the west the role is reversed and the roads pass under with the railway on embankments on top.

The landscape here is like the South Downs with high plateaux, some rolling, but some ground near Cachy bowling-green flat; to the south lies the Somme River and its marshes. To the north at Corby the River Ancre gently rises away to its source north of Albert. On the southern side of Villers-Bretonneux the land is slightly lower than the town whose church can be seen at all times. Further south the land dips away and it is in the higher of these reaches that Hangard Wood sits in a hollow. The wood is overlooked from most directions except the south where the village of Hangard is well below it in the valley. The rise beyond Hangard is higher on the eastern side than on the west, giving the Germans who held this ground the advantage here. The historian of 18th Divisional notes that 'the chief tactical features of the sector were two spurs situated north and west respectively of the village of Domart-sur-la-Luce, the high ground of the Villers-Bretonneux plateau and the Gentelles-Cachy plateau'.[231] The original British line lay on the high ground east of the wood, but subsequent lines ran through the wood, a bad position. The building of the Cachy Switch line on high ground to the west was a better sited position, being the last before the flatness of the Cachy plain. Hangard Wood, in true Great War style, was to remain a heavily contested battlefield, with thousands of lives lost for its capture and recapture.

The Somme, Avre, Noye and Ancre rivers all merge east of Amiens and offered some defence for the Allies in their plans to defend the city. This was also land untouched by the war, except for some bombing of Amiens; this was the first time the medieval city had been in range of the German guns. The target of the German guns was the railway yards at Longeau, Amiens station and the bridges over the Somme to the east of the city.[232]

Holding Villers-Bretonneux was the last card in the Allies' pack, and was to be tested in the following weeks, and the German will to advance any further tried to the limit. This battle was termed the Battle of the Avre.

The Australian forces were fresh into battle in the defence of Amiens, having been resting and re-equipping behind the lines. However the

nd were battle worn, as were
ie days. A small part of 58th
/illers-Bretonneux. The 6th
battle whilst the rest of the
portant to defend Amiens in
ont line when the battle was
of 58th Division joined the
was very useful at propping

eriod of the German attacks
ght up to Villers-Bretonneux
as the full strength battalion
ows of artillerymen and their

of a complete battalion
ose from the ground and
There was a section of
h exhaustion, away from
ss, and then turned and
upefied, they were trying

ild expect at this stage of the
es, plus an equal number of
his is the front line strength,
Amiens with the rest of the

x they found it intact, much
their way to the front:

'houses and shops were intact and roads unmarked by shell fire; only the darkness, the absence of civilians, and the presence of so many soldiers, suggested the altered circumstances... Some were accommodated in the cellars of houses, others in a cloth factory, and others again in a school.'

So the soldiers had a very comfortable first night in the town, a roof over their heads and 'a hundred and one things that could make a billet comfortable'.[235]

The 7th Battalion were in a reserve position in Bois de L'Abbé to the west of the town. They did however draw stores from a huge warehouse 'full of tinned food, wine, candles and a heap of other things in short supply.' The resulting stews were much enjoyed by all ranks. For a few short hours life was good. The key thing was that the soldiers' morale was kept up and this London Battalion was at full strength and enjoying good food and billets in the line for the first time since they had left England.

The 6th Battalion's sleep was interrupted next morning with an artillery bombardment on the town at 5.30am.

> 'No more efficient alarm clock than an unexpected bombardment has ever been invented, and in no time platoons were seeking safer if less comfortable accommodation in cellars, but in directing the men to them many officers became casualties, amongst whom was Major W. Whitehead, the second in command.'[236]

Stretcher bearers were kept busy most of that day picking up the casualties from this unexpected bombardment. One source puts the casualties of the 6th Battalion from this bombardment as 100 men including most of the company officers, so not really justifying the night in comfortable surroundings, as this diminished their strength considerably.[237] The remainder of the battalion was soon dug in around the town and in trenches immediately outside it as a reserve. At 6.30am German infantry in small numbers started forward to the Allied line, these were the German storm trooper squads whose job it was to infiltrate the British lines. This time the visibility was much better and 'these were immediately dealt with by machine guns, Lewis guns and rifles with deadly effect, very heavy casualties being inflicted upon the enemy who immediately retired slightly without persisting in the attack'.[238] The difference between this attack which failed, and the attacks of 21 March which succeeded (up to a point) is notable, this time the weather was not to the German's advantage.

Likewise at 7am the Germans attacked in mass formations, this time the British forces responded with 'an accurate barrage which was right on the dense masses of advancing enemy, cutting gaps in his formations.'[239] This accurate and heavy defensive fire from the infantry caused 'enormous losses.' At this stage 18th Division to the north was under severe attack, a panic started to spread through the British and Australian forces. This seems to have started in the 8th London Rifle Brigade of 14th Division and spread along the line as one force pulled back due to the battalion on their flank pulling back. The retreat of the 8th London Rifle Brigade opened up the flank of the Australians who lost two machine guns but eventually held their position by pulling back their left hand company. The troopers of 1st Dragoon Guards came up and operated as dismounted infantry with their machine guns and rifles and held the line on the Australians' left. Six Canadian armoured cars of the Canadian Machine Gun Squadron were brought up and held the gap in the line, knocking out the German machine guns, as no tanks seem to have been available not having the speed to get there quickly. By 11.30am the London Rifle Brigade were launching a counter-attack, having been buoyed up and turned around.

It seems to have been the cavalry that saved the potentially disastrous situation where the Germans could have out flanked the Australians and opened the way into Villers-Bretonneux. The mobility of 6 Cavalry Brigade, made up of 1st and 3rd Dragoon Guards, the 17th (Duke of Cambridge's Own) Lancers, was the key.[240] One Australian colonel reported:

> 'Seeing them gallop into action with swords and lances drawn, going to where help was most needed, enthused our men enormously. It is an honour to fight alongside such gallant troops. Their dash, their gallantry and their discipline are of the highest order. These are true British soldiers.'[241]

The brigade soon had elements of the dismounted Dragoon Guards dug in by squadrons. For the first time since 1914 the cavalry had played its part on the Western Front in the period from 21 March with the conditions of near open warfare that existed.

One interesting insight into the Rifle Brigade retirement is that it came not just from the onslaught of Germans attacking but from 'fifth columnists'. It was reported in 36th Battalion AIF that a 'British' officer came up to their position and ordered them to retire, but in usual style the Aussies refused.[242] He was wearing an officer's tunic and a private's cap and was not suitably fitted out. When questioned he was unable to satisfy their demands and show papers, and the Aussies promptly shot him.[243] If a German spy or spies were operating in the British lines, rather like during the Ardennes battles in 1944, then less stoic men than the Aussies might well fall for the deception and pull back. The historian of the 9th Battalion has a different angle on this. This is that on 9 April a 'show' was organised by the Intelligence branch 'orders were issued and everything was cut and dried, even to officers having to wear privates' tunics, but the 'show' had to be postponed owing to the fact that the Boches themselves were going to attack.'[244] It is possible that an officer involved in some intelligence branch operation was still wearing different uniform five days later. If so it was his loss. This agrees with the Australian Official Historian, Charles Bean, that the officer probably was British. The pressure on the British forces by the Germans was intense and the line, by whatever means, was tested severely.

To the north of the Roman road and the River Somme the battle was going badly. Hamel was lost despite the now stout defence by the London Rifle Brigade of 14th Division. It is understandable that new reinforcements, bought in to bolster under-strength battalions after the German attacks would not be savvy enough to see a spy and might dump their weapons and kit and retreat. That a whole battalion would fall back shows that whatever happened this was widely believed to be a direct order. The Australian 33rd Battalion was dug in at the east of Villers-Bretonneux, its strength on the 3-4 April was at about 68 officers and 411 men. It was the Aussies under General Elliot and Colonel Ferres who re-organised the London Rifle Brigade and other stragglers into a stop line on Hill 104. British cavalry was brought in and not only held the gap in the line but helped reorganise the stragglers and by whatever means held the Germans. The war diary of the London Rifle Brigade states:

'At 6.30am [the enemy] repeatedly attacked, but was driven off. Eventually he succeeded in penetrating our position and reached Battalion Headquarters in the quarry. Here a stand was made and the enemy held off for about one and a half hours. A line being re-established around 500 yards behind Headquarters.'[245]

It does not state anything about troops breaking, although it does admit that the Germans broke their lines, but nothing about German spies, Australians and the cavalry taking charge.

The attacks seem to have then lessened for a period as the Germans consolidated their gains, pushing machine gun teams ahead of their infantry to give them some protection as they dug in. The British forces followed this by pushing their own gun teams forward and a period of movement back and forward followed as both sides jostled for position.

In the afternoon on the south side of the Roman road the hard-pressed 53 and 55 Brigades of 18th Division were pushed back to the Bois de Hangard in the morning where they were able to hold the line. The Australian 33rd and 35th Battalions were then heavily engaged. The Buffs on the right were forced back in disorder with part of the 35th Battalion AIF as well. This led to the whole line pulling back at about 5.15pm and as one officer put it succinctly 'the Battalion headquarters was the most advanced position'. The Australian 34th and 36th Battalions were in reserve, as were the 6th Battalion and it was at this juncture that the command to counter-attack was passed to Colonel Goddard of the 35th Battalion AIF.

South of the Roman road Australian officers brought word of Colonel Goddard's impending counter-attack that evening and an officer and his men of D Company, 6th City of London, who were retiring due to a falling back on their right, duly informed of the immediate counter attack 'at once turned back and re-entered their trench'.[246] The Londoners and the Australians were to launch the attack to restore the line north and south of the railway. Men of 35th and 36th Battalions AIF were the main force with the Queens (Royal West Surrey) and 6th Londoners joining them. Although some officers refused to join the attack, there was a general impetus for it from all ranks.

Three companies (presumably A, B and C), a total of 270 all ranks of the Londoners, moved out of the town, turned south across the railway bridge and then deployed in sectional rushes. Two companies took part in the attack and a third held the line. D Company had been detached to reinforce the Buffs earlier in the day and some of the section's Lewis guns had been sent to the Australians whose guns were jammed with mud. This was a perilous task with one killed and five wounded. 'Thus the action was largely entrusted to the Riflemen, and worthily they responded to the call, and simple were the plan, it was entirely successful.' German soldiers 'retired, however, on seeing fresh troops coming into action, and after covering parties had been pushed forward for a hundred yards or so, digging was commenced along a line at right angles to the railway.'[247] The Australians were able to conform to this line and moved forward that night to form a new line largely unopposed. Once again the sight of fresh troops coming into sight either buoyed their own side or lowered morale on the enemy side.

Sergeant Cowherd paints a marvellous picture of this attack:

A Company, with fixed bayonets, started down the road to meet the enemy. We reached the eastern end of the town, dashed through the enemy barrage, and formed a line astride the Marcelcave road in remarkably quick time. We then saw lines upon lines of the enemy advancing, and they stopped about 400 yards from us. A few Australians joined us, and we started a rushing attack which surprised the enemy into a sudden but orderly withdrawal by stages to his old line.'[248]

This was more like something out of the Peninsular War than the Great War; advancing with fixed bayonets to meet the enemy, a true tactical advance, and, unlike so many attempts in the Great War, this was successful.

Edmonds paints this in a slightly different light, saying the 6th only formed the second line of this attack. Some sources put the numbers at one thousand Australians in the attack; however this must be the total British forces, including the depleted Londoners and Australians. A battalion at full strength was 800 to 1,000 men, but only half were ever committed to any attack. There were 270 Londoners, and possibly around 400 men in each Australian Battalion, plus the Queen's, so around 800 or 900 Australians, 270 Londoners come to about 1,200. Pedersen makes the very good point that it was only British forces in 1918 that were so under strength that they had to reduce the battalions in their brigades; the Australian forces were well manned, in early 1918 with many of the wounded of 1917 returning to the ranks after the AIF had four months of re-equipping and training.[249] Bean puts the Australian 36th Battalion in the vanguard, south of the railway, with 35th on the left, the 7th Queens on the right. The battalions were under orders to the 35th Battalion AIF and this is where the confusion may come from. But the Australian 9 Brigade was under orders of 18th British Division, Maxse's old command. Also the Queen's and 36th were south of the railway, the Londoners and the 35th to the north of the railway. This meant that the Londoners would not have been necessarily aware of the attacks north of the railway line. This explains Sergeant Cowherd's comment that 'a few' Australians joined in the attack; these must have been stragglers and troops holding the line who joined in when they saw the successful attack. The line was re-established and on the right the French had held on at Hangard Wood. Now the 6th Battalion was pulled out and 173 Brigade went into the line. The main force of the Londoners had played a small but significant part in the defence of Villers-Bretonneux during the first battle.

The Brigadier of 9 Australian Infantry Brigade praised:

> 'the splendid work of the cavalry (1st Dragoons and 17th Lancers) in protecting my northern flank by vigorous offensive action. The timely co-operation of the Queen's in the counter-attack of the 36th Battalion was of the utmost assistance and was most helpful at a very critical moment. The Sixth London Regiment proved particularly keen and willing to help in staying the enemy advance and was used to very good effect.'[250]

Although 173 Brigade had been mauled by the attacks in March, it was 'pleased with itself and all the men were very optimistic.'[251] The losses of the 4th Battalion alone had been 15 officers and 379 men between 21 March and 3 April. They stayed in the French sector longer and were only relieved on 3 April. This brigade was detrained at Longeau on 6 April, and was reinforced with the 6th Battalion King's Own Yorkshire Light Infantry and 12th Battalion Middlesex Regiment. Half the Yorkshires went to the 3rd London, the remainder of 4 officers 344 men went to the 4th Battalion. The 12th Middlesex became the 2nd London Battalion, further diluting the original battalion, not that there was much of it left. Colonel Dann had commanded the Fusilier Brigade between 24 March and 6 April when he relinquished command and resumed command of the 4th Battalion. It took over a support line at Gentelles, and received a draft of 127 'lads under 19 years of age...very keen'.

Casualties for the period 4-6 April were 30 officers and 635 other ranks for the Australian 9 Brigade and 153 officers and 3,377 other ranks (period 5 April to 27 April) for 58th Division in both battles.[252] It would be best to assume that 100 casualties were caused by the initial bombardment, 1 British machine gunner was killed and 5 were wounded, plus 50 to 80 men, something similar in proportion to the Australians. Of the two Australian battalions, the 35th had lost 3 officers and 43 men killed, and 6 officers and 101 men wounded with 44 other ranks missing. The 36th had lost 4 officers and 29 other ranks killed, and 8 officers and 126 men wounded and one other rank missing. The losses inflicted on the Germans appear to be very high, with claims of 4,000 on 4 April and 1,000 on 5 April alone.

On 11 April Field Marshal Sir Douglas Haig issued his famous 'backs to the wall' order, in which he tried to stiffen the hearts of the British forces fighting on the Western Front, but which especially applied to the battles around Amiens:

'In spite of throwing already one hundred and six divisions into the battle and enduring the most reckless sacrifice of human life, he has yet made little progress towards his goals. We owe this to the determined fighting and self-sacrifice of our troops. Words fail me to express the admiration which I feel for the splendid resistance offered by all ranks of our Army under the most trying circumstances. Many amongst us now are tired. To those I would say that victory will belong to the side which holds out the longest. The French Army is moving rapidly and in great force to our support. There is no course open to us but to fight it out. Every position must be held to the last man; there must be no retirement. With our backs to the wall and believing in the justice of our cause each one of us must fight to the end. The safety of our homes and the freedom of mankind depend upon the conduct of each one of us at this critical moment.'

On 12 April 173 Brigade was in support behind the Australians at Hangard Wood, with the French 131st Division on its right and 24 Brigade of 8th Division on its left. Also involved were 5th Australian Division on the north side of the town and 18th Division in reserve. The Allied line ran east of the town from west of Hamel in the north to Hangard in the south. The French came under attack at the Bois de Hangard and crucially lost it to the Germans at this point. All the battalions of 173 Brigade were in the front line, the depleted 2nd, 3rd, and 4th battalions, with the 7th Battalion in reserve at Cachy Switch. The 8th Battalion, like many others, was at low ebb for manpower and had to be reinforced by two companies of the Norfolk Regiment on regrouping at Amiens. The division was severely depleted by this stage and mostly had few links to its Post Office or London roots. The rest of the division was in reserve positions, 174 and 175 brigades behind 173 Brigade. So once again the whole division was committed to the front after a period of rest and refitting.

The division had relieved 5 Australian Brigade at Hangard Wood on 18 April. Major General Cator had this compliment to pay:

> 'All the fighting work they did here was splendid; one and all, from Brigadier-General Smith downwards, were all out to help and we found them first class to work with.... I have never had the good luck to be with Australians in this war, but I think I can safely say that they are one of the best fighting units I have come across.'[253]

This type of inter-unit praise was commonplace in the war, and I am sure they meant it. Bean was of course an Australian, but he was a journalist not a soldier, and although the Australian sources are of course going to praise their own forces, it is sure that the Australians had earned their congratulations. Let us hope that the Australians took the compliment to heart, because rather than a long period of rest, they would be needed again soon.

The suddenness of the attack and the withdrawal to Amiens meant that there had been little time to build adequate defences, and after the First Battle of Villers-Bretonneux the Australian line was mostly fox holes 8 yards long and 2 yards wide with steps at each end. There was no wire to speak of as the Australians preferred to fight in the open. Colonel Dann wrote: 'We got to work at once and by 24 April had a good trench dug along our whole section with good strong wire in front of it.'[254]

They were going to need it as on the night of 23 April they brought in an Alsatian deserter who gave them worrying news of a further attack.

VILLERS-BRETONNEUX

- - - - FRONT LINE 24 APRIL
-·-·-·- FRONT LINE AFTER ATTACK
-··-··- RESERVE LINES
++++++ AFTER COUNTER-ATTACK
✗✗ TANK BATTLE

A - CACHY SWITCH
B - RAILWAY CUTTING

N↑

CORBIE

RIVER ANCRE

0   YARDS   250

Hamel

VILLERS-BRETONNEUX

MONUMENT FARM

HANGARD WOOD

FRENCH SECTOR
HANGARD

BOIS D'AGUENNE

173 BRIGADE

BOIS D'AGBÉ

CACHY

A

175 BRIGADE

GENTELLES

DOMART

BLANGY WOOD

GENTELLES WOOD

LONGEAU
174 BRIGADE

RIVER AVRE

after Edmonds

Notes

228 Keeson, A. 1923 *The History and records of the Queen Victoria's Rifles* (London) p.393

229 Edmonds J.E. *Military Operations* 1918 Vol II, (London) p.126n

230 Nichols, G. *History of the 18th Division* (Edinburgh and London) p.302

231 Edmonds J.E., *Military Operations*, 1918 Vol II, p136n

232 Pedersen, in *Villers-Bretonneux*, gives the strength as 370 at the start of the battle. Pedersen goes into the battle in great detail, so for the purposes of this book I will concentrate on the southern sector of the battle, where 58th Division was involved.

233 Godfrey, *The Cast Iron Sixth* (London) 1938 p.197

234 Godfrey, (London) 1938 p.197

235 Godfrey, (London) 1938 ibid

236 AWM4 23/52/10 35th Battalion A.I.F. war diary

237 AWM4 23/53/18 9 Infantry Brigade A.I.F. report on action

238 AWM4 23/53/18 9th Infantry Brigade A.I.F. report on action

239 Baker A. 1986 *Battle Honours of the British and Commonwealth Armies* (London) p. 222 ff

240 AWM4 23/50/18 33rd battalion A.I.F. report on defensive operations April 4-5

241 AWM4 23/52/18 36th Battalion A.I.F. war diary

242 The officer they shot, 2nd Lt. G.E. Martin, 5th (attached 7th) Queens (Royal West Surrey Regt.) is listed as dying on 4 April 1918 and is commemorated on the Pozières memorial, if this was the same body and not a German in Martin's uniform. This would seem to imply he died of wounds, but there is no burial site recorded.

243 Keeson, A. 1923 *The History and Records of the Queen Victoria's Rifles*, Vol II (London) p.394

244 National Archives WO95/1895, war diary 8th Battalion, L.R.B.

245 Bean, 1941 *The A.I.F. in France* (Sydney) p.341

246 Godfrey, *The Cast Iron Sixth*, 1921 p201

247 Godfrey, *The Cast Iron Sixth*, 1921 p.201

248 Pedersen, 2004 *Villers-Bretonneux*, (Barnsley) p.40-41

249 AWM4 23/53/18 9th Brigade A.I.F. statement of action 4-6 April 1918

250 National Archives WO95/3001 extracts from diary of Colonel W.R.H. Dann

251 Edmonds, J.E. 1937 *Military Operations* 1918 Vol II (London) p.405

252 Bean, 1942 *The Official History of Australia in the War* (Sydney) p.521

253 National Archives WO95/3001 report

254 'Sturmpanzerwagen' Storm panther vehicle

Chapter 11

Gas and Armour
The Battle of Villers-Bretonneux
24–25 April 1918

The Germans sensed that this ground was tank country and that the battle for Amiens deserved fledgling armoured support as so much could be won by taking Amiens. They had fourteen tanks available, although one suffered mechanical trouble. These first 'Panzers'[255] were mostly the new A7Vs, a Goliath of a tank, and an unheard of number in one place for the Germans in the Great War. The Germans only built twenty-one tanks during the war, but did use some captured British ones as well.[256] This was to be the most truly modern battle of the First World War and it was in Villers-Bretonneux that armoured warfare would have its debut. The London Division would be right there in the crucible and for once the Official History records it directly.

The first move in the Battle of Villers-Bretonneux was the German saturation of the town in mustard, phosgene and irritant gases. The historian of the 7th Battalion history claims 15,000 gas shells were fired into the town and surrounding area on 18 April. This caused the British command to conclude that this was a diversion and the town would not be attacked but an attack at Albert on the old Somme battlefields was likely. Aerial reconnaissance however showed that this was not so and that German forces were indeed massing beyond Villers-Bretonneux and accordingly German railway centres were bombed, such as Chaulnes.

In the Bois de L'Abbé off to the west the two battalions of Londoners felt the full effects of the gas bombardment and by the afternoon had to move out to a new position not affected. The gas attack was severe and battalion and brigade headquarters were knocked out and their staff severely affected. A direct hit on the 8th Battalion headquarters caused ninety casualties, including Colonel Soutton and Major Browne, with fifty men later dying of gas poisoning. Three Medical Officers were appointed in one day, with one, Captain Massey-Miles, removing his gas mask to help the wounded and succumbing to the gas himself. Only the third, an American called Lieutenant MacBean, survived unwounded to serve with the battalion until the end of the war.[257] The divisional casualties from the gas were 1,209. The Official History describes both 8th and 58th divisions as barely reconstructed, but of the two 8th Division was by far in the worse condition, having lost double the casualties of 58th Division. Edmonds goes on to state that there were at that time no reserves for a counter-attack.[258]

The Alsatian deserter brought in by the 2nd Battalion was most forthright with his details of the coming attack. Many deserters and prisoners were taken and it seems that most if not all were willing to give away vital information, condemning their comrades to death or capture and the attack to eventual failure. Desertions from the German forces gave the information that storm troopers had taken over the front line. A British airman further supplied the evidence that the trenches near the Bois de Hangard were full of troops, which led to a long bombardment of the German front, the routes to the trenches and supply points.[259] The Londoners were with 173 Brigade in the front line once again, with 175 Brigade in reserve, having just replaced 174 Brigade, now to the rear. On the receiving end of this bombardment the German historian of the First Jaeger Battalion says that 'it was however quite immaterial where one lay; heavy shells came down almost vertically. They struck straight like hammers and crushed out life in the trenches and in the shell holes with the same indifference.'[260] German accounts use much more elegant prose than British ones, but despite that, the grim reality comes across.

Early that morning the 8th London was brought to readiness as a reserve force. It was almost entirely composed of newcomers to the battalion, one of whom stated:

'we had 'stand to' at 4am on 24 April and moved to a reserve position behind Gentelles Wood, on the way we ran into gas shelling and marched in our gas masks. Most uncomfortable as one seemed to be suffocating.... Gentelles Wood was full of 60 pounders and 4.5-inch howitzers which were firing continuously. The noise was deafening and terrifying. In front of our guns were batteries of French 75mm field guns and these were also firing.'[261]

This was part of the bombardment that so decimated the waiting German forces.

On that morning the Germans attacked with gas and a heavy artillery bombardment. This was by now no surprise to the awaiting British forces in their trenches. 'Everyone was ready and the attack was repulsed with heavy losses to the attackers. At about 7am the attack was renewed, preceded by about six tanks.'[262]

To the north they attacked the depleted 8th Division which gave up the ground easily and at great loss. Thirteen German A7V tanks accompanied the assault making it the largest German tank attack of the war. The 173 Brigade was able to repulse the German infantry attacks on it, but when the German tanks appeared they had no defence against these armoured behemoths:

'Wherever tanks appeared the British line was broken: they got astride the trenches and shot down the men in them, so that a number of the young soldiers surrendered to the following infantry. Having no tank defence weapons they could make no effective reply; one officer shot in vain with his revolver point blank at the rear face of a tank.'[263]

The main thrust of the attack was against 8th Division, but because of the German success here the flanks of 58th Division were forced to fall back to hold the line. With everything to lose the British rallied their tired divisions against yet another German attack. In case the battle was lost the Allies hoped to utilise the natural barrier of the Somme by inundating and creating a water barrier 600 yards wide east of Amiens.[264] The city had by now been evacuated by the authorities so movement of troops would be unknown to any spies based there and therefore kept secret from the Germans.

The battalions of 175 Brigade were brought into the reserve line, as fresh troops would be less tired and better equipped to fight. The new battalions in the reserve line were from north to south the 12th, 10th, and 9th battalions. At 3.45am the bombardment started and some of the messages received by the brigade sum up the action.

The 12th Battalion reported in messages to brigade at 7am:

'The valley in which headquarters are was shelled intensely with H.E. [High Explosive] and gas from about 3.45 to 6am. Still being shelled but not heavily. No news from our companies but reliable signaller of 9th says our posts have not been so heavily shelled. It seems that enemy have silenced most of our batteries. Burnside and my Adjutant wounded but the latter carrying on pro tem. I.O. [Intelligence Officer] gone forward to ascertain situation. French 75s have just started activity splendidly; Colonel Powell and Nicholls and Doctor fit. Our casualties at HQ about five badly wounded remainder uncertain. P.S. four other ranks killed; activity of artillery both sides increasing at moment of writing, valley full of gas.'[265]

This gives an idea of the vagueness of the experience at a headquarters where everything is uncertain and nothing known for sure, with gas and shelling literally adding to the fog of war.

At 8am two hours after the attack started Captain Spencer of D Company reported:

'O.C. [Officer Commanding] Centre Company of Fourth Battalion reports that enemy attacked at about 5am [sic, actually probably 6 a.m.] this morning. Attack was easy to cope with as infantry seemed to have lost direction and appeared to be poor material. Later two tanks appeared (square Boche tanks) which cleared trench by firing pom-poms into our troops.[266] Line was broken by these tanks. Officer left line wounded at 7am. No signs of enemy yet but machine gun fire heard in the distance.'

The post battle report states that following the first attacks; 'between 6.30 and 7am the enemy again attacked with six tanks, [and] forced the Battalion to evacuate its trenches. The battalion was reformed at the Cachy Switch at 10.15am.'[267]

It appears that the centre company of the 4th Battalion was attacked vigorously and cut off by the tanks which were in the vicinity of Cachy. The centre company of the 4th gave way and the withdrawal was continued to the left. A message sent by the 12th at 9am.stated; 'Enemy have pierced front line on left; our garrisons falling back on Cachy Salient. No definite news from right.'[268] Things were not going all the Germans' way. The Third Battalion Royal Fusiliers was holding out at Hangard against attacks starting similarly at 6am and held out all day 'in spite of the flanks falling back, and heavy fighting all day'.[269]

The battalion casualties were 6 officers and 219 other ranks. The French at Hangard Wood were under attack but still reported to be holding at 9.25am. A message from the commanding officer of the Rangers to his counterpart in the 9th stated that: 'French reports that Villers- Bretonneux has been taken by the Boche but that they are 'assez loin' [far enough from] Cachy. Strong reinforcements of the Foreign Legion are reinforcing French on our right.'[270] The French were bringing in the Foreign Legion as reinforcements to Hangard. At a time like that this news would hopefully have been heart warming to the Londoners as they were under pressure at Cachy.

At 9.30am on 24 April a sighting of a German tank was reported 400 yards east of Cachy. This report was made by Shepherd's Force, still in existence long after the corps and divisions had moved back from Condren.[271] The artillery batteries of 83 Brigade Royal Field Artillery were attached to Shepherd's Force and were destined to play a major role that day which affected Shepherd's Force and therefore the London Division. These were 'the first divisional troops to come under fire on the 24 [April].[272] Shepherd's Force held the line in front of Cachy, which village, owing to continual bombardment, had become a mere heap of road mending material. Both Shepherd's Force and B Battery 83 Brigade RFA made speedy acquaintance with the German tanks. When the Boche infantry broke through. one of the tanks came on until it was on top of the barbed wire and there it stuck. The German infantry was driven off by Shepherd's Force and the German tank was brought in as a trophy.'[273] They retired 500 yards and then further back to the Cachy Switch line.[274] It was here that the British reserves of artillery and infantry were able to play a part in the battle.

In a shallow valley north east of Cachy with rolling open slopes around it, to the east of the Bois D'Aquenne, history was about to be made. It was here that the third German thrust was met by the tanks of I Tank Brigade at about 9.30am. There were four German divisions against the British two, 58th and 8th Division. The front line was lost but the Cachy Switch line was held. Eventually 173 Brigade had to fall back due to the tanks and the right battalions at the Bois de Hangard had to fall back slightly due to the French doing likewise. Two German tanks were disabled, one by falling into a quarry and the other by shell fire, the other two tanks were engaged by the British Mark IV tanks, two female (machine guns only) and one male (6-pounder guns and machine guns). The German tanks put the two females out of action (but there was little they could achieve with machine guns anyway) and the German Panzers were then forced to retreat by hits from the British male tank.[275] This tank was abandoned but then later recovered after dark. Two more German tanks appeared but were also driven off by gunfire from the British tank. The British gunners had driven off the German tanks successfully.

This was the first tank battle; a brief but decisive action in which the Germans had been defeated by superior gunnery. Had the German tanks been successful they may have pressed on, although the rate of mechanical failure or ditching amongst these early tanks was very high, as shown by British attempts to use them in 1917.

At 9.35am 8th Division was withdrawing from Villers-Bretonneux and forming a line with 58th Division at the Cachy Switch line. So the work of the First Battle of Villers-Bretonneux was undone in a morning. The Germans had attacked with tanks along the railway line and easily taken the town. The soldiers of the 2nd West Yorkshire put up a defence for a time but there was little they could do with only 140 men, just over a company. The German tanks were backed up by infantry and flamethrowers, a perfect yet deadly and dreadful accompaniment. There were three main German thrusts with tanks, one into Villers-Bretonneux and the east and north-eastern outskirts with three tanks, and the second with four tanks at the Bois d'Aquenne and two at the railway station. The third thrust was to Cachy with four tanks.[276] It was here at Cachy that the Londoners were again faced by these behemoths.

From his headquarters Colonel Dann observed with a slightly different angle on the advance of the German Panzers:

'The tanks were very badly handled - some were seen describing circles and firing wildly into the ground nowhere near our positions... The tanks after some time managed to get astride our trenches and here they halted and opened enfilade fire on them.'[277]

Where these tanks met soldiers in shallow trenches there was little the infantry could do to halt them, many were killed by tanks traversing trenches with gunfire. Faced with no other means of defence soldiers of 58th Machine Gun Battalion of the London Division raked one tank with concentrated machine gun fire and caused the crew to abandon it through the splash of the bullets inside the tank, causing lethal flakes of metal to wound the crew. The machine gunners did well 'dispersing the former [infantry] and preventing the latter [tanks] from reaching the Cachy trenches.'[278]

Proof of the brave gunners' resistance was made by the fact that four of their guns (and crews) were crushed by tanks, firing till the last. Further proof of their heroism was given by a captured German crewman who testified to this. The division may have been full of youngsters, but they seem to have put up a fight. As was reported by their officers, they may have been young but they were keen and determined to do their bit. The 4th Battalion retired under pressure from the tanks to a position 500 yards further back, and then as this position left an exposed flank and a yawning gap in front of Cachy, retired back to the Switch Line by 10.15am. This gave the brigade time to consolidate and reform the line and a period of time before the German tanks could catch up, being only capable of a walking speed. At the same time an officer of the Royal Artillery was sent for further assistance in the form of two field guns to help in an anti-tank role.

Colonel Dann reported that at 'about 11am when I was at an observation post near my headquarters on the outskirts of the village, I noticed five tanks (three of British make and two of German) appearing out of the mist about 300 yards away and bearing down on Cachy. These tanks were followed closely by lines of German infantry in extended order and were moving forward very slowly...' would the field guns he had asked for arrive in time? The artillery had moved and failed to report to anybody at HQ their new position and were lost in the fog....

'As I was speaking to him a man ran up and reported the arrival of an 18-pounder gun which after considerable trouble had been located in a cemetery just west of Cachy, and been manhandled from there to my HQ.... At the same time as the arrival of the gun was reported, I saw six or seven of our light tanks coming from the direction of the Bois L'Abbé. The 18-pounder gun at once opened fire on the enemy tanks. Our light tanks passed through the line of German tanks and opened machine gun fire on the German infantry, inflicted heavy casualties on them and forced them to retreat in great disorder. The 18-pounder did not appear to hit any of the German tanks but they turned round and slowly followed their infantry.'[279]

The attack had been beaten off but 173 Brigade had been mauled twice in successive battles in March and April 1918. Once again the brigade had borne the brunt of the attack. For that day the casualties of the 4th London were 8 officers and 334 other ranks.

The way the Whippet tanks passed through the German tanks and beat up the infantry is very interesting historically, these heavy tanks were not able to fend off the lighter tanks, their visibility was not very good and the smoke and fog added to their problems. Their only gun was in the front of the tank and not able to traverse to the flanks unless the whole tank turned round. The British male tanks only had 6-pounders in the side turrets and were also slightly limited in their capabilities by this.

The German attack, supposedly a surprise, had been undone by their soldiers who when captured or deserting were ready to pass on information about it. The Londoners were involved with the Cachy Switch and it was the Hackney Rifles who were on site at the first armoured battle between British and German tanks. The Hackney men counter-attacked at 10.30am. This was held up by heavy machine gun fire from Hangard Wood, further attempts to attack were countermanded by orders and the battalion appears to have been pinned down. Losing their Commanding Officer Colonel Symonds to a fatal wound left the battalion without a leader for that day.

Now that the heavy German tanks were defeated the British could once again send in the light tanks. Aerial reconnaissance reported that two battalions of Germans were massed in trenches near Cachy. It was decided to send in seven of the light tanks, Whippets, with a maximum speed of 8mph, much faster than the 3.7mph speed of the Mark IVs. These Whippets were put under the direct command of 58th Division. The Whippets attacked the German forces here and reported slightly zealously 400 casualties on these German reinforcements but certainly that they 'completely broke up the attack'.[280] The number of German casualties is contested but certainly they would have had a massive effect on morale, not just casualties. Without the heavy tanks winning their battle, these fresh German battalions may have been able to attack the British, but with their defeat the offensive was over. North of this Germans did not attack against Shepherd's Force but advanced in small numbers with tanks. This first phase of the Battle of Villers-Bretonneux had lost the town, but gained a morale boosting armoured victory and caused considerable German casualties to the south.

Already the counter stroke was being planned and was well under way by midday. By 10am the Australian 13 and 15 Brigades were on standby to relieve the situation, and they moved at midday. Already as the two sides dug in after that morning's battle British and Australian reinforcements were on their way. The Australians were marching the 6 miles back to the front after only four days out of the line to relieve the hard pressed British forces after their near month of fighting. General Rawlinson had set a plan in motion that would relieve the town, press back the Germans and allow his III Corps divisions to be properly relieved from the fighting. General Butler, the Corps Commander now also agreed and sent a staff officer, Colonel Bennington, to see that it was carried out. This was to be the Australian's counter stroke, assisted by the remaining British forces that would have to endure the attack to enable their relief. The 58th Division had its three brigades in successive lines, behind each other, with 173 Brigade on the front, 174 Brigade in reserve and 175 behind that. This enabled the Commander, General Cator, to swap over depleted battalions with fresh ones and look after his own communications as for the first time since 24 March the whole division was in the line together.

Messages from the front line at 11.30am stated:

'Colonel Symons has been wounded leading counter-attack of A

Company to regain footing in wood surrounding U.16 central. Attack appeared to be going well but nothing definite to hand reported that enemy were withdrawing at approximately 11am. By degrees touch seems to be in steady progress towards Cachy Switch left flank has not fallen back any further.... My casualties being heavy, many surrounded and taken prisoner. Estimate present strength 150.'

The reply was sent back from headquarters to the beleaguered troops:

'Well done Corbett! Hold on. Reinforcements are practically here, and you ought to have plenty of support. Our tanks (Whippets) ought to be up to our assistance by now. Three Companies of the Tenth are going to push to their front from road U.16 central. Give them all the covering fire you can. Good luck, things are improving.'[281]

At noon in 175 Brigade the Queen Victoria's Rifles were relieved by the 11th Royal Fusiliers and became the counter-attack battalion. In the front line was 173 Brigade with the 10th Battalion in reserve as the counter-attack battalion. The 8th Battalion was ordered to come up to reinforce the line.

Due to the open nature of the warfare and the recent arrival of the war in this sector communications were easily broken and runners and messenger dogs had to be used which brought; 'valuable and frequent information from the front line'.[282] Telephone cables were unsuitable for this type of warfare unless they could be dug in underground about 6 feet deep and there was no time for such luxuries.

'The front line was a few hundred yards up this ridge and the telephone lines between the companies and headquarters ran up this ridge. These lines were being constantly broken by shellfire and I, as linesman, was sent out to mend the break each time the line went "dis [connected]." It was a hopeless task,' said one messenger.[283]

For this reason power buzzers, an early form of wireless, were used in some situations. As a general rule telephones were considered easier than telegraphs. Power buzzers could only be used in plain sight, therefore putting the signallers in quite open and dangerous situations.

The Australian counter-attack was Rawlinson's idea, but the Australian commanders insisted on no artillery support so they could achieve total surprise. This was going to be different to Passchendaele and the Aussie insistence was the correct one. They would attack in brigade strength, not into Villers-Bretonneux, but around it in a pincer movement. It would be a night attack at 10pm, leaving the town to be mopped up by British forces the following day; 58th Division would advance at the same time to the south of the town at Cachy to regain most of the ground lost that morning. The Australian forces were still under overall British command in the Fourth Army, and it was not until the Battle of Hamel in July that they would have their own command, until then they were under Rawlinson's orders.

The two Australian brigades reached their positions, but started an hour apart meaning that the first brigade suffered undue casualties and when the southern pincer started the Germans saw it as a separate attack. This actually worked in their favour. The Aussies of 59th Battalion were strafed by machine guns, which fortunately went over their heads and when the momentum was gained their officer shouted 'charge!' and 'there went up from the unleashed line a shout, a savage eager yell.'[284] German flares fired off to call in their artillery acted as illumination for the attackers, and for once luck was on the Allied side as the Australians achieved their initial objectives. This was Australia's hour and they deserved their accolades for this was a well won attack.

Unfortunately the British forces sent to start the mopping up in the town were beaten back by alert German forces in the deep railway cutting who realized that this was their only means of escape and kept it open for many hours, allowing German forces in the town a means of escape. It was not until much later that this avenue of escape was put under artillery bombardment, by which time many enemy had escaped. Edmonds questions whether the late start of the southern 15 Brigade meant that the troops who were mopping up had a harder task, and the lop-sided attack made this escape possible and the task of taking the town harder, but concludes that this is unlikely. Street fighting is difficult for any force, and it is likely that anyone trying to take the town would have found it a formidable task by dark or by daylight. If at all, the escape of some of the defenders made it easier to take the town.

The 58th Division also attacked at Cachy, moving forward to Hangard Wood to support the pincer movement to the north. This movement forward was never going to have the same intention or momentum as the Australians' pincer movement. The 4th Battalion held their positions at Cachy and the 7th Bedfordshire Regiment later attacked through them but was not able to push the Germans back from their positions between Cachy and Hangard.

The 11th Royal Fusiliers counter-attacked at 10pm in conjunction with the Australian attack at Villers-Bretonneux. This battalion, of 18th Division, brought up from 53 Brigade of that division at Amiens, were the reinforcements for 58th Division at Hangard Wood. They were not needed in the event, but as we have seen the 4th Battalion were engaged heavily at Hangard Wood. They had retreated 'but not to such a depth as the troops further north at Villers-Bretonneux'. Their casualties for the day were 4 officers and 203 other ranks missing. The soldiers of 173 Brigade had truly been tested, twice in succession, while the other brigades had been relatively untried, but casualties were still heavy. The attacks here at Cachy and Hangard Wood may not have had the dash of the advances at Villers-Bretonneux, but the flanks of the attack are as important as the centre, and once again the 58th Division had been holding the flank where it joined the French.[285]

The attack is best summed up by the actions of the 9th battalion, Queen Victoria's Rifles:

'At 9pm orders were received to counter-attack Hangard Wood at 10pm and to recapture the old front line. Company Commanders were sent for, and reached Battalion HQ at 9.10pm and left at 9.20pm. At 9.25pm the Commanding Officer and Adjutant left battalion HQ to mark the jumping off line.

'The order of attack was four Companies in line, with three platoons each in the front line, and one platoon each in support. Order of companies from right to left A, B, C, D. Three companies were got on to the jumping off line in their proper formation. There was, however, no time to get D Company into position, and the company was held in reserve.

'At 10pm A, B and C Companies started off in line, the right of A Company striking their objective. B Company first of all reached the line of the track from….. [Army coordinates]…. Having taken a number of prisoners, three machine guns, and having killed many enemies. Movement could then be seen in Army coordinate… And this was found by scouts to be some of the 3rd and 10th [Battalions] Battalion. C Company lost direction and came out through the wood on the southern side, having killed many of the enemy and sent back a certain number of prisoners.

At about 11pm prisoners began to arrive at Battalion headquarters and from information of escorts it seems that the advance was successful but that the companies had lost touch.'[286]

The line had to be consolidated during the night. 'B' Company had a difficult night as they were fired on by the enemy from the rear and had to face both directions to deal with the fire.

The brigade commentary on events is obviously distanced from the action but the 9th Battalion's history uses quotes from men who were there in Hangard Wood, men such as Lance-Corporal Sydney Stroud:

> 'Then another machine gun opened a terrific fire and we were obliged to get down and open fire with our rifles. I was expecting the left to advance while we kept the gun engaged, with the idea of surrounding it, but after waiting some time to see what was developing I decided to get back into the wood and take up position, and I then went along with a sergeant and two other men to try to get in touch as we seemed to be disconnected [from other units].... I came upon a German machine-gun post. I put up my rifle to fire but it jammed, so I called out to the men who I thought were following me to fire, but they were nowhere to be seen.... One of them [Germans], realising how I was placed, fired, wounding me in the leg. I then rushed at him and settled his business, but while I was dealing with him the other rushed off.'[287]

This is a very good account of how the fighting was for the individual soldier. Suddenly, after being part of a platoon or company, it is actually down to individual fights; rather than the large panoply of big formations, it is the small actions, by night in the gloom of the woods, lit by artillery and flares only. This is indicative of the loneliness of combat, its fear and isolation when senses are heightened, these are the descriptions which many authors base their histories on. This could not be further from the large scale attack of the Australians to the north taking place at the same time.

The Londoners came under considerable direct machine gun fire, unlike the Aussies who were lucky not to be met by such heavy fire. They still took their objective by 2.45am but then were forced to pull back 200 yards to avoid machine gun fire and a counter-attack. Tanks were required to help them close the gap in the line around Hangard Wood between the 9th London Regiment and 54 Brigade of 18th Division.

The next day was spent straightening up the line and clearing Villers-Bretonneux of the enemy. 'The day was spent in clearing up pockets of the enemy. Continuous fighting all day. Two battalions of 174 Brigade were relieved by the Moroccan Division.'[288]

The Moroccan Division had now arrived in strength. Whippet tanks were again called on in the afternoon to attack enemy troops in a trench west of Hangard Wood. This time only three were available that had survived the previous day's attack in working order. Later German counter-attacks were planned but then cancelled and only the artillery bombardments went ahead.

The casualties by brigade between 4 and 28 April were as follows. The 173 Brigade lost 18 officers and 306 other ranks, the 174 Brigade lost 117 officers and 2,345 other ranks and 175 Brigade lost 18 officers and 726 other ranks in the month of April. Total casualties for the division in his battle are therefore 153 officers and 3,377 other ranks.[289] The London Division had shown its mettle and suffered the consequences, but deserves a place in the history books for the fighting at Villers-Bretonneux.

Further attacks took place after the main battles, but were not a great success. The French Moroccan Division lost 3,400 men and 70 officers trying to take back Hangard Wood in an operation with the Australians. In a 1929 Staff College tour of the battlefields it was summed up that:

> 'The French attack on 26 April was a waste of life and only happened due to General Debeney's failure to co-operate on 24 April.'[290]

This was proof that not all Anglo-French attacks were destined to succeed. The Battles of Villers-Bretonneux had shown that the British and French forces could co-operate, but there was much work to be done. It was realized that the Germans' attention had moved elsewhere on the Western Front, and the effort to take Amiens was at a standstill. By expending his energy all along the front the German General Ludendorff made sure that all his troops were exhausted, little ground was gained, and all he had done was retake the ground given up on the Somme the previous year. Warfare was changing and tanks and infantry were starting to co-operate much better together.

Notes

255 online source Second Battle of Villers-Bretonneux, Wikipedia htt://en.wikipedia.org/wiki/Second_Battle_of_Villers-Bretonneux
256 Messenger, 1982 *Terriers in The Trenches*, (London) p.113
257 Edmonds, J.E. *Military Operations*, 1918, Vol II p.388
258 Edmonds, J.E. *Military Operations*, 1918 Vol II p385
259 1st Jager Battalion, 1st Jager Division, quoted in Edmonds, 1918, Vol II p.384n
260 IWM 2/65/139 FA9 Anonymous
261 National Archives, WO95/3001
262 Edmonds, J.E. *Military Operations*, 1918 Vol II, p389
263 Edmonds, J. E., *Military Operations* 1918 Vol II, p385
264 National Archives WO95/3008 175th Brigade report on Operations
265 A Pom-Pom was a German Maxim designed machine-gun firing a 1-inch round, like a Bofors gun

or an Oerklion cannon; source Marix-Evans, 2010 *Somme 1914-1918*, *Lessons in War* (Stroud) Photos p.96-97

266 National Archives WO95/3008 175th Brigade report on Operations

267 National Archives WO95/3008 Rangers message sheet

268 National Archives WO95/3001 War diary

269 National Archives WO95/3008 message sheet

270 Shepherd's force consisted of two companies 2nd Northamptonshire and one company 1/4th Suffolk Pioneers at this stage under Major Shepherd of the 6th Battalion Northamptonshire Regiment. In Edmonds it is referred to as the 2nd Northamptonshire, since this type of arrangement was so common at this stage of the war. He does mention a Carey's Force earlier in the First battle at V-B.

271 By Divisional troops the text means artillery that was at the behest of the Divisional Commander, General Cator, rather than the individual Brigadiers, or indeed Army troops that served the whole Fourth Army.

272 Micholls, 1922 *History of the 18th Division*, (Edinburgh and London) p.321

273 Edmonds, J. E., 1937 *Military Operations*, 1918 Vol II (London) p389

274 Edmonds, J. E., 1937 (London) p.389

275 Edmonds, J. E., *Military Operations*, 1918 Vol II (London) 1937 p.390n

276 National Archives, WO95/3001 report on operations

277 National Archives, WO95/3008 war diary

278 National Archives, WO95/3001 2/4th London report on operations

279 National Archives, WO95/3008 war diary 175 Brigade

280 National Archives, WO95/3001 messages

281 National Archives, WO95/3008 war diary 175th Brigade

282 Messenger, *Terriers in the Trenches* (London) 1982, p114

283 Bean, C. The A.I.F. in France, 1918 Vol. V (Sydney) 1941 p.602

284 O'Neill, *The History of the Royal Fusiliers in the Great* War (Eastbourne) p.259ff

285 National Archives WO95/3008 175 Brigade report on Operations

286 Keeson, C. *The Records and History of Queen Victoria's Rifles*, Vol II, (London) 1923 p.404-5

287 IWM Library, C.W.G.C. *The 58th Division in France and Flanders,*

288 IWM Library, C.W.G.C. *The 58th Division in France and Flanders,*

289 IWM 76/60/1 The papers of Brigadier Page – Staff College Camberly tour, April 1929

290 Edmonds J.E., *Military Operations*, France 1918 (London) Vol III, p.193

Chapter 12

Goodbye Old Man – Fortunino Matavia and the Battle for Chipilly 8 August–20 August 1918

Further German offensives at the Lys against the Portuguese Division, against the French at Kemmel and the Scherpenberg, near Ypres, in April 1918, and the Aisne in May now diverted attention elsewhere. These were the great German attacks that followed in the early part of 1918. The Amiens sector quietened down, but it still simmered, not resting entirely. The official history says of this period 'during the comparative quiet following these enemy offensives in the sectors of the front not directly concerned in meeting the German attacks there was no cessation of activity: bombardment and counter battery harassing fire on batteries and roads at night, small operations and raids'.[291] For the division though a period of complete rest and reorganisation was at last provided.

The Londoners moved to Saint-Riquier on 26 April and then moved towards the west of Albert. They began to work on the trench and defence system at Baizieux and the defence of Henencourt Chateau, a useful strongpoint if the Germans attacked, until relieved by 18th Division on 2 June. On 10 June it went to Cavillon and then between 11-15 June was involved in training. On 16 June it relieved 47th Division in the line west of Albert. For the next four months the division was to have regular contact with its sister division, as they were able to forge a friendship that had been too long in the waiting since their split in late 1914. The crucible of this new friendship was to be the old Somme battlefields of 1916, the first time the 58th Division had fought on this ground.

On 7 May the division was moved by bus with the following composition in the 173 Brigade. The headquarters was moved in three buses, the men of 173 Light Trench Mortars and snipers in five buses, the 2nd Battalion in twenty-five buses, the 3rd Battalion in twenty-nine buses, the 4th Battalion in twenty-five buses, the 505 Field Company RE in six buses and 211 Field Ambulance in eight buses. This is obviously a move of manpower alone and none of these figures include any equipment or stores which would have come separately by horse transport, lorry or railway. The movement of what was left of the brigade took 101 buses, quite a convoy.

Back in the front line it was evident that not much had changed, the usual cycle of reliefs, stand to, trench raids and counter raids continued, the attack on The Hairpin in 47th Divisional area on the 8-9 May is such an example. For now the division was to operate in reserve as a counter-attack unit should the Germans attack and break through, thus allowing it vital time to continue its recuperation. On 16 May the 6th Battalion were in the line at The Hairpin, which had been raided by the Germans in early May. They buried about twenty-five German bodies and found the 'trenches battered about and shallow'.[292] Their period in the lines was marked by much agitation about the 'almost daily expectation that the enemy would attack on the Albert to Arras front. Prisoners captured in the sector were apparently convinced that these were the enemies' plans and actual dates were passed down to units'.[293]

However nothing out of the ordinary was experienced during their time in the line, patrolling found the enemy normal and, aside from a gas attack on the rear lines, artillery fire was at the normal intensity. On 21 May the 8th Battalion was expecting an attack on its positions which did not materialise. While the defensive nature of the front was continually being checked, offensive operations were being planned, in this case a part of the enemy lines including a quarry behind their front line suspected of being home to a German dugout, was being reconnoitred for a raid by the 8th. An abortive patrol of this position took place on 25 May and was fired on, however it was believed that useful information was gained. Over the next month the training would continue as the battalion moved behind the lines to continue their preparation. The division was relieved in the line by 18th Division on 31 May and marched back to Daily Mail Woods at Mirvaux, a rest area behind the lines, where they would practise their upcoming raid in secrecy.

On their way back towards the front line on 9 June these troops joined the 174 Brigade as they marched past the III Corps Commander, Lieutenant General R.H.K. Butler, on their way to a church service. These open air services were held on Sundays for troops out of the line. On 10 June they were in the town of Picquigny and on 18 June in the front line at Bresle. Three days later a patrol under Second Lieutenant Hatcher from the 174

Brigade went forward to reconnoitre the enemy barbed wire but was hampered by mist, while another patrol under Second Lieutenant Knell and one other rank went out and spent a day concealed in standing corn in no man's land, staying there until noon on 22 June. The information gained showed that the raid could achieve its aims; the battalion was pulled out of the line for final training.

At 5.30pm on 26 June all officers and NCOs were briefed about the scheme and a field taped out to represent the area was visited and familiarised. For the other ranks of the battalion company training concentrated on trench warfare skills such as bombing squads and bayonet fighting and movement over the ground in attack formation was practised. This was well as many of the men would be young replacements who had never undertaken a large scale attack in daylight. However this last minute training must have been spotted by the Germans who added to the reality of war by firing a shell killing four and wounding eighteen men of D Company. This was not a good omen, but a final patrol by Lieutenant Knell was uneventful, although the raid might have been delayed for several weeks if they felt their cover was blown by practising so close to the front lines.

At this point Brigadier General Higgins retired from his command and was replaced by Brigadier General A. Maxwell in 174 Brigade. On 1 July the 8th Battalion relieved the Third Battalion in support: A Company was in Dodo Trench, B was in Hills Row, C in Darling Reserve left and D in Darling Reserve right. This was the period of the Australian attack on Le Hamel, a notable success for General Monash. The 9th and 12th Battalion in support were in the line next to the most northerly of the Australian forces. The Australians mounted a raid to support their own troops at Le Hamel, the Londoners co-operated by mounting a Chinese attack; this time there was no use of dummy figures but instead an artillery barrage with shells and gas projectors; the result of this was a prolonged and heavy German counter bombardment which caused fourteen casualties; four killed and ten wounded.

Sergeant Wyatt was fatally wounded as was Rifleman Petherick, one of the favourites of B Company; 'a typical little Cockney, always cheery. He was in charge of a gun team at the time and was getting his gun ready, and cheering up the rest of the section when he was hit. He had both arms and legs broken. He was cheery until the last and died the same evening in the Advanced Dressing Station at Montigny.[294]

They had an otherwise uneventful tour in the front line and were relieved by the 10th Battalion, on 17 June German airplanes bombed the battalion cookers at 2am, killing three and wounding two more. On 22 June the raid was on and the men were warned it was to be a battalion-size raid of four companies with 19 officers and 453 other ranks taking part. Three companies, A, B and C would attack, with D in reserve and support.

The exact time of the raid is unknown, but it was daylight and the enemy were literally caught napping, which suggests early morning, as the Germans were wearing forage caps and did not have their equipment with them. The fact that the men of the 8th lay in no man's land prior to their attack suggests early morning. The barrage was not very good, with rounds falling short and the timing going wrong, but the general effect was good. The right hand assault party under Captain R.R. Poulton found no problem in entering the enemy trenches, taking three prisoners and capturing a machine gun. However the party attacking The Quarry was caught in enfilading machine gun fire and came up against a stout defence making it impossible to get through the enemy wire. They lost both platoon leaders killed or wounded. The centre company under Captain E.C.K. Clarke got to the German trench easily and killed ten Germans, taking fourteen prisoners and two machine guns, they were able to exploit their success and help out the flanking companies. On the left Captain A.S.C. Thomas MC succeeded as well. It seems that in this attack no prisoners were taken and they got into bombing and bayonet fighting, killing forty enemy soldiers. One dugout was partially cleared but time ran out and the Royal Engineer demolition parties were unable to achieve much across the entire attack and the raid ended with a rapid withdrawal. Most casualties had been caused on the flanks of the attack as men were caught by enfilading machine guns. That was the problem of a daylight raid: the smoke barrage was ineffectual or non-existent and the men were clearly visible.

The raid was short and sharp, and the incredible thing is that after this rapid cut-throat attack a truce was followed and stretcher bearers were able to operate for a time in no man's land to gather the many wounded. Despite this not all could be retrieved and some had to be left out.

> 'To collect our men in no man's land our Medical Officer [Captain Barwick] and Padre went out towards the German line displaying a Red Cross flag - they successfully negotiated a cease fire for one hour with the German commander. Then all hell let loose on our front line and supports.'[295]

The result of the attack was a high casualty list for both sides, the British casualties were 2 officers and 10 other ranks killed and 4 officers and 105 other ranks wounded. A total of 121. The battalion claimed about 100

German casualties and 17 prisoners, so really it was about even for both sides. The men of the 7th and 10th battalions, and the 131st Regiment US Army were all involved in helping bring back casualties, so it involved the wider brigade as well.

Patrols of the enemy front lines were frequent occurrences and anything could happen in these night time forays. On 26 July a regrettable incident occurred when a patrol of the 6th Battalion with some Australians attached was disorientated in no man's land. Led by Second Lieutenant Neville it attacked an Australian listening post by mistake and suffered casualties as a result. In the same period a patrol of the 7th Battalion was lying low near the German positions but was betrayed by bright moonlight and bounced sustaining seven casualties. On 26 July the relief of part of the division was begun by 47th Division.

The Germans started to withdraw in the Ancre Valley on 27 July and ultimately established their position on the east bank of the Ancre. The 47th Division was able to push forward patrols into the ruins of Albert. South of the town on 58th Division's front the German withdrawal was noted on 2 August, when a large explosion in the quarry behind enemy lines indicated that something was up. Patrols sent out cautiously showed that the enemy had indeed left his front line. The ebb of the German attacks had now slowly turned into a gentle flow backwards; a small adjustment of the lines to a more easily defensible line on the Ancre River gave a better line to defend. That is not to say that the Germans were going to give up ground easily and without fighting, the whole outcome of the war was still in the balance.

On 2 August 1918 the division commenced being relieved by 12th Division: 35 Brigade relieved 174 Brigade in Round Wood; 173 Brigade in front line right and 37 Brigade relieved 175 Brigade in front line left which moved back to Vignacourt, north-west of Amiens, to rest and train, as part of the normal trench warfare routine. The other two brigades of the division were still on the front line and involved in the German attack of the 6 August. This was a brief rest as by 8 August the new offensive was to start and two battalions of the brigade were required as reserves to 12th Division in the front line.

Marshal Foch, in command of the Allied forces on the Western Front, now wished to counter-attack the Germans who had been in the ascendancy since 21 March. His objectives were similar in scope to the German attacks since March. He was to attack first on the Marne with French forces to move the Germans away from Paris and stop them using a long range gun on the city.[296] Secondly he would attack in Picardy and the Somme with British

RIVER SOMME

CANAL DU NORD

MOISLAINS

MONT ST QUENTIN

PERONNE

CERISY

47th DIVISION
58th DIVISION

58th

AUST

AUSTRALIAN FORCES →

47th DIVISION
58th DIVISION
SAILLY

BRAY

CHIPILLY

0 kilometres 5

WOODS

AFTER MAUDE 1922

————— FRONT 8 AUGUST
—··—··— " 22 AUGUST
—x—x— " 24 AUGUST A.M.
—o—o— " 24 AUGUST P.M.
—···—···— " 1 SEPTEMBER
—x—x—x— " 2 SEPTEMBER

A- MALARD WOOD
B- CELESTINES WOOD
C- GRESSAIRE WOOD
D- LES TAILLES WOOD
E- BOUCHAVESNES
F- HAPPY VALLEY

and French forces, thirdly in the Argonne with the Americans and finally in Belgium, around Ypres.

The London Division, and III Corps, had been moved to the left flank of the Australians from the right flank where they had fought at Villers-Bretonneux. They would fight here in the battles of Amiens and Albert, on the flank of the Australians from Dernancourt to Peronne.

The Germans attacked with fresh forces on 6 August against 18th and 58th Divisions, taking over 200 prisoners, none of them knew of the impending attack, and therefore the Germans suspected nothing.

'The attack had happened when the leading company of the 8th London Regiment, coming in to relieve the 2nd Bedfordshire [18th Division], was stuck in the trenches, deep in mud, 600 yards from the front line.'[297]

There is no recorded account of the action, but it appears that there were attacks and counter-attacks throughout the day, with a final counter-attack by the 8th Battalion at 9pm on 7 August and by the 11th Battalion Royal Fusiliers. Territorially the Germans only gained 800 yards, but more importantly they did not know of the Allied offensive pending on the Somme, despite capturing many prisoners.

The Canadian Corps had been secretly moved to the old lines of 58th Division at Villers-Bretonneux, so now the offensive was to be made with the two best Corps, the Australians and Canadians. The task of the Londoners was to clear the high ground north of the Somme River which would otherwise allow the Germans to fire into the flanks of the Australians as they advanced eastwards. They were to keep pace with the Australians who would otherwise be unable to advance.

This would involve taking the difficult terrain of the Chipilly Ridge, bluffs and the villages around it. Bean, the Australian official historian, states that:

'the Australian attack would be straight forward in one contingency, that failure of the difficult protecting attack on the heights north of the Somme and their offshoot, the Chipilly Peninsula. With these in their hands, the German gunners could shell in flank and rear the Australians advancing past them along the slopes south of the river.'[298]

They would be given armoured and aerial support, but the main offensive by the Australian and Canadian Corps, initiated by the French attack at Montdidier, was to have the majority of support by other arms of the services. This was open ground and the problems of open warfare were the lack of cover, 'our machine guns were positioned just behind the crest of a ridge, it not being a trench system... during the night we worked feverishly digging in with the little entrenching tools which all soldiers carried and scooping out the soil with our hands'.[299]

The great advance on 8 August started in dense fog reminiscent of the German attacks in March, at 4.20am with a simultaneous barrage and attack. The British had realised that in attacking Malard Wood (Bois Malard) a frontal assault was useless, so they opted to surround the wood. 'We rushed forward with yells and shouts which were drowned in the deafening roar of the guns.' Seven tanks were to proceed with the infantry in the advance to Malard Wood, one of them to Sailly-Laurette and Chipilly. 'I found one tank with which was one of our officers and a number of men of both 6th and 7th Battalions, we helped them to clear out one or two enemy posts,'said machine gunner P.G. Ackrell.[300]

The conditions were once again thick mist but at least it was daylight now, the mist aided the attackers but also slowed them down as the tanks were not able to assist at the beginning. A note in the report on the attack states that both the terrain and the bombardment tended to draw troops downhill and to the south. Generally the advance was successful and not resisted, but on the right opposition was met, alleviated by the arrival of a tank near Sailly-Laurette.[301] The 6th Battalion had fought hard all the way to Malard Wood. The objective of the 7th Battalion was the high ground to the north-east of Malard Wood, with A, B and C Companies attacking together on the left flank and D Company detached to occupy the north-west corner of the wood.[302] The 7th took a ravine near the wood which was full of dugouts and German supplies. Malard Wood was taken but the enemy remained in control of the Chipilly Spur dominating the Australian advance to the south. Sailly-Laurette was taken early on by the 10th, who then attacked Chipilly but were forced to withdraw to a position just outside it. A Company of the 1/4th Suffolk (Pioneers) was engaged in digging in on the flank to protect the main force.

Finding the right direction in the mist was virtually impossible and in the end all the soldiers drifted to the right. However a composite force was made and the gaps filled, the battalion reorganised and Malard Wood was defended. Once again men experienced the isolation of the advance in the misty conditions and one officer, with a small group of five men, wrote:

'there was a small party of the 7th and 8th battalions... digging in. Passing them we pushed on to the quarry, which was the main landmark given to our company, and to our surprise we found no one there at all.... It all felt weird and strange, the mist was thinning, and we could see further, not a man could we find.... So we went on again, but quite soon we spotted in another wood a fairly large group of Boches with horses and field guns.'[303]

They had penetrated through the enemy lines and reached the gun lines, with a measure of caution they decided that the best course of action was a tactical retreat, back to the rest of the battalion; they had to fight their way back with a brief skirmish.

The lead attack formation was 174 Brigade with 173 in the second line. The task of 173 Brigade was to pass through the 174 which had made the initial attack and form a new front line. The colonel of the 7th Battalion found a body of the 2nd Battalion wandering through the mist and was able to use them to advance through the wood to its eastern edge where they formed a front line. They had the assistance of a tank and a light trench mortar battery. The 173 Brigade and 3rd Battalion also set off but lost direction in the fog, before 174 Brigade were on their objectives. Things went wrong and battalion headquarters became the forward unit, pressing on and assaulting various positions, but had numerous casualties including the adjutant. They persevered and captured seventy prisoners and four machine guns.[304]

The position achieved by 10am was that the 7th Battalion was established partly at their objective and a group of the 6th were at the quarry near the edge of Malard Wood, where the officer had failed to find his men. The west edge of the wood was held by elements of both battalions, but there was no connection between the two fronts. The wood was not occupied by the enemy, but neither was it garrisoned by British troops. This situation was cleared up by moving sixty-three officers and men of the 8th to reinforce the 7th on the left flank. One company of the 6th was sent to the south end of the wood to connect with the 7th Battalion. The 2nd Battalion requested that two companies pushed through the wood to make it secure. There was no fighting here as there had been at Hangard Wood, and the wood was easily secured.

After this move the brigade were reorganised and men sent back to their respective units as they had been very mixed up after the attack. The mist had helped the attack, but luckily the Germans were so beaten that they did not counter-attack, but fell back. The attack had been unexpected and the Canadians and Australians south of the Somme River had advanced at Villers-Bretonneux and pushed the Germans back 8 miles or more. The

Canadians at Cachy took over the former front from the French that the Londoners had occupied a few months previously. The attacks north of the Somme had pushed the line back a few miles and this conformed to the edges of the wedge pushed into the German lines further south. Likewise the French to the south had advanced in a measured way to aid the Canadians.

Ludendorff termed 8 August 'the Black Day of the German Army' as they had been attacked all along the front and had given up ground with high casualties. From the first moment that the Allied air forces had been able to operate that day they had reported the German forces to be in retreat eastwards over the Somme bridges.[305] An aerial bombardment was ordered but was largely ineffective in destroying the bridges and holding up the forces trying to escape over the river.[306] For the Allies the actions of that day meant a great change of morale:

> 'It produced such a swing of mood that it would stand high for those involved amongst the war's unforgettable experiences.'[307]

In this grandiose scheme the Londoners had achieved their objectives to a degree, they had been hampered as much as aided by the mist, and had helped achieve something greater than their own modest advance by being on the flanks of the Australians, as they had at Villers-Bretonneux.

The Chipilly memorial to the London Division states that:

> '58 British Division was one of the only English Divisions, co-operating with the French Army and the Australian and Canadian Army Corps, which managed to penetrate the German defences between Le Quesnoy and Montdidier on 8 August 1918, which determined the German retreat which ended in the Armistice of 11 November 1918.'[308]

The original is in French as the division had fought with the French and Foch was the Allied Commander. The Americans are not mentioned as they were in reserve on the 8th and only saw action on 9 August.[309] They were attached to the London Division as a reserve force, and are therefore included in this formation. We have seen the effort that the division put in on the 8 August, on 'the Black Day of the German Army'. They showed fortitude, self-sacrifice and bravery that day. This day was seen as the turning point of the war on the Western Front and is the reason that the memorial was built at Chipilly, not just for the achievements of the Londoners, but for the joint effort and the magnitude of the Allied effort that day. This was the start of an offensive all along the Allied front, there would be no turning back or retreat after that day, although there would be some hard fought battles.

On 9 August the success of the previous day was to be followed up by an attack on Chipilly Spur itself. This was originally scheduled for dawn but then rescheduled to 4.15pm and later to 5.30pm as some forces were not ready, although not all commands were aware of this.[310] The problem here was the terrain; there were very steep descents and almost vertical ascents. No bombardment was ordered and the infantry was to advance in artillery formation, that is spread out. The 6th Battalion attacked at 4.15pm as they did not receive news of the delay. The battalion at this time was only ninety-six strong after the previous day's casualties. It was reinforced by a patrol of the 7th Battalion on its left flank, with the rest of the battalion waiting till 5.30pm for the general attack. The attack was met by severe fire from Celestines Wood (Bois des Célestins) and from the dominating ridge, but was helped by two companies of the 10th Battalion, which aided it from Malard Wood.

The 10th Battalion worked south-eastwards, using the steep slopes for protection but on facing severe machine gun fire they asked for extra artillery support. The attack was supported now by the Australians from the south who sent a patrol to get into the village under cover of a smoke screen. Working round the spur the Australians and Londoners rushed the German machine gun posts with help from K Battalion of the American 131st Regiment. The village was taken along with 200 prisoners and 12 machine guns.[311] It had truly been an international effort and Chipilly village was taken by 8pm.

The general attack on Chipilly Ridge went ahead at 5.30pm with the following order of battle from left to right: the 8th battalion, the Rangers, 3rd and 1st Battalion with the American 131st Regiment in support. Again Celestines Wood was reported clear of Germans, however the commanders took no chances and kept their flanks reinforced with machine guns and flanking companies. Three tanks co-operated with the advance, one suffered a punctured exhaust, one was burnt out and the fate of the third was unknown. Despite claims that the village was clear the right flank of the advance was heavily fired on and suffered consequently. The fire came from Celestines Wood and Chipilly Ridge itself and caused many casualties, the infantry subsequently went to ground and the advance temporary stalled until Chipilly village had been taken by 8pm. The assault did not come to a complete halt and some initiative was used by British forces. Captain Idris of the 6th Battalion met a large force of the 3rd Battalion and the 131st US

Army Regiment, troops assigned to the advance as reserves. He assumed command of them as they were somewhat unsure as to their role. These reinforcements were most welcome at this stage. The British noticed how the Americans were tall, big men, whereas the British were old men and boys, overshadowed by the American's stature. This was a tangible reminder of the arrival of American forces in Europe, here to help the London Division and they made all the difference when used correctly.[312] Captain Idris deserves credit for taking command here and making the most of his forces.

> 'The machine gun fire from the ridge was terrific, and the enemy's artillery was firing most effectively, and there was no possibility of making further progress. Appreciating the situation Captain Idris realized that an entirely new attack would have to be launched if the position was to be gained.'

Idris sent the battalion back to their jumping off point.

> 'He then returned himself to the starting point to organise a second attack, and soon he found advancing through the wood large numbers of American infantry, whose confused knowledge of the battle and ignorance of what was expected of them suggested that he should use them for the purpose. Assuming command of them, he at once explained to them what had to be done. The American officers were only too glad that someone on the spot should tell them where to go and what to do, and in a very short while the Americans, and what was left of the 6th, were formed into a long line awaiting his signal to start the advance. He gave it and they moved forward, nor did they stop. Down into the valley they went, and up the other side, onto the crest, the Germans in full flight.'

The American troops had been extremely useful, and their numbers had made the difference at the crucial moment. Chipilly ridge had been taken. They took with them the survivors of the London battalions. One of the Americans, Corporal Jake Allex, won the Congressional Medal of Honour, for like many others, when all his officers had become casualties he took the offensive and took a machine gun post and fifteen prisoners, when his bayonet broke he used the butt of his rifle.[313] The war diary of the London Division stated that the 'attack went splendidly and by 11pm all objectives had been captured'.[314] However British forces had been mauled again in this attack, the casualty numbers added to the ever increasing list. The 7th had suffered 12 officer casualties and about 300 other ranks.

The Colonel of the 7th was unhappy with the arrangements made for the wounded in regard to stretcher bearers who were not allowed forward of the Regimental Aid Post even if the front was quiet. Even the stretcher bearers were being rationed, it was up to the attackers to get their wounded back to safety.[315]

Carrier tanks were used to bring up ammunition and reinforcements and some supplies were even supplied by parachute courtesy of the Royal Air Force. The effect of the attack had been to buoy the soldiers to ever increasing feats of endurance, not to limit it. The Germans now were prone to surrender or flee if attacked strongly enough. The battalion could be happy with what they had captured in two days fighting: 500 prisoners, ten trench mortars, twenty-five machine guns, ten heavy machine guns, three 5.9-inch howitzers and four field guns. The acquisition of all these armaments, the trench mortars in particular, was ample reward for the loss of similar equipment in March. They had suffered though, as the colonel knew full well, 300 casualties in the ranks and 14 officers. Included amongst these were some long standing officers such as Captain Halley-Jones and Sergeant Bill Neben, both of whom had served with the battalion since it arrived in France or, in the case of Neben, since 1914. In terms of medals, Colonel Johnstone received the Distinguished Service Order, Captain Berliner and Peppiatt, and Lieutenants Fraser and Pinnock, the Military Cross. Twenty-four Military Medals were also handed out amongst the ranks. A junior NCO, Corporal Chetland, on becoming in sole charge of his platoon, since all other officers had become casualties, was awarded the Military Medal for courage, initiative and devotion to duty.[316]

An anonymous source, who had been wounded at Villers-Bretonneux and had missed the actions at Chipilly stated that the battalion 'as such had sustained heavy losses, nearly all my friends had gone...so now I was the sole survivor of the thirty odd London Rifle Brigade signallers [5th] who had joined the Post Office Rifles [8th] in the previous January.'[317]

On 10 August patrols reported that Tailles Wood was clear of the enemy. Progress was made and by 1pm the old Amiens Defence Line had been captured by 58th and 12th Divisions. This action brought to a close the Battle of Amiens (the French term it the Third Battle of the Somme). The line was stabilised on 11 August and on the 14 August the division was relieved in the line by 47th Division for eight days until the 22 August. The Germans had been pushed away from Amiens and the old defence line of 1916 was the base of the Allied line for the moment.

The casualties for the London Division in the period 7-15 August (noon) were 23 officers killed and 84 wounded and 4 missing, 264 other ranks killed and 1,597 wounded and 434 missing: a total of 2,406 casualties. This is against 6,205 for III Corps, 9,074 for the Canadians and 5,991 for the Australians. The total was 22,202 for the three Corps. Ten per cent of these were the London Division, almost half from the Canadians. American casualties are not established. The Germans had around 75,000 casualties, or around three times as many as the British, with many more being prisoners of war.[318] The figures do not include the 200 British casualties incurred by the German attack on 6 August.

The Canadians had suffered the most casualties in the Battle of Amiens. With this battle won, the advance became an Anglo-French push along the whole front from Arras to Montdidier. For the Londoners they were seeing a large number of young drafts and continuing casualties killing a number of well known and established figures within the division.

Notes

291 National Archives, WO95/3009 report on the Hairpin sector

292 National Archives, WO95/3009 report on the Hairpin sector

293 Keeson, C. *The History of Queen Victoria's Rifles*, p.419

294 Messenger, 1982 *Terriers in the Trenches*, (Chippenham) p.116

295 The ill fated and under strength 8th Division, which had fought at Villers-Bretonneux, was amongst the British forces sent to the Marne for a 'rest', only to be attacked again soon after.

296 Bean, 1942 *Official History of Australia in the War* (Sydney) p.519

297 Bean, 1942 *Official History of Australia in the War* (Sydney) p.495

298 IWM, MISC 11955 the papers of Ackrell, P.G.

299 ibid

300 National Archives, WO95/3005 6th Battalion report

301 Planck, 1946 *The History of the 7th (City of London) Battalion*, (London) p.198

302 Godfrey, 1938 *The Cast Iron Sixth*, (London) p.223

303 O'Neill, *The Royal Fusiliers in the Great War*, (Darlington), p.287

304 Beyond Peronne the Somme river turns south and therefore the German retreat would have been across it. They were retreating from the Australian and Canadian onslaught.

305 Edmonds, J. 1945 *Military Operations*, 1918 Vol 4, (London) p.83-84

306 Brown, M. *The Imperial War Museum book of 1918*, (London) pg. 190-1

307 58th Division Memorial by Henri Gaquie, is based on a popular painting by Fortunino Matania, 'Goodbye Old Man' c.1916.

308 Holt, T and V, 1996 *Major and Mrs Holt's Battlefield Guide to the Somme* (London) p.170-1

309 This action is covered in full in Edmonds, *Military Operations* 1918, Vol 4 pg.108ff

310 Edmonds, 1945 *Military Operations*, 1918 Vol 4, (London) p.109f

311 This shows one way of using the American forces, breaking them up amongst British Divisions. This was found useful by the British commanders, but not for the American General Pershing, who wanted an all-American army under his own command.

312 Marix-Evans, M. 2010 *The Somme 1914-1918*, (Stroud) p.222

313 IWM library, quote in The 58th Division in France and Flanders , CWGC

314 National Archives, WO95/3005 report on Operations

315 Planck, 1946 *The History of the 7th (City of London) Battalion*, (London) p.201

316 IWM MISC 2165/139 Anonymous

317 Edmonds, J.E. 1945 *Military Operations* 1918 Vol 4 (London) p.158-9

318 National Archives WO95/3009 report on operations

Chapter 13

Peronne and Peizieres
20 August – 27 September 1918

The next attacks were called the Battle of Albert, from the 21–23 August, just as the first two weeks of the 1916 Battle of the Somme was called the same name. The emphasis had moved away from Amiens and onto the old battlefields of the Somme, fought over with so much sacrifice in 1916. For now the brigades of the London Division were under the command of 47th and 18th Division in a reserve role, they would take turns advancing along the north side of the Somme on the flank of the Australians. The Australian 3rd Division kept a force of varying size on the north bank of the Somme, on the direct flank of the 58th Division, which allowed cooperation with their forces to the south of the river, in much the same way that 58th Division had straddled the Oise River in March.

In the intervening period the battalions spent some time training and new tactics were the order of the day.

'Always throw in reinforcements and reserves into places where progress is being made and not into places where you are held up. The further you progress where you are successful the more difficult it will be for the enemy to hold out in the other places.'[319]

The 173 Brigade spent 20 August behind the lines training with half-limbers as mock tanks, all tanks being involved in the great advance. The brigades were under orders of the divisions in the line, as above, 173 Brigade was posted to Mericourt, 174 at the disposal of 18th Division and 175 Brigade to the 47th Division. The latter was to attack on 24 August at Happy Valley, a position formerly behind British lines in 1916 and used as a supply line and rest area, hence the name. The area was used as a railway supply route in 1916 and railways had been built here around the circuitous contours. However the area was full of dugouts which had to be cleared of enemy and posed a real problem in the attack. The 47th Division suffered both through the heat of the summer days, lack of water and through the fact that the 'Germans had anticipated our attack and redistributed in depth in order to meet it. A systematic counter-attack had been ordered to start as soon as this redistribution was complete.' It is worth noting that captured British soldiers would give nothing away; the historian of 47th Division reported that a 'captured sergeant refused absolutely any information'.[320]

The Londoners of both divisions knew now that the Germans were on the back foot, and that it was only a matter of time before they were pushed back. This difference in morale, between the Germans at Villers-Bretonneux and the British after the 8th August was of great importance.

On 24 August 175 Brigade was used by 47th Division for a renewed attack on Happy Valley which they had failed to take. An anonymous source in the 8th Battalion wrote of the experience that 'this was my first time over the top and I was very nervous. I fitted my magazine and fixed my sword [rifle regiment term for bayonet] and prayed and waited for the barrage to start'.

Overhead an intense thunderstorm soaked the soldiers and added an air of tension in the summer heat:

'When the barrage opened up and we went forward it was a most unpleasant experience, we stumbled into shell holes up to our knees in mud and water, tripped over barbed wire and other objects. We didn't care what happened, we were so thoroughly fed up and wet through. Fortunately there was no opposition as the enemy must have withdrawn the night before.'[321]

The relief must have been overwhelming.

The 9th Battalion was drawn up for a night attack on Happy Valley starting from positions just behind their own front line. The colonel of the 9th wrote that:

'owing to the brightness of the moon I feared that the enemy would see the troops assembling for the attack and cause considerable trouble and many casualties. In fact the enemy's machine guns were very active especially on the left in front of A Company.... It is probable that he did see movement [even] if he did not put it down to an impending attack.'[322]

Night attacks could work in the attackers' favour, and usually did, but there were still many risks. They were thought generally favourable though, and throughout the summer campaign, as we have seen, they were usually favoured over daytime operations. The attack started at 1am and considerable opposition was met in Happy Valley and some stiff fighting took place. Some German machine guns were rushed and taken and their crews killed. The main part of the fighting seems to have been led by B Company's Captain Bowler and Sergeants Ridgeley, Keats and Dunn, and D Company met similar opposition led by Second Lieutenant Powell:

'After the valley had been captured the mopping up was carried on with under difficulties owing to the night being much darker and the dugouts being difficult to find.'[323]

Some problems indicative of night operations were met with including a large gap to the left of the 9th where it did not link up with the 12th Battalion on their left and indeed 47th Division further north. In fact it took up to twenty-four hours to extract more than a hundred enemy soldiers despite the fact that the area was swarming with British troops moving forward.

The soldiers holding the line during the day of 24 August were unable to safely reorganise as they were frequently left very close to machine guns and snipers who had not been taken during the night advance, the ground was open and it was impossible to move without casualties. One significant casualty was Captain Ralls, who had been in command for a number of days, killed by one of these snipers whilst accompanying the colonel to a conference. When the battalion headquarters moved up that day they suffered from 5.9-inch and 8-inch artillery fire. Since they were based at a cross roads in a sunken road by a railway line, they made an obvious target, and had to retire to a better position which, while still under some artillery fire, was at least protected by a bank. A later attack planned for 4.30pm was postponed until 2.30am on 25 August.

Now the line was handed back to the 58th Division staff, meaning that the soldiers and staff would be rested but a brigade would still be in the line. This system of rotating brigades and staffs would maintain a fresh impetus in the attack and advance as general war weariness was a draining factor on all involved. The 140 Brigade of 47th Division was used again by 58th Division with 175 Brigade for the attack on 25 August at Heilly with 173 Brigade in close support:

'Very little opposition was met with from the enemy but some difficulty was encountered at first in getting to the objective, owing at first to the fact that the gully east of Happy Valley was difficult to cross having high and very steep banks, also the gully having several turns in it tended to throw the troops off course... a thick mist came down, making it impossible to see more than a few yards.'[324]

Passing through the former brigades, 173 Brigade became the lead unit. The objective now was Bonfray Farm and the north of Billon Wood and

Maricourt, all scenes of intense fighting in 1916. The 4th Battalion was compelled to deploy when attacked near Billon Wood, but with severe fighting all day, the greater part of the wood was secured.[325] The fighting was continuing and the Germans were still able to bring fresh divisions into the battle, as 47th Division noted to the north of the 58th Division. On 26 August 173 and 174 Brigades advanced over ground to the east of Billon Wood, being heavily shelled from Maricourt and Crest Avenue. The attacks continued in the following days, with brigades being relieved on an almost daily basis, Fargny Wood and Clapham Farm being the objectives. Fargny Wood was not taken immediately but eventually held on 27 August.

A breakthrough force was created to strike if and when it was needed. Due to stiffening opposition it was not possible to use in this role and it was reorganised as a vanguard force. The method was now to have an advanced guard, or vanguard, pushing forward. This was formed on 25 August by two troops[326] of the 1/1st Northumberland Hussars, one section of 86 Brigade Royal Field Artillery and one section of the Machine Gun Corps under Major Crossbie. The infantry complement were made up of the 4th Battalion London Regiment. This made for a more fluid and mobile all arms force with good firepower. Also available were six Whippet tanks which, as we have seen before, had a better speed than the heavier tanks and allowed greater flexibility.[327] This vanguard was able to pursue and catch up to the Germans in retreat, and if tougher opposition was met the main forces of infantry and artillery would be brought into play. In the event the force was not able to break through and the line was held in some form. This change of tactics really marks the move into the last phase of the war, open warfare and the substantial retreats of the last months of the war.

Now the advances had to coincide with the divisions to the north and south, the forces to the south being the Australians. The battle was on for the ancient fortified town of Peronne and a dominating hill to the north-east, Mount St Quentin. The Australians were to assault these positions, but the two London Divisions were to the north, playing their role in the advance attacking Bouchavesnes village and Moislains Wood. General Monash had changed his mind about the Australians attacking across the Somme River as being too potentially costly and instead wanted to attack from the north which precipitated a forward move of 58th Division. He allowed sufficient forces to probe across the river and build bridges to keep the Germans diverted from the main attack from the north first to Mount St. Quentin and second into Peronne itself. The Australian attack on Peronne is one of the major achievements of the end of the summer battles of 1918. The

Londoners to the north played their role in supporting this by their advances. That a private of the 1/22nd (Queen's) of 47th Division won the Victoria Cross shows the continuing good spirit and determination of the men.[328]

The role of the 47th and 58th divisions was to attack Bouchavesnes and Moislains in an easterly direction, giving the Australians the room they needed to manoeuvre from the north in a southerly direction along the eastern side of the river. By advancing forwards the London divisions opened up the axis of advance for the Australians. These objectives were reached by the 173 Brigade passing through 174 Brigade to co-operate with 47th Division on the left and the 3rd Australian Division on the right. A German headquarters and staff were captured intact. Posts were established along the front line. The signs were that the division was now exhausted, as were many of the Australians, many of their platoons down to half strength.

The Australians had to cross the Somme River by bridges behind 58th Division, move north-eastwards and attack Mount St. Quentin. This was a surprise night action which was made in the style of the counter-attack at Villers-Bretonneux by a relatively small group of soldiers charging up the hill and taking the objective quickly. The ground was not held onto immediately due to a counter-attack, but once reinforced they took and held the position. Peronne was to be taken by the Australians in a similar assault from this open flank of 58th Division. As the division was exhausted the divisional front was handed over to the 74th (Dismounted Yeomanry) Division, fresh off the train from the Middle East via the south of France.

On 6 September the division again replaced the 47th Division with 175 Brigade as the lead unit. By 7 September the divisional artillery had pulled out and 175 Brigade with a few men of XXII Corps cavalry pushed on as an advance guard to Saulcourt Wood and village. In this way ended the division's five month liaison with the Australian forces and their month long service with the 47th Division. They had contributed to the right flank of the Australians at Villers-Bretonneux and the left flank in May, June, July and August. The division had co-operated well with Australian and American forces to win local victories in the long hot summer of 1918. They had fought at the first tank battle, survived trench raids and pushed 22 miles along the strategic heights of the Somme bluffs at considerable cost in lives; many of the new boys to the front and many of the old soldiers of Bullecourt and even Loos and Cambrai had given their lives.

The front line was now back in front of the Hindenburg Line, where it had been in 1917. The territory west to Amiens had been cleared of the Germans, but now the Hindenburg Line had to be crossed again. The Allies

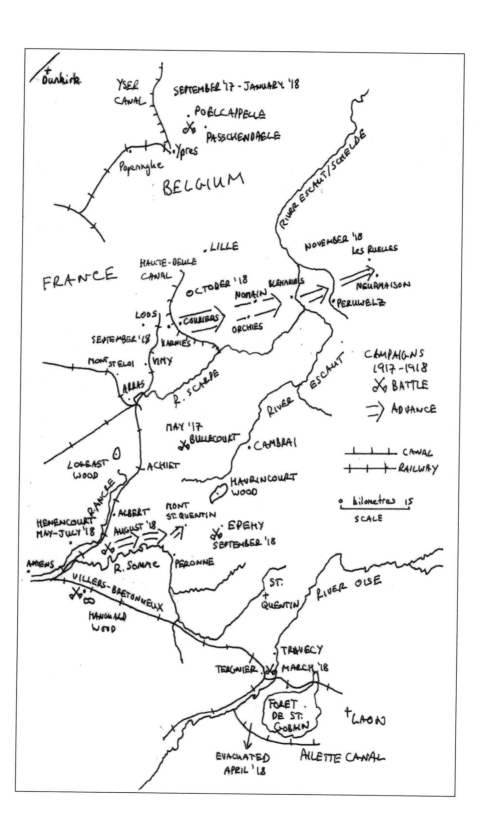

had failed to do this in 1917 at the battle of Cambrai, would they be able to do it in 1918?

The London Division was now in front of Epehy, an outpost of the Hindenburg Line, in fact behind the old British front line. The fighting before the main Hindenburg Line battles in which the Londoners were involved was termed the Pursuit to the Hindenburg Line. The preliminary to the Battles of the Hindenburg line lasted from the 12-26 September. The hard fighting for the actual line was in October 1918 and did not involve the Londoners. The pursuit stage involved two battles that were part of the approach, the Battle of Havrincourt and the Battle of Epehy; it would be in the latter that the Londoners were involved.

There were two canals in the area that made the battle here important for both sides, the canal La Tortille and the canal du Saint-Quentin. These both were carried in tunnels through the uplands of the plateau. It was over this ground that the British approached the Hindenburg Line in September 1918. At Havrincourt, where 58th Division had been in July 1917, it was the 42nd (East Lancashire) Division that was involved this time. The Germans were trying desperately to stop the British approaching the Hindenburg Line. The Londoners were now approaching Epehy-Peizières from the south-west. The Battle of Havrincourt Wood was the first in the two battles that would dictate the approach to the Hindenburg Line. The Londoners had been here in 1917 at one of their first actions. This time it would be the New Zealanders, 37th and 62nd divisions that would fight there. The Germans vigorously counter-attacked the British here, and the battle was not easily won.

If anything, after the excellent forward progress of the British Army in August, the German resistance was stiffening as they reached their old defences. This was Germany's west wall in 1917 to 1918 and there was little in the way of defences after it, but many canal lines to be crossed. The Hundred Days was all about surmounting these obstacles, a series of defence lines around the Hindenburg position and then a series of canals, such as the canals around La Fère which the Londoners had defended in March 1918. The taking of the vastness of Havrincourt Wood would allow the British to occupy the land between the two canals, and approach the Hindenburg Line unhindered, building transport lines and supplying their front line troops whilst clearing the ground to the south.

The London Division was brought in again on 7 September to attack Epehy. In this they would see stiff opposition in the form of the German Alpine Corps, an elite unit of the Kaiser's forces who were holding the villages of Epehy and Peizieres. These two villages lay in front of the

Hindenburg Line and had formed part of the British line in 1917 to 1918. The Germans expected an attack here for two reasons.

'In the first place Ronssoy, Lempire, Epehy, Peizière were very strong, having been thoroughly prepared for all-round defence and provided with good wire and dug-outs by the British in the winter of 1917-18; and the area around them, which had formed part of the battle zone of March 1918, was a maze of trenches. Secondly, it was of vital importance to retain this front, as it covered the tunnelled portion of the Saint-Quentin canal, over which a tank attack could therefore be made without meeting the then insuperable obstacle which the canal provided elsewhere.'[329]

This was the trouble with relying on defensive zones in the Great War, when they were captured they were difficult to retake. The canal tunnel from Venhuile south to Bellicourt ran several miles beyond Epehy, and it was at the canal line that the main defence line ran although the former British trenches to the west had been repositioned and the wire re-laid and expanded to form a formidable defence line in front of the main line.[330] The British were approaching from the west and trying to take the villages. For the British it was vital to take this position or face a difficult canal crossing. The battle for Epehy would take the rest of September 1918.

The approach to Epehy was from the direction of Bouchavesnes, to the south-west, the line now resting in the area of Guyencourt, Saulcourt and Villers-Faucon villages. The first attack was by 175 Brigade on 7 September relieving 140 Brigade of 47th Division. The 10th Buffs of 12th Division were on the left flank of the 10th Battalion and the 9th Battalion on the right. The objective was the two railway lines to the south of Epehy around the hamlet of Sainte-Emilie. The intended advance was over some 7,000 yards and crossed open farmland with some woods, notably Saulcourt Wood, the objective being the high ground east of Sainte-Emilie.

Soon the attack of the brigade was held up by machine gun fire from Guyencourt, Grebaucourt Wood and Saulcourt Wood. The response to this was a couple of machine guns and a shrapnel barrage of the wood by two 18-pounder fields guns of 62 Brigade Royal Field Artillery and brigade artillery[331] which was followed up by A Company of the 9th Battalion attacking the wood. Grebaucourt Wood was being bombarded by enemy artillery as soon as 'C' Company had entered into its shade. Patrols sent out in the direction of Epehy were still unable to advance due to machine gun fire from Jean Copse and Capron Copse. The 9th mopped up the woods and cleared Jean Copse. B and C companies were detailed to help mop up Jean Copse and advance towards Sainte-Emilie, whilst maintaining contact with 74th Division advancing on Villers-Faucon on the right.

The leading companies of the 9th attacked the spur overlooking Sainte-Emilie where they came under heavy machine gun and artillery fire from the direction of Epehy; instead of retreating they pressed ahead rapidly down the slope towards Sainte-Emilie and the protection of the railway embankment.[332] To the north 12th Division had failed to take Epehy and therefore the line was not straight, instead the Londoners were in a salient to the south of the village. The rest of the day and that night were taken in consolidation as the brigade had made a long advance. Some realignment of the line was to take place and the 9th were to advance again that night to take a line of trenches to the north-east. In fact it was established that the 9th were the most easterly advanced of all British troops in France at that moment.

The casualties of the battalion were 3 officers and 116 other ranks. The brigade was to be relieved by 74th Division, but even this was not undertaken easily as the relief took much longer than anticipated as enemy fire kept the incoming troops pinned down behind the Londoners.

This had been the easy part. The approach to the Hindenburg line was relatively straightforward. Now the British had to retake their old defences. By a strange quirk of fate Epehy was attacked by the same 12th Division which had lost it in the March offensives many months before. For the moment the British held the line, the transport and supply system endeavouring to catch up with the forward troops after a considerable advance. The brigade was to be rested and then brought into the line again three days later, but this time their stay in the front line was quiet and treated by the men as an extended rest. The 10th held the line for another day and were then relieved by the 4th Battalion Suffolk Regiment on 11 September. Casualties for the 10th were one officer died of wounds, and four wounded; other ranks were 32 killed, 98 wounded and 9 missing, one gassed.

On 10 September 173 Brigade was to attack Epehy and Peizières. They managed to take the village of Peizières but had to fall back to their original position due to the tenacity of the Alpine Corp's snipers and infantrymen in the ruins of the village. The men of the 2nd and 4th battalions were driven out. The attack of 175 Brigade similarly ended in failure.[333] Brigadier General Cochran of 173 ordered the soldiers on the ground to stop organised attacks and instead use the Stokes mortars to demolish each post and infiltrate each position, creeping forward that way.

On 11 September the battalion was in the line again and the British brought up the special companies of the Royal Engineers to discharge gas into Epehy.[334] The first steps had been taken and the battle for Epehy and Peizières was beginning, 58th Division would be in the battle from the beginning.

On 8 September 174 Brigade was to attack with the 7th and 8th battalions, passing through 12th Division, with the Sixth Battalion in support. The skirmishing line was to advance up to the barrage at 7.20am and the assaulting battalions went forward at 7.30am.[335] All four companies of the 8th were involved and advanced to within 1,000 yards without difficulty but then came under heavy machine gun fire, having captured Wood Farm. D, C, and B Companies entered Peizières and Epehy. Without flanking support however they were forced to fall back to Tottenham Post, a former British observation bunker, leaving some small groups of men in the village. In this exposed position they were supported by 62 Brigade Royal Field Artillery under Major Roney-Dougall who moved his guns up to within 800 yards of the front line to support the battalion.

The attack of the 7th Battalion was very similar in that they met heavy opposition from German machine gun fire. They were able to take some prisoners of the 10th and 14th Jaeger Battalions but their own casualties were considerable, although mostly wounded rather than killed. Their companies ended up under cover in shell holes, a sunken road and some in trenches. For the moment the day was going the Germans' way. The strength of the companies of the 7th was at this time only about thirty men each, about a quarter of nominal strength. The only answer to this lack of progress was to attack the following morning and share men amongst the assaulting battalions. They were to 'hold the line at all costs,' and did as requested until relieved by 10 September by the 12th Battalion.[336]

The 12th Battalion relieved 173 Brigade, with the 8th Battalion attached, on the night of 10-11 September. The relief was completed with some difficulty as the posts were spread around in a somewhat haphazard fashion. A further attack ordered for 3am was cancelled when it became clear that it could not be achieved under the conditions in the line at such short notice. The difficulty of the relief itself was made clear by the loss of Lieutenant Gillespie who walked into a German post in the dark and was killed in the ensuing fighting. The line itself was problematic with Tottenham Post being held almost in isolation of the main line. Complaints were made at a brigade level, but the corps commander insisted that the line be held as it was at that time. The 12th Battalion was disposed in the line with A and C Companies in the front line and D company in 'Tottenham Post some two to three hundred yards in advance and entirely isolated'. B Company was in support in the rear of the three other companies.[337] On 11 September the 9th and 10th Battalions were brought in to take over from 173 Brigade, and the 12th came under orders of their own 175 Brigade once again.

The Germans saw the isolation of Tottenham Post and realised they would be able to wrest it back if they isolated it with an artillery barrage. By 9am on 12 September a furious machine gun barrage kept the Londoners in the trenches and a box barrage around the post kept reinforcements away from it.

> 'After a stout resistance the garrison were driven out, captured or killed. Sergeant Moore with about thirty men fought their way back to the battalion, while Captain Anderson, Lieutenants Clarke and Baker were captured and Beeching killed. An attempt by Lieutenant Sievewright proved unsuccessful, the enemy machine guns being too strongly posted.'[338]

The battle for Tottenham Post was fierce and it only fell to the Germans after desperate fighting.[339] Their casualties between 6-10 September had been 2 officers killed and 4 wounded, 141 other ranks killed and wounded.

The 7th Battalion meanwhile had faced casualties from machine gun fire; they had captured some prisoners and had established a post in a sunken road to the south west of the village. The fighting had reverted to old style trench warfare and the inability of the commanders to give ground meant that the soldiers on the ground paid for their decisions. The brigade was relieved in the front and returned behind the lines to rest.

The battle here can be summed up by the following statement by the colonel of the 7th Battalion:

> 'The number and the character of the troops holding Epehy were of a different order to those previously encountered in recent fighting. A determined and organised defence was put up by a higher class of troops who did not make the facile surrender customary recently. Their morale and general attitude were in a much higher plane.'

He says that in comparison the soldiers of the 6th and 58th Division in general, were 'tired and weak in numbers and the bulk of the officers and men inexperienced in any form of warfare'.[340] Such were the British casualties in 1918 that few of the London men, replacements or otherwise, would have the depth of experience against such highly trained troops as the Alpine Corps. The Londoners had not yet taken Peizières and the struggle would go on.

For a few days the battle petered out with little going on as both sides recovered and reorganised. On 18 September the attack was renewed with an artillery barrage and 58th Division was to take Peizière whilst 12th Division took Epehy. This time 58th Division was to have more support. The reason the ground was so valuable was that tanks could operate here without having to bridge the canals, and it was given two tanks, a brigade of Field Artillery and one of Garrison Artillery under the Divisional Commander of Royal Artillery, Brigadier General J. Maxwell, which gave them access to heavier guns and howitzers.[341] The tanks were of some use but drove into Epehy and opened fire on the British troops of the 12th Division holding the ground there.

The battalions had been training whilst they were out of the line and the battalion chosen to mop up the enemy positions was to be the 2/24th Battalion. The 2nd Battalion was to attack the village with a final objective of Poplar Trench with the starting time of 5.20am. By 8.30am it was seen from a summary of reports that 'the final objectives of D, A and C companies had been taken, but there were reports of the enemy still holding posts in the village. However these were left to the 2/24th London Regiment, whose role was to mop up the village'.[342] The former three companies had been to hold the Brown Line in the village whilst B Company pushed on to Poplar Trench. It seems that B Company had not reached its objectives and had dug in short of them.

At 2pm the battalion commander of the 2nd received his orders to gain possession of Poplar Trench, using elements of the battalion under Captain A. Wright and, in addition, a company of the 24th. The 12th Division had failed to take Epehy on the right and were ordered to renew the attack at 8.15pm through the village to Prince's Reserve Trench and their final objective of Chestnut Avenue. On 12 September 175 Brigade relieved 173 with the 4th Suffolk pioneers attached. The 8th Battalion was put at the disposal of 74th Division to the south but with an order that they were for defensive use only. They were trying to push to the objective but the village was still being mopped up and they could not advance whilst the enemy lurked there. The only sign that the village was actually taken and held over the next few days was that the German artillery started to bombard it, which seemed to be significant, as they thought they had lost the position.

On 21 September 175 Brigade attacked Dados Lane and Dados Loop and held Kildare Avenue and Sprint Trench. On 22 September the attack was continued by 175 Brigade in conjunction with 33rd Division, however the line remained unchanged and the division was relieved by 12th Division.

The final attack of the operation to capture Epehy once again fell on 175 Brigade. The brigade attacked at 5.30am on 22 September and considerable casualties had been suffered on the approach march, often with all the junior officers wounded in any given platoon. This and the prompt German counter barrage as soon as the Londoners went over the top resulted in many losses and the attackers were enfiladed from both flanks by machine gun fire. The flanking attacks had failed to advance and the resultant pressure on the 12th Battalion forced them to go to ground where they were. Many ideas were sought at the headquarters as to how to help the troops advance the line and a potential raid with a bombing party was abandoned as impractical. In the end the 9th Battalion and the 4th Suffolks were sent forward to help consolidate the position.

The Germans were not going to let the Londoners off lightly, they counter-attacked around 10am [12pm according to other sources] on 23 September:

> 'A party of the enemy about fifty strong came down the sunken lane running north-south through [army coordinate] unperceived under the cover of the bank and forced an entry into Dados Lane and Dados Loop and started bombing outwards. The situation at once became serious as the supply of bombs taken in the attack began to run short and the enemy began to push outwards in both directions.'

Supplies were rapidly gathered to send up bombs and Lewis gun ammunition to the men of the 9th.

> 'After considerable fighting particularly on B Company's front the enemy were driven back, leaving two wounded prisoners in our hands and the position was re-established.'[343]

Subsequent interrogation found that the Germans were from the 2nd Guards Division. Particular bravery was shown by Rifleman Rossi who 'went forward by himself and drove them back with hand grenades, leaving about five or six dead behind them. After that Sergeant Hart went forward with a small party of men and again drove them off'.[344] Both Sergeant Hart and Rifleman Rossi won the Military Medal for their courage that day. The officer casualties included Second Lieutenant Lacey who died of wounds. Lieutenant Hodgson 'had some hard fighting as the enemy nearly reached his Company headquarters'.

It had been a close run thing for the Londoners and even at the last the Germans had kept up the pressure on the division; they were not prepared to give up Epehy and Peizières without a substantial fight. The battles of Amiens and Albert had cleared the Germans off the old Somme battlefields, the battles of Havrincourt and Epehy had approached the defensive line of the Hindenburg Line. Now it had to be broken through, something that the Allies had failed to do in 1917.

Notes

319 Maude, 1922 *The History of the 47th (London) Division* p. 189
320 IWM archives Anonymous MISC/2165/139 FA9
321 National Archives, WO95/3009 Ninth Battalion report on operations
322 National Archives WO95/3009 report on operations
323 National Archives WO95/3009 report on operations 9th Battalion
324 IWM library, C.W.G.C. *The 58th Division in France and Flanders*
325 National Archives WO95/3009 Accounts differ as to whether this was two troops or two squadrons of cavalry. This may be due to the fact that it was originally a breakthrough force of two squadrons but was reformed as a vanguard with two troops of cavalry.
326 Maude, A. 1922 *The History of the 47th Division in the Great War* (London) p.188
327 Pte Harvey's V.C. was 47 Division's second of the war, and the only surviving recipient. The other being Lance-Corporal L. Keyworth in July 1915 (Posthumous).
328 Edmonds, J.E. 1945 *Military Operations*, 1918 Vol IV (London) p.483
329 Mitchison, K.W. 1998 *Epehy* (Barnsley) p.51
330 Derviche-Jones, *History of the 8th Battalion Post Office Rifles*, 1914-1918 p.34
331 Cuthbert-Keeson, *The History and Records of Queen Victoria's Rifles*, p.436
332 Edmonds, J.E., *Military Operations*, 1918 Vol. IV p.455
333 National Archives, WO95/3009 war diaries
334 National Archives WO95/3005 report on operations
335 Derviche-Jones, *History of the 8th Battalion Post Office Rifles*, 1914-1918, p. 34 courtesy of B.P.M.A.
336 Wheeler-Holohan, A. *The Ranger's Historical Records*, p.234ff
337 Wheeler-Holohan, A. *The Ranger's Historical Records*, p.236
338 IWM library C.W.G.C. *The 58th Division in France and Flanders*
339 National Archives WO95/3005 statement of operations
340 Edmonds, J. *Military Operations*, 1918, Vol IV. p.488
341 National Archives, WO95/3001
342 National Archives, WO95/3009 report on operations
343 Cuthbert-Keeson *The History and Records of Queen Victoria's Rifles*, p. 442

Chapter 14

The Phantom Division
30 September–11 November 1918

The breakthrough of the Hindenburg Line was made by the Canadians and New Zealanders near Cambrai in October 1918 with help from 46th (North Midland) Division. This time the Allies had captured the full set of maps covering the defences and this allowed a tactical and strategic approach to be made by the Dominion forces charged with breaking through the line. For 58th Division, though, a proper rest was ordered and the men spent time at Ligny-Saint-Flochel near Saint-Pol, Aubigny and Savy-Berlette near Mont-Saint-Eloi. They were behind the lines now, protected from the battlefields by the comforting embrace of Vimy Ridge.

On 30 September 1918 the division moved into the line near Loos as part of the VIII Corps (First Army) under Lieutenant-General Aylmer Hunter-Weston.[345] The division was pretty much exhausted and was put here to rest allowing fresher troops to take up the offensive. It could advance and still had men in its ranks but was never again the sharp-edged sword that the Canadian and Australian forces continued to be. Loos was a quiet sector where the trench lines had not moved since the Canadian attack on Hill 70 in 1917. This had been a sector where much mining and counter-mining had taken place but this does not seem to have been a problem now as this warfare was not used any more. The landscape was dominated by the buildings associated with the coal mining of the district and the huge craters of the underground war. The trenches, though, were pristine and clean even having piped water laid on and taps. 'It was heaven; I remember the march into the line was through a number of tunnels all lit by electric light,' said one soldier of the 8th Battalion.[346]

The section of the front was near the Hart and Harrison Craters, just north of Lens, and east of the Double Crassier, a famous landmark in that part of the front. The tunnels, or subways, were constructed either separately or including coal mining tunnels that abounded in this part of the front, although the mining tunnels were much deeper. 'Canteen tunnel' was used

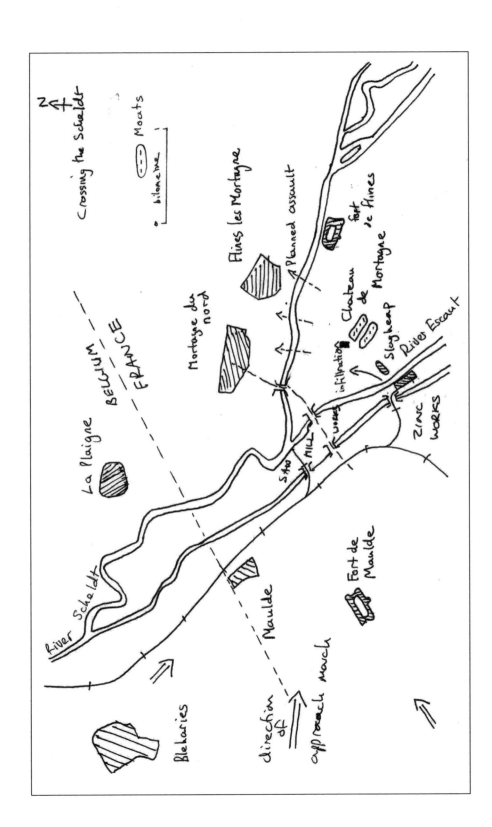

Crossing the Scheldt

N

- o kilometre
- --- Moats

Blaharies

River Scheldt

La Plaigne

BELGIUM
FRANCE

Maulde

direction of
approach march

Fort de Maulde

Montagne du nord

Flines les Mortagne

Planned assault

Saw mill

works

infiltration

Château de Mortagne

Slagheap

River Escaut

Zinc works

Fort de Flines

Mortagne

as a Brigade Headquarters, whilst the battalion headquarters of the 7th Battalion were in Hythe Tunnel.[347]

The Germans regarded the division as a good formation. The British had captured intelligence papers about the 58th Division after their move to the Lens sector. In this the Germans report that '58 Division is considered an excellent storm division. They were twice engaged in the fighting between the Somme and the Scarpe last month, during which period they sustained exceedingly heavy casualties'.[348] The divisional commanders who saw this captured report were no doubt surprised and pleased to be seen as such a good unit. This was proof that they had come a long way from the doubt that Maxse had shown them in the run up to the Wurst Farm Ridge attacks. They would continue to have a presence even when the war ended and long after. For the moment there was still a war to be won and they would advance from Loos eastwards with the rest of the Allied armies.

The main fighting in early October was occurring further south near Cambrai led by the Canadian and New Zealand Divisions. The effect of this was that as the line pushed forward to the south, the Germans retreated and the line had to conform. The first move was on 3 October, and 173 and 174 brigades advanced as the German position was partly evacuated. However for 175 Brigade the path of their advance lay through the town of Lens which had been saturated with gas, presumably by the Germans to delay the Allied advance. It was not worth incurring casualties to occupy the town until the gas cleared. Advancing around Lens 174 Brigade took the Cité St Auguste after some opposition and crossing the 50-foot deep railway cutting that crossed the path of their advance. After this Lens was evacuated by the Germans and 175 Brigade went into reserve.

An order stated that 'the enemy is retreating in a north-easterly direction, with strong rearguards'. A soldier of the 8th Battalion reported that:

'it was a case of leapfrog. One day we were in front, and then the 7th took over the following day, then the 6th and so on. We were told that the Germans had gone back and that there was nothing for miles.'[349]

The line settled down for the infantry, but it was the divisional artillery now that was used extensively to support the main attacks further south. The artillery was lent to XIII Corps of Fourth Army which used thirteen brigades of field artillery to support the attacks of 50th (Northumbrian) Division on Le Catelet. The weight of artillery fire was seen as important in the taking of the Beaurevoir Line. Two days later they still had eleven artillery brigades aiding 50th Division. Meanwhile 58th Division was still in the line but this was a quieter period whilst the centre of the First and Fourth armies bore the brunt of the fighting.

The 173 Brigade returned to the advance on 9 October as it supported 12th Division in taking Noyelles on the 9 and 10 October. Confusion seems to have occurred on the 11 October as the order to advance did not reach the division until 9.35am when it was due to start earlier in the morning. The Londoners were ordered to capture Harnes Fosse, which they eventually achieved and were on the line of the railway by 4pm when Harnes was occupied. This had not been a good day as it was crucial that the line advanced consistently; it was not until 7am the next day that the previous day's objectives were consolidated. The village of Annay was evacuated by the Germans and the brigades advanced to within a thousand yards of the Haute Deûle Canal. This would be the first canal to be crossed in the next three weeks, which would take all the ingenuity of the engineers and infantry against the German resistance and the destruction of bridges. The last canal and river to be crossed would be the Scarpe and Schelde canal.

The 7th Battalion was ordered to take Courrières on 13 October as part of the attacks by 37 Brigade of 12th Division:

> 'The Germans were shelling the village, and all the men could do was to dig in. B Company's headquarters in a cellar was shelled very heavily, and they had to move *"tout de suite"*. No sooner had they done so than the enemy scored a direct hit - a lucky escape.'

Casualties to the battalion were light but there was no let up and the advance was not going all the Londoners' way. The failure of an officer, Lieutenant Powl of D Company of the 8th Battalion, to secure prisoners who had voluntarily surrendered led to further casualties. Waving them back to headquarters, he continued, but the Germans, unguarded, returned to their positions and opened fire. Number 14 Platoon was advancing in the rear of Lieutenant Powl, and were all found by the canal bank dead, wounded or reported missing (presumed captured). The 8th Battalion suffered over 100 casualties in the area.[350] But these were by no means the only ones: against best advice the General Officer Commanding 58th Division, Major General Ramsay, came to Courrières at 3.30pm on 15 October and advanced towards the bridgehead, where his aide de camp, Captain Sir William Farquhar (Baronet) was shot dead by a sniper.[351]

The division was transferred to the I Corps on 14 October. On this day they were opposite a large chemical works, distillery and associated German positions on the south side of the Haute Deûle canal. An artillery barrage preceded the attack at 5.30am. The 2nd Battalion attacked the positions and took them but was unable to hold on. D Company withdrew after meeting heavy opposition, C Company gained the canal bank, and B Company met much opposition from the distillery and houses in the village of Vert Gazon. Fighting patrols were put out that night and revealed at 5.30 in the morning that the enemy had evacuated it overnight. The advance continued and the first inhabited villages were close by. The military formation that had been used in August was adapted for the advance guard and included a battalion of infantry, one section of 18-pounders from the Royal Field Artillery, one section 4.5-inch howitzers, one section Machine Gun Corps and a platoon of corps cyclists rather than cavalry.

Even now the division was still to have new experiences. On 17 October the first civilians were encountered. The occupied villages to the east of the Hindenburg Line were reached where the Germans had not evacuated the civilian population after four years. The 9th Battalion approached as 'civilians were filling in many craters and making rough bridges to allow us to pass by [more rapidly]'.[352]

The 2nd Battalion entered the town of Mons-en-Pévèle:

'after it was evacuated by enemy on the 17 [October]. About 400 civilians, women, children, and men above military age, were still in residence. Except for hardships subsequent upon military occupation and the curtailment of liberty they appear not to have been badly treated. All cattle and horses had been sent away and food was scanty. The town was undamaged. Nearly every house flew the tricolour.'[353]

The 7th Battalion recorded 'the inhabitants gave the troops a wonderful welcome; the band played in the street and after they had rendered the Marseillaise the people showered them with flowers'.[354] The village of La Petrie was the first to be approached by the men of the 2nd Battalion which stated 'enthusiastic reception of inhabitants, liberated from four years under the Germans'.[355] Yet the population was sometimes cautious and feared the Germans would return. At the village of Nomain 'the inhabitants here appeared to be greatly cowed, and feared that the Boche, who had retired only at midday, would return'.[356]

After initial concern, though, the villagers saw that it was a final liberation and the advance turned into something of a triumphal progress. On approaching the village of Péruwelz after crossing the Escaut the 9th Battalion reported that:

'the entire population of which some nine thousand, flung itself upon the battalion as we entered. It became impossible to move, and as the first arrivals we were naturally in the thick of it. As one of the first officers to enter, with every available space on my horse bedecked with flowers, I must say that the square presented a most wonderful sight. The noise was too great for anyone to hear what anyone else was saying. The mayor was addressing us, or so we understood, in terms of welcome, the band was playing, everyone was shouting, while mounted officers were pulled off their horses and carried shoulder high round the Place.'[357]

This was a fitting tribute to the men who had fought and survived, perhaps wounded several times, through the two years the division had seen action. The war was not over yet and the division faced a major barrier in the form of the triple watercourses of the Scarpe, Escaut and the Canal du Centre at Péruwelz. This was guarded by the Fort du Maulde on the west bank.

The Fort de Maulde, rather like the forts at Liez and Vendeuil in March 1918, were ancient forts to protect this part of France and the river crossings. These were now garrisoned by the German rearguards. The Londoners approached the fort cautiously and Corporal Merriman won the Military Medal whilst leading a reconnaissance.

'He was in charge of three scouts preceding a platoon, when nearly through the enemy wire three enemy machine guns opened fire at close range and wounded his three scouts. He succeeded in getting all three scouts back to safety and obtained valuable information.'[358]

These were held by the Germans for several days against the Londoners to give their main forces the chance to retreat in orderly fashion. The Germans were in no mood to give up yet. This was an organised withdrawal, not a disorganised rout.

The crossing of the Scarpe at Mortagne was achieved by the 7th Battalion by the following methods.

'A pontoon ferry had been established opposite the slag heap [of the zinc works]. A Company [who had established the ferry] were relieved by D Company who had moved up from Cense de Chocques, commenced crossing the Scarpe with one section of machine guns and two light trench mortars attached at 11pm. The crossing was complete by 1.50am, the pontoon carrying between eight and ten men at a time. The whole force was concentrated at the slag heap. A patrol was sent to examine the cottage at J.10.C.5.3

[army coordinate] and reported it empty. One platoon at once set out for the road junction and another for Chateau Mortagne.'

The area was cleared up efficiently, much aided by a thick morning mist. One officer was wounded and missing and one other rank killed.

The closest thing to an atrocity occurred during this period when the Germans appear to have bombarded the newly liberated towns of Bleharies and Rongy with poison gas on 7 November, knowing full well that civilians were in these towns, despite propaganda to the contrary. The medical teams of the London Division were later praised for their aid to the children and other civilians caught in this act of barbarity. The medical records do not show what the civilian casualties were caused by, only that civilians started to receive treatment on 20 October. The records show the average to be twenty civilians being treated every day, with a initial peak of twenty-seven on 24 October followed by a drop and then a peak around the start of November, with up to fifty-four being treated daily. Of these a small number were sent to hospital in Lille for further treatment. Civilian treatments continued, with a drop in numbers on 8 November when it fell to a few a day.

From this data we can surmise that gas may have been active in the area in early November, but it may be that civilians had maladies the Germans were unable to treat and that these civilians came forward when they were liberated. The army was changing from an offensive force, to a liberator, to an army of peacetime.

The 6th Battalion was trained for an assault crossing of the L'Escaut Fleuve, and practice was carried out at [a] Mortagne chateau moat with prefabricated rafts made out of barrels and tarpaulins from a local brewery. The far side of the river was heavily defended and this was going to be a costly assault for the 6th Battalion. Colonel Benson protested at this attack reasoning that the softening up of the enemy positions would take weeks of artillery preparation and it would be inordinately costly in lives. Despite his protests the order was to be carried out, but then at the last moment the Germans retreated and the attack never had to be carried out. On 8 November A Company of the 2nd Battalion was to cross and occupy Lalaigne; C Company Belloy and L'Hommois, and B Company as support and to assist the Royal Engineers as carrying parties reconstructing a bridge over the river. Thankfully, despite a desultory high explosive shelling, there were no casualties at the crossing.

The morning of 11 November started off with most of the division on the march as they moved forward to keep pace with the retreating enemy.

For many battalions the morning was a relentless march along the roads. The columns were on the move all morning and it was only after midday before they stopped. Some did not rest until 2.30 in the afternoon. It was then that they heard the news. The message ran:

> 'Hostilities cease 11.00 today aaa Troops will stand fast on the outpost line already established aaa All military precautions will be observed and there will be no communication with the enemy aaa Further instructions later aaa Acknowledge Ends.'

Some seem to have been calm and detached about the news of the Armistice. such as the men of the 12th Battalion who were more concerned about the whereabouts of the ration cart.[359] In others 'the boys gave a yell; their first reaction to the news was to change their tin hats for soft caps'. They admitted that 'it seemed too good to be true, perhaps an enemy trick'.[360] A poignant touch was added by the 9th Battalion which recorded that their buglers sounded the 'Stand fast' and 'Cease fire'.[361] Those battalions that were calm during the day seem to have realized the enormity of the news by the evening when quite a party was held.

The division held its line, having reached the area south of Chievres and north of Herchies, just to the north of Mons. They billeted in the vicinity of Peruwelz to the north-west of Mons. The men attended parades, undertook training and much education work was provided to make them fit for life outside the army. Many men had left school, joined the army and did not have the skills for employment in the wider world. Some men joined composite battalions that went off to 47th Division in the Army of Occupation on the Rhine. The army now saw its role to educate the men, and prevent them getting bored, listless and resentful. There was a lighter side to life and dancing and boxing were in demand. One of the highlights of the stay here in March 1919 was the visit of the King and Prince of Wales for which quite a fête was held with flags and streamers adorning the towns. No doubt the soldiers lined the streets, forming an honour guard and escort.

There was no way that millions of men could be returned home immediately as the labour market would not have been able to cope. So instead there was a gradual trickle of men back to Britain, a slow demobbing of thousands of men returning to civilian life. For the wounded a slow recovery, or for some a continual decline leading to later death many years down the line, caused by injury or gassing endured on the front line. Many of the last casualties of the war are buried in Tournai Allied Cemetery

Extension where they were reinterred after the war from the small cemeteries made near the L'Escaut Fleuve.[362]

The casualties of the division for the last month since 27 September were remarkably light, at 10 officers and 200 other ranks, though a high proportion were caused by the zealous use of gas by the retreating enemy. Compared to any of the previous two years they were the lightest casualties for any period in serious combat.

* * *

With the demobilisation of the London Division at the end of June 1919 the 58th Division vanished from the Official Army lists. Their casualties had amounted to a minimum of 1426 men killed, 3124 wounded and 2475 missing. Other Territorial divisions continued to have an impact in military history. The 51st Highland Division became one of the most famous units of the Second World War, being left behind at Dunkirk, reformed and fighting again in Europe as a fully armoured division. However 58th Division had a minor but important role to play as a phantom division in 1944 under the Operation Fortitude deception plan, lulling Hitler into thinking that the real second front would be anywhere but Normandy. In this guise, along with General Patton's phantom First United States Army Group (FUSAG), it made sure the landings in Normandy eventually succeeded by keeping forces at bay in northern Europe and Scandinavia. The men of the Great War Division would have been proud of this role.

The 47th Division was broken up and reformed as searchlight units, anti-aircraft units and stayed in the UK for the majority of the Second World War, also playing a role in the phantom armies. Many of the units kept on a proud history of this, and certainly recently there was a signals unit named after 47th Division. Most of the units live on as only company or platoons of these two once great divisions. The Victoria Cross recipient of the Post Office Rifles, now Captain Alfred Knight, served in the Second World War, gaining the Military Cross as an officer.

On paper the division was reformed as part of the Twenty-first Army Group, and was known to German headquarters from April 1943 to April 1945. It was in existence as a phantom division as part of this ruse. It was picked due to the fact that information suggested that the Germans believed it existed in the Windsor area in this mid-war period, so it seemed sensible to continue this belief and send them information as to its whereabouts. The temporary rebirth of the division was proposed, really only being formed of a few scattered wireless units of 12th Signals unit. This phantom division with associated wireless traffic was at the heart of the deception. This was identified with a new divisional symbol, the stag's head, which is a rather Scottish emblem that had nothing to do with the division's London roots. The Germans believed that 'in the same area is 58 English Infantry Division [sic] which was hitherto assumed to be west of London in the Southern Command. Since there has been for some considerable time no confirmation of the presence of this division in the latter area its transfer to Scottish Command at the beginning of this year must be presumed.'

The division was moved accordingly to feed the German Staff's analysis and reappeared in March 1944 as part of II British Corps at Stirling and back in its Great War guise as part of Fourth Army, based at Edinburgh under General Sir A.F.A. Thorne. Other units of this army were the VII Corps based at Dundee, with 52nd (Lowland) Division at the same place, 55th US Infantry Division in Iceland, and the XV Corps in Northern Ireland composed of 2nd, 5th and 8th US Infantry Divisions. This whole army was the centrepiece of the early Fortitude North deception to threaten a landing in Norway, possibly a link up with the Soviet Red Army through North Norway.

Intelligence from Germany noted that:

'we must reckon with four to six active divisions in this area (Scotland and the North). The shipping reported in east Scottish waters corresponds approximately to the tonnage which would be necessary with the tonnage to transport this force. Troops and shipping available to the enemy command would therefore allow the latter to embark forces in Scotland to strength of four or five divisions. One or two American divisions from Iceland might be added to this number.'[363]

In fact the Germans were convinced that an extra division, the 50th (former Northumbrian or Tyne Tees) Division also was attached to this grouping of northern armies. This was all very well, so the division existed in the minds of the German General Staff, but what effect did this northern army have on the war. In the short term the Germans promoted 'an intensification of aerial reconnaissance over the whole of the North Sea area is indispensable. This measure appears to constitute the only means of avoiding surprises such as those of the Sicily and Nettano landings'. This is very interesting, as the Germans believed the Northern forces existed and that an assault might be made, they did not think that they were being fooled again. They did not believe that the American forces were in Iceland, and put these in Scotland as well. Of course the Sicily landing deception, Operation Mincemeat, is very famous, but the Germans had to believe that the Norway landing might take place. How many airplanes were tied down in Norway by this ruse in unknown, one would have presumes they would be Condors, long-range reconnaissance aircraft, and medium bombers. A post war reassessment of Fortitude North says that German garrison figures in Norway in Spring 1944 only increased by one division, that of the 89th (Infantry) Division, not an elite division. Whilst the deception worked, it had no real impact. The impact might not be felt in Norway, but further south a greater deception was brewing.

While the Germans were guessing where the second front would fall in the spring of 1944 the wireless traffic moved the division south. This was information coming from sources the Germans trusted and believed in, their very own spies based in the British Isles. These spies, such as GARBO, BRUTUS and FREAK, were in fact double agents working for the British, and once again are famous. They played their part in keeping 58th Division alive: on 4 June 1944 GARBO reported that in Doncaster he had reports of units with the sign of the 58th British Division and a few of the II British Army Corps, latterly reported in Scotland. This was just before Operation Overlord, and the move south would give the Germans to believe that something was brewing, but not imminent. On 14 June BRUTUS reported that 'the British II Corps is now included in FUSAG and has headquarters at Louth. It is composed of 55th and 58th divisions with headquarters at Skegness and Horncastle respectively. I have heard that they are due to leave shortly for Kent'.[364]

Even after D-Day the 58th Division were playing a part, and playing a supporting role for their colleagues ashore in Normandy. The deception was continued and strengthened as the 58th Division joined General George C. Patton's fictional FUSAG threatening the Pas de Calais from Kent.

The former training areas of 58th Division in Suffolk were occupied by real troops during this period. As the centre of Suffolk was filled with American bomber bases the US 6th (Armoured) Division was based at Woodbridge on the old camp ground of the Queen Victoria's Rifles at Bromeswell Heath.[365] The flooded river valleys of the Suffolk coast were filled with dummy landing craft and German command, fuelled by Hitler's belief in the Pas de Calais threat, and still believing that Normandy was a feint, now fell hook, line and sinker for Fortitude South, General Patton's Army in the south-east. This plan, even cleverer in its inception, was to put the Allies' most well-known general, the temporarily disgraced General Patton, in charge of the phantom army threatening to land at the heavily fortified Pas de Calais. Hence 58th Division was on the move again between 14 and 17 July, this time to Dover, only 20 miles away from France.

As reported by GARBO this was a road and rail move, taking three days to move to Dover, just as the inland battles in Normandy heated up around the city of Caen. The ensuing deception worked so well that elite German forces were kept back specifically to defend the Pas de Calais, meaning that the Normandy bridgehead could be expanded. At this point Patton himself was brought into France and punched a hole in the German left wing and sped across northern France, enveloping the German forces, almost annihilating them when he closed the pocket with the British and Canadian forces at Falaise. The German High Command still believed in the forces lying in Kent, and so Fortitude South was continued into the Autumn of 1944 and the spring of 1945.

Just before the landings at Arnhem under Operation Market Garden 58th Division was moved into FUSAG as part of the Fourth British and Fourteenth US Armies. BRUTUS communicated to German Command in October 1944:

> 'am sending details obtained at Wentworth. I was told that 61st and 80th divisions have been withdrawn from VII Corps but that they remain at Wye and Canterbury respectively. Headquarters of the VII Corps are now somewhere to the south of Newmarket and include 5th British Armoured Division and 58th British Infantry Division.'[366]

And now although the British kept the division alive, they now whittled down its potential involvement in the European theatre of operations, for the last time. On 15 November 58th Division moved to Leeds and on 19 January 1945 became a draft finding unit to put troops into the army units at the front. It had its last orders in April 1945, and with the war all but over, it lost its phantom status and passed into oblivion once again and sadly for the last time.

General Eisenhower wrote that the enemy 'was completely misled by our diversionary operations,'[367] so the phantom divisions played their part, a fitting tribute to the men who had inhabited that division between the years 1914 to 1918 and still lie in the fields and cemeteries of France and Flanders.

As this book was being written the Territorial Army, as it is now known, is in the process of being enlarged, whilst the regular Army is being made smaller. This reflects Britain's place in the world, with a smaller and smaller standing army. This also would have amused the Great War Territorials as most of them passed away during the Cold War, when Britain still had a large standing army. The Territorial Army still has to fight in Britain to be taken seriously, with even ministers saying they are 'playing at being soldiers'.[368]

The trail of the London Division is a long one and, like many other Great War divisions, they moved around between sectors of the Western Front quite frequently. The nature of the warfare was so exhausting and depleting that often the divisions had to come out of the line to be rested and reorganised, receiving many hundreds of reinforcements. In the Second World War this happened, but to a lesser extent, and few generals would have wanted to see such slaughter again. The most famous generals of the Second World War were in the Great War as junior officers, but rising through the ranks, such as Bernard Law Montgomery, who had served not in 58th Division, but in 47th Division as the chief of staff during the Chipilly battles.

The memorial to 58th Divisional at Chipilly is quite modest and smaller than one might imagine from photographs. It sits across the road from the church at a road junction in the village. It was at Chipilly on the Somme, where they were so torn and ravaged by the machine guns and artillery they faced, that the division chose to build their memorial, although many more of their men lay in Flanders, mute testament to the sacrifice of the Londoners. It was here that the officers felt the division had its finest moment, finding cohesion as a unit in the turning point of the war, and deserving this joint memorial to the decisive battle of 8 August 1918.

At Chipilly they chose to have a French sculptor, Henri Gaquie, to build their memorial, showing not a single soldier but also a dying horse. Beyond their achievements at Ypres, it was beside the French at Saint-Quentin that the division had its finest hour, under French command. But it was not a memorial just to the division, the memorial is dedicated to '58 Division, one of the only English divisions, which co-operating with the French Army and the Australian and Canadian Corps, managed to penetrate the German defences between Les Quesnoy and Montdidier on the 8th August 1918, leading to the German retreat and ending in the Armistice of 11th November 1918.' This was what the men of the division wished to be remembered for. Of course by the time the division was at Chipilly they had been heavily reinforced with men, or boys, from all over the country. It is also fitting that the Poelcappelle Cemetery was designed by Charles Holden, creator of the London Underground Map, for it is here that most of the Londoners lie, in unknown graves, or simply missing and therefore on the Tyne Cot Memorial.

The divisional memorial at Chipilly has as its design a soldier cradling a wounded and dying horse. There are various incidents that might be the cause of this idea. Of course dying horses were a common sight on the transport lines of the war, so there is nothing unusual about the theme. Early in the war this had been brought to the popular imagination by the painting 'Goodbye Old Man' by Fortunino Matania. This had been used in various forms in support of the Our Dumb Friends League which was the home of the Blue Cross Fund to help horses and other animals in wartime. It became the Blue Cross in the 1950s.

A film showing British and French troops at the battle of Villers-Bretonneux shows men of the London Division shaving and resting behind the lines, it also shows a brief clip of two dead horses that were drawing a wagon. The sight was obviously a common one but why did it end up as the memorial? Another event is a whole team of dead horses hit by artillery and recorded in the Australian Official History east of Villers-Bretonneux.

A different and telling incident as to how and why this was the memorial for the soldiers, after all, not horses, is recorded in the history of the Queen Victoria's Rifles. Battalion Quartermaster Sergeant Mark Brawn, serving at the time with the Bedfordshire Regiment, 'one of the most popular non-commissioned officers that ever served in the Queen Victoria's Rifles, was killed 1 September 1918'. He was attached to the Royal Naval Division. Lieutenant Hawkings who was present at the time of his death, wrote:

> 'It was about two miles south of the village of Henin, behind the Queant-Drocourt Switch Line. At about 10pm a few low flying Boche planes came over dropping bombs. One of these caught the Bedford's transport lines, killing or maiming sixty horses, and also killing a NCO four men and poor old Mark. His old comrades will always remember him as one of the best, [and] will be glad to know that his death was instantaneous.... I halted by the transport lines and there met him. I had just left him when the bombs fell.'[369]

Death could come on the lines or behind the lines at any moment, and of course with hindsight the later deaths of the war seem more fruitless and pointless than the millions beforehand. This is the sort of incident that would stick in the mind of the soldiers and might lead to the memorial at Chipilly.

The statistics show that approximately 1.05 million men served in the forces from London. Of these about 130,000 died on service, roughly 26,000 in the London Regiment.[370] The 58th (London) Division's share of the total was around 7,000 casualties. Many of these were wounded several times and returned to combat. An estimate of the dead from 58th Division is a minimum of 3,400 to 5,600. This is a lasting tribute to the men of the division that no modern pen can emulate. They had survived the worst of the Third Battle of Ypres, the German attacks of March 1918 and the Allied counter-offensive; they had worked with tanks and fought at close quarters with the enemy. Even when disbanded they found a presence to deceive the enemy when the next European war was fought.

Notes

344 A.W. Hunter-Weston had commanded the 29th Division at the Dardanelles and the Somme in 1916

345 IWM archives, MISC 2165/139 FA9 Anonymous soldier of the 8th Battalion

346 Similar examples can be visited on the Canadian Memorial site at Vimy Ridge.

347 National Archives, WO95/3006

348 Messenger, 1982 *Terriers in the Trenches* (Chippenham) p.124

349 National Archives, WO95/3006 reports on action

350 Captain Farquhar is buried in Fosse 10 Cemetery Extension, Sains-en-Gohelle, CWGC.

351 WO95/3005 war diary

352 National Archives, WO95/3001 war diary

353 Planck, D. 1946 The History of the Seventh Battalion the London Regiment ((London) p. 210-11

354 National Archives WO/95 3001 war diary

355 National Archives WO95/3001 war diary

356 Cuthbert-Keeson, *The History and Records of Queen Victoria's Rifles*, p.452

357 Wardrop, J. *Tenth Battalion London Regiment*, unpublished, Courtesy of Hackney Archives

358 Wheeler-Holohan, A. 1921 *The Ranger's Historical Records*, (London) p.246

359 Planck, 1946 *The History of the Seventh* (London) p. 214

360 National Archives WO95/3005 war diary

361 cwgc.org.uk Tournai Allied Cemetery Extension. The existing cemeteries on the L'Escaut-Schelde canal are from May 1940.

362 National Archives WO 208/4374 Operation Fortitude Deception plan- lessons learnt

363 National Archives WO208/4374

364 The Sutton Hoo treasure had been found on the eve of the Second World War but proper excavation had to wait until after the war.

365 National Archives WO208/4374

366 Rankin, N. 2008 *Churchill's Wizards* (London) p.408

367 'Philip Hammond on the future of the TA; I don't want people playing at being soldiers' The *Sunday Telegraph* newspaper, October 15th 2012, and letters 22nd October 2012

368 Cuthbert-Keeson, *The History and Records of the Queen Victoria's Rifles*, p.434

369 IWM 98/17/1 the papers of B.F.J. Chapman 2/7th Battalion Killed 8th August 1918

370 Winter and Robert, 1997 *Capital Cities at War* (Cambridge) p.63ff

58th (2/1 London) Division

173 Brigade (2/1 London Brigade)*

2/1 City of London (Royal Fusiliers) replaced by renamed 3/1st Battalion 1915

2/2 City of London (Royal Fusiliers) replaced by renamed 3/2nd Battalion 1915

2/3 City of London (Royal Fusiliers) replaced by renamed 3/3rd Battalion 1915

2/4 City of London (Royal Fusiliers) replaced by renamed 3/4th Battalion 1915

2/24 County of London (The Queens) joined 11 September 1918

214 Machine Gun Company

173 Trench Mortar Battery

174 Brigade (2/2 London Brigade)

2/5 City of London (London Rifle Brigade)

2/6 City of London (City of London Rifles)

2/7 City of London (London Rifles)

2/8 London Regiment (Post Office Rifles)

215 Machine Gun Company

174 Trench Mortar Battery

175 Brigade (2/3 London Brigade)

2/9 London Regiment (Queen Victoria's Rifles)

2/10 London Regiment (Hackney Rifles)

2/11 London Regiment (Finsbury Rifles)

2/12 London Regiment (London Rangers)

215 Machine Gun Company

175 Trench Mortar Battery

*2/1 London Brigade went to Malta, Gallipoli and then Egypt 1915, returning to France in 1916 when it was broken up to provide reinforcements, mostly for the 47 Division.

Divisional Troops
1/4 Suffolk Regiment Pioneer Battalion (1918 only)
206 Machine Gun Company (until 2nd March 1918)
58 Machine Gun Company
100 Machine Gun Company

Divisional Mounted Troops
1/1 Duke of Lancaster's Own Yeomanry
A Squadron Hampshire Carabineers

Divisional Artillery
CCXC (2/I London) Brigade Royal Field Artillery joined September 1915
CCXCI (2/II London) Brigade Royal Field Artillery joined September 1915
CCXCII (2/III London) Brigade Royal Field Artillery joined September 1915
(last became an army brigade in January 1917 included 1 Glamorgan RHA and 1 Shropshire RHA)
2/IV London (Howitzer) Brigade Royal Field Artillery – broken up July 1916
1 London Heavy Battery, Royal Garrison Artillery, left March 1916
2/1 London Heavy Battery, Royal Garrison Artillery, remained in England
58 Divisional Ammunition Column Royal Field Artillery

V.58 Heavy Trench Mortar Battery, Royal Field Artillery (personnel to X.58 and Y.58 March 1918)

X.58 Y.58 and Z.58 Medium Mortar Batteries, joined March 1917, Z broken up February 1918 and reorganised

Royal Engineers
2/1 London Field Company, left for 1 London Division February 1916
2/2 London Field Company, left for 1 London Division February 1916
511 (1/5 London) Field Company joined 16 November 1915
503 (2/1 Wessex) Field Company, joined 22 February 1916
504 (2/2 Wessex) Field Company, joined 23 February 1916
58 Divisional Signals Company

Royal Army Medical Corps
2/1 London Field Ambulance, left for 1 London Division 21 February 1916
2/2 London Field Ambulance, left for 1 London Division 21 February 1916

2/3 London Field Ambulance, left for 1 London Division 21 February 1916

2/1 Home Counties Field Ambulance, joined 22 February 1916
2/2 Home Counties Field Ambulance, joined 22 February 1916
2/3 Home Counties Field Ambulance, joined 22 February 1916
58 Sanitary Section, left for VIII Corps 30 March 1917

Other Divisional Troops

58 Divisional Train Army Service Corps (509, 510, 511, and 512
  Companies ASC)
58 Mobile Veterinary Section Army Veterinary Corps, joined 21st
  November 1915
249 Divisional Employment Company, formed 23 June 1917, broken up
  22 April 1919

Appendix 2

Personnel and Casualties

General Officers Commanding 58th (2/1st London) Division

Formation	Major General W. Fry
4 May 1915	Brigadier General E.J. Cooper
5 September 1916	Major General H.D. Fanshawe
6 October 1917	Major General A.B.E. Cator (sick 10/5/1918)
10 May 1918	Major General C.G. Higgins (acting)
21 May 1918	Major General N.M. Smyth VC (sick 10/6/18)
10 June 1918	Brigadier General C.G. Higgins (acting)
13 June 1918	Major General F.W. Ramsay

GSO 1

Formation	Lieutenant Colonel H.A. Boyce
21 September 1916	Colonel F. St.D. Skinner
1 June 1916	Lieutenant Colonel F.W. Radcliffe
5 September 1916	Lieutenant Colonel T.H. Nunn
21 March 1917	Lieutenant Colonel J.E. Turner
13 November 1917	Lieutenant Colonel R.H. Mangles
13 July 1918	Lieutenant Colonel C.M. Davies

Brigadier General Royal Artillery

Formation	Brigadier General G.S. Duffus
11 February 1915	Colonel F.T.M. Beaver
13 January 1916	Brigadier General E.J. Granet
10 May 1916	Brigadier General R.W. Fuller
25 August 1916- 20 December 1917	Brigadier General E.J.R. Peel
15 January 1918	Brigadier-General J. McC. Maxwell

Assistant Adjutant and Quartermaster General

3 November 1914	Lieutenant Colonel St. G.L. Steele
3 May 1916	Lieutenant Colonel A.G.P. McNalty

Commanding Royal Engineers

Formation	Lieutenant Colonel G.W. Walters
13 March 1917	Lieutenant Colonel E.M. Newell
17 July 1917	Lieutenant Colonel W.H. Kelly
21 November 1917	Lieutenant Colonel A.J. Savage

2nd/1st London Brigade

29 December 1914 Colonel E. Fitz G.M Wood (brigade broken up by Feb 1915)

2nd/2nd London Brigade

Formation	Colonel Sir T.S. Cave
24 November 1914	Brigadier-General W.C.G. McGrigor

2nd/3rd London Brigade

19 January 1915	Colonel G.B. Stevens
6 February 1915	Colonel G. Pleydell-Bouverie

173 Brigade
(3rd/1st London)

10 May 1915	Colonel H. Cholmondley
9 January 1916	Brigadier General G.P.S Hunt
20 April 1917	Lieutenant Colonel P.W. Beresford (acting)
21 April 1917	Brigadier General B.C. Freyburg V.C. (wounded 19/9/1917)
19 September 1917	Lieutenant Colonel W.R.H. Dann (acting)
3 October 1917	Brigadier General R.B. Worgan
22 July 1918	Brigadier General C.E. Corkan

174 Brigade
(2nd/2nd London)

24 November 1914	Brigadier General W.C.G. McGrigor
21 April 1917	Brigadier General C.G. Higgins
10 May 1917	Lieutenant Colonel C.B.Benson (acting)
21 May 1918	Brigadier General C.G. Higgins
13 June 1918	Lieutenant Colonel C.B. Benson (acting)
14 June 1918	Brigadier General C.G. Higgins
2 July 1918	Brigadier General A Maxwell

175 Brigade
(2nd/3rd London)

6 February 1915	Colonel Pleydell-Bouviere
17 January 1916	Brigadier General C. de Winton
25 August 1916	Brigadier General H.C. Jackson
19 March 1918	Brigadier General M.E. Richardson
12 July 1918	Lieutenant Colonel E.G.H Powell (acting)
2 August 1918	Brigadier General Maxwell-Scott (temporary)
10 August 1918	Brigadier General H.W. Cobham (temporary)
21 August 1918	Brigadier General H.W. Cobham

Source – Becke, A.F. *History of the Great War, Order of Battle of Divisions, part 2a* reprinted 2007 (Uckfield)

War Establishment comparison Home service v Foreign service

57th (West Lancashire) Division 1915 versus 58th (2/1st London) Division 1918

All Ranks	17,212	11,035*
Horses and mules	4,156	1,838
Guns	44	48
Trench mortars --		36
Stokes	--	24
Medium	--	12
Machine guns	24	400
Vickers 24		64
Lewis	--	336
Carts and vehicles	768	870
Cycles	491	341
Motor Cycles	16	44
Motor Cars	13	11
Motor Lorries	5	3
Motor Ambulances	21	21

*This figure is October 1918 when the division was exhausted and understrength
Source Becke.

Divisional Casualties 1917-1918*

	Officers	Other Ranks	Total
Killed in Action	266	1,160	1,426
Wounded	218	2,906	3,124
Missing	4#	2,471	2,475
Total	488	6,537	7,025

* These are minimum figures from battle casualties reported, and the true figure will be higher including trench holding periods and general sickness. The relatively low number of ORs killed in action is compared with the high number missing.
# figure just August 1918 – other missing officers included in other ranks and totals killed in action/missing.

Central Force

This was a home service force originally termed General Force, this was changed to Central Force in August 1914. The force was a group of three armies, Mounted Division (Bury St Edmunds), First Army (Bedford), Second Army (Aldershot), and Third Army (Luton). In February 1915 this was changed to two mounted divisions, and First, Second and Third Armies, a total of eleven Territorial Force Divisions and three cyclist battalions. In November 1915 it comprised two mounted divisions, three armies including eight divisions, one armoured train, two heavy batteries, ten cyclist battalions and one infantry battalion. In 1916 the Force was scrapped and its soldiers reorganised under Viscount French into Northern and Southern Armies.

Source Becke.

Appendix 3

Bibliography

Anonymous *The History of the old 2/4th Battalion (London)* 1919

Arthur, Max *Forgotten Voices of the Great War*, (London) 2002

Aspinall-Oglander, C.F. *Military Operations, Gallipoli Vol II* (London) 1932

Baker, A. *Battle Honours of the British and Commonwealth Armies* (London) 1986

Baynes, *Far From a Donkey, The Life of Sir Ivor Maxse* (London) 1995

Bean, C. *The A.I.F. in France 1918 Vol V* (Sydney) 1941

Becke, A.F. *Order of Battle of Divisions Part 2b, The 2nd Line Territorial Divisions* 1937 reprinted (Uckfield) 2007

Brown, M. *The Imperial War Museum book of 1918* (London) 1998

Cuthbert-Keeson *The History and Records of Queen Victoria's Rifles, Vol I and II* (London) 1923

Commonwealth War Graves Commission, Cemeteries and Memorials in Belgium and Northern France (Clermont-Ferrand) 2004

Coppard G. *With a Machine Gun to Cambrai* (London) 1980

Derviche-Jones, *History of the 8th Battalion Post Office Rifles, 1914-1918*

Edmonds J.E *Military Operations France and Belgium 1917 Vol I* (London) 1940

Edmonds J.E. *Military Operations France and Belgium 1917 Vol II* (London) 1948

Edmonds J.E. *Military Operations France and Belgium 1917 Vol III* (London) 1948

Edmunds J.E. *Military Operations France and Belgium 1918 Vol I* (London) 1935

Edmunds J.E. *Military Operations France and Belgium 1918 Vol II* (London) 1937

Edmunds J.E. *Military Operations France and Belgium 1918 Vol III* (London) 1939

Edmunds J.E. *Military Operations France and Belgium 1918 Vol IV* (London) 1947

Edmunds J.E. *Military Operations France and Belgium 1918 Vol V* (London) 1947

Fenton-Jones, *The Story of the Tenth (Hackney) Battalion* (London) 1917

Fraser-Tytler N. *Field Guns in France* (London) 1922

Gittins, S. *The Great Western Railway in the First World War* (Stroud) 2010

Godfrey *The Cast Iron Sixth A History of the Sixth Battalion London Regiment* (London) 1938

Gough, H. *The Fifth Army* (London) 1931

Henniker, A.M. *Official History: Transportation on the Western Front* (London) 1937

History of the Post Office Rifles, 8th Battalion City of London Rifles (Aldershot) 1919

Holmes, R. *The Western Front* (London) 1999

Holmes, R. *Tommy* (London) 2004

Horne, Alistair *The Price of Glory, Verdun 1916*, (London) 1962 and 1993

Major and Mrs Holt's Battlefield Guide to the Ypres Salient (London) 1997

Marix Evans, Martin *Passchendaele, The Hollow Victory* (Barnsley) 2005

Marix-Evans, Martin *The Somme 1914-1918, Lessons in War*, (Stroud) 2010

Maude, Alan *The History of 47 (London) Division 1914-1919* (London) 1922

Maurice, F. *The History of the London Rifle Brigade, 1859-1919* (London) 1921

McCarthy, C. *The Third Ypres, Passchendaele, the Day by Day Account* (London) 1995

Messenger, C. *Terriers in the Trenches* (Chippenham) 1982

Middlebrook, M. *The First Day on the Somme* (London) 1971

Middlebrook, M. *Your Country Needs You* (Barnsley) 2000

Mitchell, T.J. and Smith G.N. *Official History, Medical Services* (London) 1931

Mitchison K.W. *Gentlemen and Officers: The impact and experience of war on a Territorial Regiment 1914-1918* (Uckfield) 1994

Mitchison, K.W. *Epehy-Hindenburg Line* (Barnsley)1998

Micholls, G. *The 18th Division in the Great War*, (Blackwood) 1922

O'Neill, H.C. *The Royal Fusiliers in the Great War* (Eastbourne) no date

Passchendaele, The Untold Story, Prior and Wilson (Yale) 1996 and 2002

Pedersen, *Villers-Bretonneux*, (Barnsley) 2004

Planck, C.D. *The History of the Seventh Battalion in the Great War* (London) 1946

Repington, *The First World War, 1914-1918*, (London) 1920

Riddoch and Kemp, *When the Whistle Blows* (Yeovil) 2008

Saunders, A. *Fortress Britain* (Liphook) 1983

Vaughan, E. *Some Desperate Glory* (Barnsley) 2011

Wardrop, P.J. *Tenth Battalion County of London Regiment* (Hackney) unpublished

Wheeler-Hollohan and Wyatt (eds), *The Ranger's Historical Records from 1859 to the Conclusion of the Great War* (London) 1921

Winter J. and Robert, J.L. *Capital Cities at War* (Cambridge) 1997

Unpublished Sources

Imperial War Museum

The Commonwealth War Graves Commission, 58th Division in France and Flanders, Compiled from Official Sources

Young, W. With the Post Office Rifles in France and Flanders, 1915-1918 (MISC 88/57/1)

Wardrop, History of the Tenth Battalion 1914-1918

Primary Sources

National Archives WO95/2995-3009

Magazine Articles

Clayton, 'The Paget Locomotive' in reprint of *Railway Gazette* No. 2 (1945) Courtesy of the National Railway Museum, York

Appendix 4

Poetry

Trench digging
'Gobblecock Hall!
Gobblecock Hall!
We're going out to Gobblecock Hall;
With spade and with maul,
Wire cutters and all,
We're going to march out to Gobblecock Hall!

And when we get there,
When we get there,
Trenches to dig revet and repair,
Britons prepare!
Germans beware!
Trenches to dig revet and repair.

And that isn't all,
That isn't all;
We've got to march back from Gobblecock Hall,
Oh! Peter and Paul!
King David and Saul!
We've got to march back from Gobblecock Hall!

Foxhall Heath

There's a certain place called Foxhall Heath
Near good old Ipswich Town
And if I could only but escape
I'd ne'er go back again.

The place is noted far and wide
A Depot for recruits
Trench digging and route marches
Which wears out all your boots.

The scenery is beautiful
You should see some of the hills
Where we go through a performance
Which the poets call 'Swedish Drill'.

We rise every morning at half past five
Just when Reveille blows
And practise rapid marching
In charge of NCOs.

Sometimes we go shooting
To try and earn our bounties
But some of the shots I fired myself
Could be found in several counties.

Foxhall Heath is alright in its place
With its valleys and its hills
But I would rather be in France
Or else the Dardanelles.

To find a place like Foxhall Heath
Many miles you'd have to roam
But I wish the war was over
And I was back at home.[371]

Sergeant Alfred J. Knight VC

For most conspicuous bravery and devotion to duty during the operations against the enemy positions.

Sergeant Knight did extraordinary good work, and showed exceptional bravery and initiative when his platoon was attacking an enemy strongpoint, and came under fire from an enemy machine gun. He rushed through our own barrage, bayoneted the enemy gunner, and captured the position single handed. Later twelve of the enemy with a machine gun were encountered in a shell hole. He again rushed forward by himself, bayoneted two and shot a third, causing the remainder to scatter.

Subsequently during an attack on a fortified farm, when entangled up to the waist in mud, and seeing a number of the enemy firing on our troops, he immediately opened fire on them without waiting to extricate himself from the mud, killing six of the enemy.

Again noticing the company on his left flank being held up in their attack on another farm, Sergeant Knight collected some men and took up a position on the flank of this farm, from where he brought fire to bear on the farm, as a result of which the farm was captured.

All platoon officers of the company had become casualties before the first objective was reached, and this gallant NCO took command of all the men in his own platoon and of the platoons without officers. His energy in consolidating and reorganising was untiring.

His several single-handed actions showed exceptional bravery, and saved a great number of casualties in the company. They were performed under heavy machine gun and rifle fire, and without any regard to personal risk, and were the direct cause of the objectives being captured.

Other medal awards to 8th Battalion 20 and 21 September 1917
Lieutenant-Colonel Derviche-Jones DSO
Lieutenant (acting Captain) Heeton MC
Second Lieutenant (acting Captain) Lanes MC
Second Lieutenants Kelly, Tregelles, Mortimer, Chancellor, Armstrong, MC

Second Lieutenant Richardson bar to MC
Sergeants Francis and Harris DCM
Corporal Solomon bar to MM
Sergeant Murray MM
Corporal Seager MM
Lance Corporal Gibbs and Needley MM
Riflemen Dixon, Mitchley, Soper, Wright, Todd, Sprakes, Payne, Ebbs, Macintyre, Drew, MacKenzie, Roper, White MM

Note: For a full list of medals received by men of the division, please see individual unit Battalion Histories in the bibliography

Model Patrol at Spider Crossroads

'The enemy were taken completely by surprise and when the sentry was shot they were all in their shelters or dug-outs and most of them asleep. The post at Spider Crossroads apparently a picket in their line of resistance relying on the warning of sentry groups stationed at two to three hundred yards in front. The sentry group seems not to have been sufficiently alert as the patrol went out, but was aroused by the firing and heard the patrols return.'

Medal Awards
Distinguished Service Order
Second Lieutenant Henderson

Distinguished Conduct Medal
Corporal F.T. Chapman
Lance Corporal W. Britten (also Belgian Croix de Guerre)

Military Medal
Lance Corporal H.W. Scott
Privates- F. Brand, J. Stout, W.E. Johnson, J. Hubbard, L. Rudelhoff, T. Menzies, A. Bennett, T. Andrews, H. Wilkins, W. Murphy, A. Perkins, G.F. Tomkins, J. Gower, T. Adlam, H. Billingham, E.J. Richardson.

Unfortunately Chapman and Menzies were in hospital at the time of the award ceremony and Brand and Adlam were not available. Other awards were made for the operations at Ypres at the same time.

Battle Honours of the 58th (2/1st London) Division and London Brigade Royal Fusiliers* 1914–1918

Gallipoli	1915-1916*
Egypt	1915-1917*
Bullecourt	3-7th May 1917
Ypres	31st July – 10th November 1917
Menin Road	1917
Polygon Wood	1917
Second Passchendaele	1917
Somme	1918
St Quentin	21-23rd March 1918
Villers-Bretonneux	24-25th April 1918
Amiens	8-11th August 1918
Albert	21-23rd August 1918
Scarpe 1918	26-30th August 1918
Bapaume II –	31st August- 3rd September 1918
Hindenburg Line	12th September-9th October 1918
Epehy	18th September 1918
Sambre	4th November 1918
Pursuit to Mons	4-11th November 1918
France and Flanders	1914-1918

* denotes 1st London Brigade Royal Fusiliers Battalions 2/1, 2/2, 2/3, 2/4 Royal Fusiliers, which were moved to Malta, Gallipoli, Egypt in 1915 and returned to France as reinforcements to the 47th

All that Remains

Memorials and archaeology connected with the 58th Division

There are many cemeteries across France and Belgium, and indeed Turkey, that have the graves of the men of the 58 (2/1st London Division). Graves are always to be recognised by battalion and date of death as well as knowing which troops were in the vicinity at a given time. This means that the divisional history always has to go back to the battalion level and therefore the regimental level. The use of the term division becomes academic to a certain degree except in knowing which battalions were likely to have been at a certain place at any one time.

Locations – Mouse trap farm bunker - private
London – individual battalion and/or regimental memorials
Ipswich – sites of camps and trench digging such as Purdis Farm
Belgium – Tyne Cot Memorial
France – Pozières Memorial, Arras Memorial
Somme – Memorial at Chipilly

Chipilly memorial by Henri Gauquie, is owned by the Executive of the Greater London Reserve Forces Association.

Poelcappelle CWGC designed by Charles Holden, London architect who designed the tube map, a fitting tribute for what is very much a London cemetery.

Epilogue

The 58th Division (BEF) Memorial Trust Fund

The author is indebted to the Trustees of the Memorial Fund for their support and their permission to include a short history of the fund in this volume.

On demobilisation of the division in June 1919 the then commanding officer, Major General F.W. Ramsay had in his control money that had been made from profits of the divisional entertainment canteen and barber shop. This was not public money and was placed in trust in the names of certain officers of the division, namely Major Generals Ramsay, Sir Charles Corkran and Brigadier General W. Cobham.

Part of the capital was invested in the Divisional Memorial at Chipilly on the Somme to represent the deeds of the battle of 8 August 1918. Excess funds were to be used for charitable distribution within the London area.

In July 1936 the remaining funds were invested in the 58th Division (BEF) Memorial Trust Fund with £4,000 invested in 4.5% Conversion Loan Stock and £2,000 in 4% consolidated Stock. By 1984 this had risen to £14,000 in value, partly due to the use of funds for distribution to charitable causes, but it was realised that this was a 'miserable performance' for the fund. Under the trusteeship of Colonel Mike Dudding this was turned around and the capital stood at some £20,000 in 1998.

Under changes to the banking sector the Trustees resisted the fund moving to Manchester in the 1990s in order to stay loyal to the London roots of the Trust. At the same time changes in the army led to the fund being controlled by the Territorial, Auxiliary and Volunteer Reserve Association for Greater London (TAVRA G-L). In August 1998 the 80th anniversary was marked by a visit of the trustees to the memorial, a service of commemoration, a drinks party to which all the inhabitants of Chipilly were invited, followed by lunch for the British and French delegations. Visits were subsequently made to local French and British war cemeteries. The importance of the action at Chipilly was invoked in a speech by Colonel Dudding:

> 'It took the 58th Division four days to capture Sailly Laurette and Chipilly and the high ground to the north of these villages. The cost

in casualties was significant – 287 killed, 1,681 wounded and 438 missing. The divisional record of awards for bravery between July 1918 and the end of the war runs to 180 pages, of which 90 relate to the four days 8-11 August 1918. This was the fiercest fighting experienced by the division during its service in France (January 1917 to November 1918). For this reason the divisional war memorial was erected in Chipilly some years later.'

The Trust continues to maintain the memorial under the auspices of the Reserve Forces and Cadets Association for Greater London (RFCA G-L). A service is planned for 2018 to commemorate the centenary of the battle.

Index